# BEWARE
# OF THE DOG

## Rugby's Hard Man Reveals All

# BRIAN MOORE

**SIMON &
SCHUSTER**

London · New York · Sydney · Toronto

A CBS COMPANY

First published in Great Britain by Simon & Schuster UK Ltd, 2010
This paperback edition published by Simon & Schuster UK Ltd, 2011
A CBS COMPANY

9 10 8

Simon & Schuster UK Ltd
1st Floor
222 Gray's Inn Road
London
WC1X 8HB


www.simonandschuster.co.uk


Simon & Schuster Australia
Sydney


PICTURE CREDITS
Courtesy of the author: 1, 2, 3, 4, 6, 8, 11, 28, 31, 33, 34, 35
*Halifax Courier*: 5
John Philburn: 7
Colorsport: 9, 10, 13, 14, 15, 16, 17, 19, 20, 21, 23, 27, 30
Getty Images: 12, 24
Mirrorpix: 18, 22,
Offside Images: 25, 26
Reuters/ HO Old: 29
Gary Bailey: 32


A CIP catalogue for this book is available
from the British Library.


ISBN: 978-1-84739-651-8


Typeset by M Rules
Printed and bound by CPI Group (UK) Ltd, Croydon, CR0 4YY

**Brian Moore** won sixty-four caps for the England rugby team between 1987 and 1995. He played in three Rugby World Cups and won the Grand Slam in 1991, 1992 and 1995. He went on two British Lions tours. Originally a qualified solicitor, he writes for the *Sun* and the *Telegraph* newspapers and is a co-commentator for international rugby matches alongside Eddie Butler on BBC TV.

**Further praise for *Beware of the Dog***

'An intense but well-considered study of the psychology of the international sportsman'
*Sport Magazine*

'A courageous warts-and-all memoir'
*North East Times*

'Remarkably candid'
*Daily Express*

To Imogen and Larissa for making me feel complete

# Contents

# Preface

Why write another autobiography, given that the first one covered the important parts of a career in rugby now long past?

I wanted to write the previous book myself, but in 1995 I had neither the time nor the ability. Some may say the latter still escapes me, but at least I know I can only blame myself. Stephen Jones, who wrote the first book, did a very good job, yet even he will agree that he could never fully capture my personality. I hope this new book does that and, whatever the impressions gained by its reading, this one is closer to whatever I am.

The first autobiography was written against the background of a prospective retirement and a divorce. Both events are and were immensely emotional, and coloured the tone of that book. The events and experiences in the intervening years have given me a different and, I believe, more accurate insight into earlier matters that has altered my thoughts about them and their importance. Towards some of these matters, I have softened my attitude; towards others, I have toughened it; whilst other matters, new matters, have only become apparent relatively recently.

In many ways, this book is darker than its predecessor, and this is inevitable given that a number of events are revealed here for the first time. Even at this point, I do not fully understand how my character has been defined by these incidents, or how they contributed to past actions and decisions that appear illogical and sometimes self-destructive. Perhaps I will never discover their full significance, but at least I now have some insight and realise that they are powerful influences in my life.

As a former international sportsman, I have had to confront the difficult fact that, when only half my life has passed, the abnormal and extreme sensations I experienced during my sporting career have gone for good and nothing will ever replace or match them. Inevitably, this loss is not easily absorbed and tends to make everything thereafter seem mundane.

With the passage of time, I am unable to explain why some of the things in the following pages have remained in my memory and others, which once seemed more important, have faded. That is just the way it has turned out.

Finally, I have to explain the references to Gollum in the book. I am a Tolkien nerd and, having read *The Silmarillion* and *Unfinished Tales of Middle-Earth* and *The Complete Guide to Middle-Earth*, I believe I have earned the right to that epithet. However, it was not until I saw Peter Jackson's brilliant translation to the screen of J. R. R. Tolkien's epic *Lord of the Rings* that the relevance became apparent to me of Gollum, who is what remains of an ordinary hobbit after years of change wrought by his carrying of the One Ring.

In *The Two Towers* part of Tolkien's book, there is detailed a conversation between the two contrasting parts that make up Gollum's psyche. As I watched this scene, it so accurately described the conversations that take place within my head that I decided that Gollum was the name I would attach to my *alter ego*.

One of the consequences of events in my early life was the accentuation of the 'dark' side of my character. I am not alone in having contrasting sides to my nature. Most people have a negative side, but it will surface infrequently. In my case the arguments between the two sides are real and powerful, they are a daily running battle. There is hardly anything that Gollum will stay silent about, and though I did not name him/it until relatively recently, I now see that he has been with me from my earliest years.

The above paragraph will not be comprehensible until the rest of the book is read but, if you stay the course, I hope you agree with my assessment of Tolkien's character and its applicability to me.

# Prologue

## The Field Trip

In 2008, I was asked to go to the Child Exploitation and Online Protection (CEOP) Centre in Vauxhall, London, to see the astonishingly worthwhile and traumatic work they do in tracking and prosecuting online child abuse. It is an uncomfortable fact that 70 per cent of child abuse is domestic. When you have children and see their utter vulnerability, their unalloyed joy at seeing your face in the morning, you cannot imagine that any parent could harm their offspring. Child abuse is one of the last taboos; rarely spoken of in any circumstances, other than with outrage to 'string 'em up', periodically prompted by media reminders that bad people are out there.

There is no easy way to tell this story, so I suppose it is best just to take it chronologically. I will leave the fallout for later.

I was at Whitehill Junior School, and although I cannot remember whether I was nine or ten years old, I was in what was called Year 3. An overnight field trip was going to Stoodley Pike near Todmorden, West Yorkshire, a monument erected in 1854 to commemorate the defeat of Napoleon. Unusually for Yorkshire, it was paid for by public subscription. I don't suppose it occurred to them that, of all the places Napoleon would *not* bother to visit, Todmorden would be in the top one.

These days the trip would not have taken place due to concerns about the youth of the students, but what could be amiss? A respected teacher, member of the church and a family friend – who would you trust more? Sharing a tent with three other boys and the teacher didn't seem amiss either, nor did the night-time story-telling. Though the word 'sex' was woven into the story-lines, it was something that, even at that age, we had sniggered about.

In retrospect, much of the pain, much of the shame, lies in the fact that at the time I couldn't recognise what is obvious to an adult, and that at the time the experience was partially fun. I have not seen any of the other boys since leaving for senior school but I sometimes wonder if they were able to exorcise the effects more successfully than I was.

Bragging about the size of your cock is something that few men need much encouragement to do. So when it was suggested we all get them out and compare it was mildly embarrassing, but nothing threatening. Of course his was much bigger, a fascinating erection when you are that age. None of us declined the invitation to 'touch it', 'move it about a bit'. It was almost flattering when he asked us to do the same; it felt naughty, there was a vague *frisson* that we were doing sophisticated, grown-up things.

Though intellectually I can rationalise the reason why we, I, was not appalled and did not protest, it has been almost impossible since to rid myself of the feeling that I should have done something.

He said it was a dare as to which of us would taste the sticky stuff on his cock, but when none of us actually volunteered, boys were chosen and forced. When it was my turn, it stopped being a bit of fun. I didn't see what anyone else did because by then I was numb.

Similarly I can remember some of the times we were lured into the classroom storeroom to be reassured that it wouldn't go so far this time. We need only show him, maybe let him touch, or touch him. He was deviously clever, and that is what would happen, but as described above, wanking just seemed naughty and felt good. The fact that the physical response was not one of repulsion was the thing that was to cause me the greatest shame and pain thereafter.

These incomplete accounts would be rich fare for a defence QC when cross-examining at a trial. The natural conclusion is to disbelieve partial testimony. That I cannot recall all the details of the field trip and the other occasions may lead you to doubt the veracity of what I am writing. All I can say is that some bits are impossibly real, viscerally so; others partially so; other elements that I know must be there, because of the time factor, are simply missing. This amnesia is not deliberate; indeed it is sickeningly frustrating. Part of me wants to remember, to complete the picture; the other part dreads doing so for fear of what may emerge.

Though it is tempting, I do not think there is now any point in naming the man. He is dead, and why should anyone innocent connected with him bear his shame? No matter what the *Daily Mail* says, this sort of thing is not commonplace, so only those who are involved professionally or victims can understand why it can take anything from a few weeks to a lifetime for people to come forward and complain. I cannot speak with certainty for anyone else, but I am sure all, most, or some of the following will resonate with any still-silent victims. Some may even take this to their grave.

What were the reasons for my silence? First, by a long way, is the shame and guilt at the fact that I did not resist. Did I deserve it, encourage it? Surely any normal boy, even of that age, would know what was unfolding and would struggle, or at the very least protest? Additionally, to other people, after the first time the subsequent episodes indicate willingness, or at least a lack of coercion.

I can rationalise the explanation given to me: at that age, my emerging identity, which would develop from child to man, necessarily involved my first contact with sexuality. As I didn't fully comprehend what was happening or the extent of the wrongdoing, it meant I would respond physically because there was nothing in my head that registered the situation as being nefarious. Yes, I understand all that, but I do not feel it; that is the vital point about resolving things. If I, or anybody else, cannot learn to go beyond the purely rational and get to the bottom of the emotions that have been lying deep inside the unconscious, it is impossible to move forward.

At the time I cannot remember asking these questions, even in a childlike way. What was happening was illicit and although I believe I felt it was not normal, it was with a figure of authority. When I finally began to understand a little later that what had happened to me was indeed wrong, I faced the difficulties other children confront in this situation. Who would believe my word against that of a teacher and family friend? I felt I couldn't tell, partly because of this, but also because of other reasons which to the reader might seem improbable.

In other respects this man was pleasant and fun. He was a good teacher. What if I told and he was taken away? That might upset my parents. I felt I could not tell my parents because of the friendship they had with him; also because I had not fought back, and at least initially had enjoyed some of the acts. Any mother or father would be mortified and feel guilt if their child felt they could not so confide. This guilt is wrong because they are also victims of this man. A person's social setting also has an influence on how they deal with such things and whether they tell anyone. My family were, and are, decent people. They are known by many in the church and from other connections. I thought of the incredible furore that would ensue if I told them. There is absolutely no fault that can be aimed at my parents – but still they would always have felt ill about this.

There is a part of me, the child, that responds as a child does by crying, 'Where were you?' Then the rational appears and it very reasonably states that they could not have known and it is very wrong to say such things. As there has been no resolution, the resentment continues, but the whole thing is made worse by the fact that I now have the added guilt of making such accusations – albeit in my head – against my innocent parents.

A number of times I came close to telling my parents, but I just could not get the words out. Instead I stayed silent and cursed myself for not being brave enough to speak out. The nearest I came to disclosing what had happened was when I found out he had been invited to drop round to our house. Although I tried, I could not tell them and instead stormed out of the room. At the time, my parents wondered what on earth had provoked such a response. They put it down to the stroppy behaviour of a child. They, like everyone else, could not have imagined it related to such dark matters.

There would clearly have been repercussions if I had told. I do not just mean the immediate ones – police, social services, family. There is something else that is hugely powerful in dissuading a child from making a complaint: I have no doubt that, whilst everybody would deny this, the revelation by someone that they have been abused leads to a subtle tainting of that person. So difficult is the subject that, if you have been abused, you feel tainted by association with the awfulness of the crime. 'People will think I deserved it, invited it, enjoyed it,' you tell yourself. Rape victims often feel the same way, but in my case I have to add to these acts the fact that they were same sex. Nudge, nudge, wink, wink, and not just from the uneducated. Hands up all those reading this who intellectually sympathise with me but who also have somewhere inside them a devil that sniggers before it can be buried by the decent thought. Don't worry: even though I experienced the above, it is the same for me. That is why I know this is a fact, not my imagination.

Only recently, however, has a further point come to me, and in a way it is as bad, if not worse, than the acts themselves. The ability and desire of the perpetrator to continue to smile, laugh and extend heartfelt best wishes to all – to me, my parents and siblings, mutual friends – requires extended cruelty. Not content with the things he had done, he also relived them by this façade: the warm chat at social and church meetings, that leering smirk at me over the shoulder of someone he was talking to. In doing this, he was reliving the acts and receiving smug satisfaction from knowing that not only had he violated me, he was violating my family – particularly satisfying as they remained oblivious to his mendacity.

The CEOP visit in 2008 left me stunned. Their tour took me to all departments, starting with the people who log every report from those who have pressed the 'report' button on a website in order to report something they feel is suspicious; from there, I progressed through the different departments, just as a particular case would, each section adding and refining the case for attention in whatever manner is thought necessary.

As the departments began to deal with cases that were thought to involve criminal behaviour, the gravity of the work began to unfold. Of all the departments, the people who work in the victim and abuser identification unit appeared to have the most challenging jobs. Identifying the people involved by minute scrutiny, for hours on end, of every frame of film, every photograph, often revealing the most horrific offences against very young children, must be severely taxing. The people work in pairs and, I understand, have to have regular counselling to retain their sanity. I asked if they ever became inured to the things they saw, and they said no. They felt it was absolutely necessary for them to retain the element of revulsion at these despicable acts so that they could maintain their focus and the will to catch the offenders.

When I left the building, I sat on a wall nearby and didn't move for half an hour. I never even raised my head as I stared at the ground. I thought about the many images I had seen and the courage of the people who dedicated their hours to preventing as many children becoming victims as possible. This triggered thoughts of my own experiences. Though not as extreme in nature as some of the cases witnessed, it was nevertheless abuse. I sobbed, trying to turn my head away from anyone walking by. When this was not possible, I walked down the road and found a small park where I had a chance to compose myself. I made a decision not to keep private that which I had buried for so many years, and to seek assistance in dealing with the consequences that I now realised had affected me so deeply that in many cases I had not even realised what had happened and why.

The CEOP visit gave me the courage to ask for help, though being helped is a searing experience in itself. I thank all who work at CEOP for giving me their examples of bravery to follow.

Once I had taken the decision to write about these experiences, I had to face the moment when I would let my mother read the text. The days before this took place were amongst the most difficult of my life. I was distracted, incoherent and frightened. I knew that the revelation would cause pain; who amongst us would not do almost anything to avoid inflicting this on a parent? Many times I concluded that I could not do it, but fortunately I was able to hold on to the feeling that this was absolutely necessary for me to have any chance of dealing with this issue. Furthermore, a prescient point was put to me by a professional counsellor: as a parent, would you be more hurt by the discovery of the facts, or by subsequently finding out that your child had felt unable to discuss this with you? It would be the latter, unquestionably.

After my mother read this chapter, she was naturally very upset but told me that a few years ago my fourth-year teacher at the junior school had made a comment to her about my abuser to the effect that he had been told what went on during these camping trips, but not until many years after retiring.

I cannot explain why, but not until this moment had I realised that, at the time these events took place, my mother was working as the Whitehill Junior School secretary. The depth of this man's deceitfulness was then laid bare for the first time. The ability to interact with a parent of a boy you were abusing, as if nothing was untoward, requires chilling dispassion.

What had previously been in my head a one-way question – my mother asking, 'Why didn't you tell me?' – was thus reciprocal. For many of the reasons previously listed, we explained to each other why we had not been able to raise the matter. Confirming all I knew of her, my mother dealt with things quietly and with compassion. Nothing she could say will resolve all the effects of these incidents, but at least from the moment I told her, I genuinely felt that I could start to move on.

# 1

## My Family

Not being born in the county, strictly speaking I do not qualify as a Yorkshireman, but being resident from the age of eight months I feel like one. I still have a recognisable accent, which I have no intention of losing. I also occasionally display the clichéd traits of one brought up in 'God's Country'. For example, calling a spade a spade and speaking your mind can be laudable, but sometimes it means insensitivity and not listening to anyone else.

I brush over my birth in Birmingham, largely because of the accent, and because I spent only a few months in the city before I was adopted in circumstances that were not to become clear until over thirty years later, and then in dramatic fashion. Having been placed for adoption, I stayed for a few months with foster parents and, through the National Children's Home, was seen by a couple from Halifax. Forms were signed and I was off to start being a Yorkshireman.

Ralph Stuart Moore and Dorothy Moore, both children of Methodist lay preachers, had two girls of their own, Catherine and Elizabeth, and an adopted daughter, Ai-Lien. To attempt some balance in this female-dominated environment, I was adopted.

Subsequently my brother Paul was adopted to keep me company, and our final sibling, Gwen, was adopted much later.

It was not my parents' intention to gather such a large flock; rather, one decision led to another, gathering an independent momentum. As I understand it, things went like this: my parents, wanting, but not able, to have another child, Ai-Lien (Chinese) was adopted as a baby and was four years younger than Elizabeth. My father was then outnumbered severely and they decided it would balance things up if a boy was adopted: me, Anglo-Malaysian and two years younger than Ai-Lien. Being the only boy, attention was lavished on me by my three older sisters. My parents then decided it would be good for me to have a brother, so along came Paul, of Welsh-Pakistani origin, and two years younger than me. This series of adoptions was natural in one sense: each addition was younger than the other siblings. I think that helped. Gwen, who is Chinese, was adopted when she was seventeen and, as such, had a much more difficult task in assimilating herself into an already large tribe, and although we have always remained civil, she never fitted in in the same way that we, the three adoptees, had done. Inevitable, I suppose. In any event, we were a 'rainbow' family long before Madonna and Angelina Jolie came on the scene.

There was very little discussion of our differing ethnicity, which was never hidden from us. When we were old enough to understand, my parents told us things about each of our non-English countries. I remember having a book about rubber plantations in Malaysia, and I pictured jungle tigers stalking the land. This probably explains why one of my favourite pieces of poetry is 'The Tyger' by William Blake. From this distance, I realise that the approach that was taken by my parents was to raise us as English and no different from any other children. Once they had told us about our ethnic origin, they provided information about it, but only when we pushed the topic. I think this was the correct approach.

Today no parent would be allowed to adopt children with such disparate backgrounds because ethnicity is seen as such an important 'right' for the child. Moreover, according to friends of mine who have gone through the invasive and often patronising interrogations of an adoption worker, race and racism is stressed so hard that at times it is forgotten that the child will live in England, under English law, with English traditions.

It is now deemed politically correct to revel in and be proud of your background, but in my case and that of many others, I believe this approach is overstated and possibly harmful. Although I had to listen to others' moronic jibes of 'Chink' and the like, I always felt English to the core. When I did find out about Malaysia, it was interesting, but not relevant to growing up in Halifax. Being part foreign is a difficult issue for children anyway. When I was young I looked far more oriental than I do now, and I was taunted because of it. Had I had my differences and not my similarities accentuated, the feeling of alienation would have been far worse. What would have been the benefit to me of trying to actively celebrate my 'Malaysian-ness'? I don't feel Malaysian, I don't live there, and my ethnic origin never impinges on my everyday life.

The barmy race theorists may denounce this as a betrayal of that part of me that is not English. Further, that my attitude hides a shame or embarrassment about this fact. Neither of these points carries much weight. I never hide the fact that I am half Malaysian, nor have I ever felt ashamed of it, but nor do I think it very relevant to who I am, other than aesthetically and because Malaysians are famous for being brilliant between the sheets. Had my difference been stressed, I might well have conveniently blamed all my setbacks on the racism of society; or I might have been one of those devastatingly misguided people who will not let anyone forget that they are from such-and-such a country and proud of it, and what do you mean you don't know anything about the place, you colonialist, imperialist racist?

Within the context of our family, a 'differentiated' approach would have undoubtedly led to a sibling's origin being added to the arsenal of abuse that all kids throw at each other when they fall out. Yet none of my siblings ever said, 'You're not my real brother', because they never felt that was the case. These words can lead to shame, but as race was never an issue with any of us, it was never used in a negative way – *ergo* we didn't feel it was a stigma. In addition, the fact that I had siblings of different race and got on well with them meant I could never accept the lies of real racists who insist that with such diversity comes inevitable conflict. How could this be true when I lived a life that proved otherwise?

Having Malaysian roots is no better or worse than having roots from any other country, foreign or English. But frankly, who cares? The dissimilarities I had/have with my family are because of my different emotional make-up and the experiences – positive and negative – that I have had, not for any other reason. That this is so attests to the remarkable wisdom of my parents.

So. Then we were six. I have no idea how my mother and father coped, but cope they did, and rather successfully. I was always told that I was adopted. When I did not know what that meant it didn't bother me; when I did, I was familiar with the fact. For many years I thought that my adoption was of no consequence and had no effect on me. I was wrong, as I will try to explain later.

Both mother and father, the latter now sadly deceased, were also Methodist lay preachers and, as you can imagine, the church played a major role in all our upbringings.

Methodism is traditionally non-conformist and strictly so. The core values of the Methodist tradition are described in *The Character of a Methodist* by John Wesley as:

1. Rejoicing over the goodness of God
2. Belief in the power of prayer
3. Belief in purity of heart and holiness
4. Keeping the commandments of God
5. Glorifying God in all that is done
6. Doing good, for the body and soul
7. Belief in the unity of the church

I have failed on all counts.

Although devout, my parents were not moralisers and always surprised me with their ability to adapt to changing attitudes without sacrificing their values. Throughout the seismic social changes that took place around them, they did not, like some, become censorious. They never said, 'Things were better in my day', and they retained their optimism, always trying to see the good before the bad. Their faith sustained them through the crises that all families have. The fact that they were each one of five children themselves meant the extended family and its attendant problems required some dedication.

At the age of fourteen, as I was developing into my version of the 'I know everything; you're wrong' teenager, I announced to my parents that I did not believe in God and I would not go to church any more. This declaration was not based on anything approaching knowledge, but rather a feeling that I didn't agree. My subsequent study of the Bible for two years at A' level would later enable me to bang on about inaccuracies and contradictions in the text, the multiple revisions to the Vulgate Bible (the official Latin version of the Bible of the Roman Catholic Church), and the fact that many of the Gospels remain unauthenticated. But because I didn't have a dangerous little bit of knowledge at the time, my parents were saved from being lectured by a know-all fourteen-year-old.

As on many occasions when a predictable response was expected – this time, of disapproval and possibly anger – my parents surprised me with their ability to disagree profoundly, but not lecture me and to accept that with which they did not concur. They said that they were disappointed, not for themselves, but for me, because throughout their lives so many burdens had been lightened and resolved through their faith; my decision to reject such help would leave me to face similar things alone. If their response was unpredictable, mine was not, though I fortunately didn't voice my thoughts that this was all nonsense. I have since moved from atheism to agnosticism as it seems to me to be the only intellectually honest view: just as they cannot prove the existence of God, I cannot disprove it. As I get older, I do wish that I had faith and was able to accept its comfort. My world would be less frightening. But I cannot and it is my loss.

We lived in a medium-sized terraced house in a district of Halifax called Illingworth. For a long time we were two to a bedroom because of the numbers. I did not get my own room until I was in the sixth form. My earliest memories are of stone-flagged floors in our house and empty roads. At the time, Illingworth was not the rough place it was to become, and it had large open spaces. Mixenden, close by, had once been a beautiful valley, but it was the first district to be affected by social engineering and it had hundreds of inferior social houses built on its fields. It had the first tower blocks ever built and all were filled with the poor and problem families. (Incidentally, it became the first ward to elect a BNP councillor some years later.) A few years later, Illingworth 'benefited' from the Mixenden experience and large council estates were built around us. One, Abbey Park, became a symbol of how not to build communities, eventually being torn down and begun anew.

Halifax had been a mill town, with some large factories and many light-engineering firms. In the 1960s the indigenous textile industry was dying in the face of cheaper foreign competition. One of the main employers, Crossley's Carpets, had a huge factory complex at Dean Clough, just outside the town centre, which employed hundreds of people, but it was to go the same way. However, as neither of my parents was directly tied to manufacturing we did not have to face the spectre or reality of unemployment. Dean Clough now houses more employed people in its small business units than it did in its days of pomp. The big difference is that they are all in service or public-sector jobs.

Unlike neighbouring towns such as Bradford and Huddersfield, Halifax's town centre retains a coherent architectural theme. You may not like the stark Yorkshire-stone buildings, but at least they are complete and not interspersed with 1960s prefabricated office blocks or, worse still, cut through by a dual carriageway. In fact,

now that the accumulated pollution that turned Halifax's buildings black has been cleaned, they exude the solidity you would
expect from a former industrial Yorkshire town. The credit for the
retention of so much history has to go to Halifax Council. So useless and indecisive was it in the era when all things new were
adopted that it failed to agree and implement any major scheme
for redeveloping the town centre. Thank God they argued and
bickered like true Yorkshire folk.

I do not have many clear memories of my very early years,
though I am glad I do not remember having a shave with death
when I was four. At that time Meccano sets had metal screw-
drivers; they don't now, for good reason. Whilst building a
structure that, to my mind, was the equal of the Clifton
Suspension Bridge, I stuck the screwdriver into a live power point
and electrified myself. By chance, my father happened to be only
a couple of feet away and, on seeing me stiffen, had the presence
of mind to kick me away from the power point. I escaped with
bad electrical burns to my hands and wrists.

This was the first of a number of potentially serious scrapes
from which I emerged alive and whole. I realise now that only
fate – or would my parents say God? – kept me from the catastrophic injuries suffered by others. Some years later we were on
the way to a family holiday in the ruggedly beautiful Shetland
Isles. Having crossed a dual carriageway in the centre of Aberdeen
to look in a shop window, I heard my father shout to me that our
bus was coming. Without looking, I ran straight out into the road
from behind a parked bus. A car in the outside lane of the oncoming traffic screeched to a halt. A clearly shaken driver leapt out and
proceeded to give me the loudest road-safety lecture in history. For
having saved my life, that man may now not be very popular in
Scotland, but his driving within the speed limit and his sharp reactions almost certainly prevented a serious collision. Think of it: I
could have died in Scotland.

Climbing trees is natural to most kids and when I was ten I was
no different. This was before you had to do a risk assessment

before embarking on any activity in which you might graze your knee and which is carried out at any height above four inches. Unfortunately, on one climbing jaunt I fell backwards and landed flat on my back from what must have been a good fifteen feet. I suffered no more than shock, bruising and being winded. In my university days a fellow student fell only eight feet whilst climbing and ended up paralysed from the waist down.

For the sake of completeness, I will mention my most recent dice with death, though this happened when I was supposedly grown-up. One evening, in 2005, I went to bed and placed a tea-tree light on the large, 'old-style' TV in my bedroom. I thought that, having a metal base, it would not pose a hazard and would eventually expire whilst I drifted off to sleep.

Suddenly, I woke up to see the TV in flames and my bedroom filled with acrid, thick, black smoke that was beginning to make me cough and retch. Most people who die in fires are killed by the toxic fumes before they are touched by the flames, and although I am no expert, I think that, had I been asleep for as little as one minute longer, I could have died in my sleep. I got out and the fire was contained in my flat, leaving the flat above undamaged, but for weeks afterwards I coughed up black solids from deep within my lungs.

Until I announced, aged fourteen, that I no longer believed in God, I attended church with my family every Sunday, and for a few years twice on Sunday. Moreover, through Illingworth Moor Methodist Church, I played in whist drives, helped on old people's trips to the seaside and went carol-singing. My father was a Licentiate of the London College of Music in singing, a level of musicianship that I didn't realise was so high until I looked it up. He could play several instruments – anything guitar-like or key-board-based instruments – and was able to pick up tunes with little effort. We were all musical. My mother was the church organist; Catherine played the clarinet; Elizabeth, the violin; and Paul, a number of instruments as well as being a very, very good rock drummer. He was later to join the Royal Marines Band at Deal in Kent. All this meant that I was lucky enough to hear a wide range of music when growing up; from classical to the Hawaiian guitar, folk to progressive rock, it was all there.

We were Yorkshire's answer to the Partridge Family, either as the Moores or as part of the church. We gave a number of local performances, though strangely no record executives seemed interested. We terrorised old people's homes with songs and sketches, but I seem to remember a few of the audience were so senile they understood not one jot. Lucky them.

As for me, I played the piano, to a fashion, but at the mature age of eleven I announced I would not be doing any more lessons and that I wouldn't regret it anyway. Wrong, wrong, wrong. However, I did have a good singing voice and won an Eisteddfod held in the Halifax Civic Theatre, singing 'Have You Seen My Little Dog?'. Oh, the shame of it. When my voice broke it never retained its previous clarity and, though I can still sing, it is with nowhere near the ability promised.

My father was a schoolteacher who worked in the specialist area of mentally and physically handicapped children, at Holly Bank School on the outskirts of Huddersfield. He did this until his retirement and I do not know how he had the empathy and most of all the patience to spend so many years in this difficult environment. 'Special needs' is the present term for such children, but the original description was better. These were not kids with mild dyslexia, or minor attention-deficit disorders, but ones with severe disabilities that required much specialised care.

I remember visiting his school only once and it upset me so much that I couldn't return. All I saw was the awfulness of these children's predicaments. My father had the necessary discernment to be able to separate the disability from the humanity of each child, seeing what they could do, as opposed to what they could not. In fact, father's gentle and patient manner suited this type of teaching; that plus the fact that it allowed him to talk all day.

By saying the latter I might be giving the impression that he liked the sound of his own voice, but that is not what I mean. Rather, he was the type that would start a story about going to the shop for something and it would wend its way in a meandering fashion with lots of digressions, and eventually this was so frustrating that I often wanted to shout, 'Get on with it!' At the time, it drove me crazy. I wish now that I could hear just one more of these stories.

When I recently watched a few minutes of one of today's seemingly endless reality TV documentaries, it dealt with people who had obsessive-compulsive disorders. This one was about people who obsessively tidy things. I laughed fondly, because I wondered what they would have done had they been my mother. She could have throttled my father daily because he was always mending things. In fact he really could mend almost anything: TVs, radios, computers, anything electrical and all manner of other things. But his storage systems were non-existent. His workplace for mending things – which in our house in Raw Lane, Illingworth, was in the cellar, part of his bedroom, part of the sitting room and most of the garage – was . . . well, to say it was cluttered would be like saying the Great Depression was an economic blip. Thousands of transistors, cables, plugs and other spare parts were strewn around in an order that only he could determine and which led him to complain that he couldn't find anything if anyone ever had the temerity to move something to enable them to carry out a trivial task. Like make space on the table to eat.

Dad was a compassionate man, but was not one comfortable with discussing intimate things. He loved me and was kind, and I feel tremendous guilt for having sometimes wanted him to be a different type of father. Though he would watch me play, he was not a sporting dad, nor a forceful leader. Why should he have been? It is a remaining source of pain to me that I could not fully accept him for the exceptionally good and normal family man that he was. Like so many children, I wish I could have found a way to talk to him about how I felt. He would have understood; he would have forgiven me.

When he died in 2007, hundreds of people took the time to write to my mother to mark his passing. All had their own story of how he had helped them in some small way or mended something for them. It was not until I read those letters that I understood the enormous impact my father had had on those he met. Similarly, until he died, I had thought an obituary in a national newspaper, hundreds of anonymous letters and perhaps mentions on TV were a better estimate of a person's worth. This failure of perspective is something that caused me trouble in the past and still does.

My mother has this single description attributed to her by many people who meet her: serene. Through many years of change, after raising six children and being the core of our family, she remains supremely positive. There are so many things I could write, but there are a few stories that are examples of the manner in which she has mixed pragmatism with an ability to retain her own values.

When I was still a sixth-former, my girlfriend came to stay overnight. As we had insufficient space in our house, she was to sleep in the small single bedroom and I had to sleep on the landing. During the night, Mum had obviously got up to go to the bathroom and discovered I was not where I should have been. In the morning, when challenged about this, I tried to lie but it was so apparent that I gave up. She told me that she did not want me sneaking about and, worse, lying about it. Furthermore, she supposed that there was nothing we couldn't do before six o'clock that we couldn't do after it, and therefore we could share a bed. From a Methodist lay preacher in her late fifties, this was a remarkable concession. She then casually requested that I might be more careful with where I put the Durex, as leaving them strewn in the bottom of the dustbins didn't really make a great impression on the binmen.

When she was in her early seventies, I found out that she had been helping out on the Abbey Park estate in a centre that was dealing with addicts and youths with various social-delinquency problems. When I asked her about this, she merely said that everybody had some sort of problem and if she could help, she would. This was in between continuing to play the organ at church and doing Methodist Committee work which at one point took her on a visit to Ghana. She would not recognise these things as being anything other than an ordinary person trying to help others, and indeed that is all they are. However, if there were more people like her, the world would be a more decent place.

That I have always felt different from the rest of my family is perhaps not surprising, given that I don't share their genes. The environment in which I was raised was loving and kind. I was not deprived, though we were not rich, and there were rarely arguments – brotherly skirmishes excepted. Yet I cannot recall a time, for example, when I was not competitive, often regarding ridiculously irrelevant matters. Nobody else in my family is remotely similar in this respect. An add-on to this competitiveness is a stubbornness that has proved both useful and unhelpful throughout all phases of my life. The refusal to relent is rewarded in sport and sometimes in business, but it is destructive in relationships, and if it becomes directed at oneself it is exasperating. Furthermore, it is exhausting. I need mention here but briefly the way this trait aided my rugby career: the refusal to accept that my size would render me unable to be successful at international level; an unwillingness to be cowed by various threats of deselection from the RFU. Both these characteristics ultimately stem from contrariness.

As a further example of this stubbornness, I once stood for a week at every break time with my face against the wall outside the masters' staff room because I refused to apologise for comments I had made during a games session that I felt strongly were justified. Had I understood that, by apologising, I was not betraying an important principle (and in the grander scheme of things, there were other, more important issues), I would not have been punished at all.

I suppose it was around the age of thirteen that the interests I pursued, sporting and otherwise, started to create a significant gap between me and the rest of my family. From that age onwards, that gap was to grow and eventually become something that I felt made me so dissimilar that I was completely different from them all. I had nobody who could explain to me that this was partly a feeling experienced by all teenagers and partly a feeling caused by issues surrounding both sexual abuse and adoption. At the time, it just felt lonely.

During that period, I could express myself only through rage and shouting, often concerning things that ordinarily did not merit such extreme reactions. This element of rage, which I have always had in my behaviour, this edge which tinges much of what I do, would surprise and, looking back, frighten people around me, making them wary in my presence.

Another repercussion of all the sport I was now doing was that I was attending various sports clubs – and, as a result, drinking alcohol. Whilst both my parents did drink, it was so seldom that they would have been considered teetotal by most people. During my childhood, as far as I was aware, they never once went to the pub. At the time, I did not realise how unusual this was. But all their time was spent at church, with family, or with friends, and they were perfectly happy with that and never at a loose end. In contrast, the state in which I sometimes fell through the door was not one that anyone else in the family ever found themselves in, and whilst I imagined I was being witty, the reality is that this was very unlikely.

The expected response, taking into account my parents' background and the principles to which they adhered, would have been condemnation and demands that, whilst I lived in their house, I was not to repeat this or similar behaviour. Why they chose not to react in this way, I know not. Perhaps they realised, correctly, that it would have had the opposite effect: my natural reaction to being admonished and lectured is to fight; all the more so if I know I am in the wrong. The possibility of self-destruction does not seem to stop this, even when it is fully considered. What they did instead was make their feelings known, gently but firmly, and then say no more, hoping that this would appeal to any sense of decency I had and lead me to moderate my actions. Most of the time, this worked.

This was not the way they dealt with all of us. My brother, Paul, had a far harder time, but that too appeared to work. This ability to discern the best approach to what were very different children is another thing that I marvel at, now that I am a parent. Letting your children make their own mistakes is something that is at times necessary, but the risk involved is that they may do something that causes them serious harm. No parent wants to see this happen and I go through mental contortions trying to decide which course of action is correct with my own children and how much freedom to give them.

My parents' acceptance of how different I was from my siblings means that I have always felt guilty about not being as thoughtful or attentive as my brother and sisters, but they accepted without disapproval that this was, and is, what I am. I think they had an inkling, though they could not know its extent, of the irrational sudden panic that I would, and still do, get into before a big family get-together. It must appear from the outside that I dip in and out of the family unit when it suits me and need to be able to leave when I want.

My own difficulties apart, we remain a reasonably close family considering we are now scattered around all parts of the country. I live in south-west London, whilst Ai-Lien lives just outside Dallas, Liz in Knaresborough, Paul in Maidstone, Cath is still near Halifax and Gwen is in Essex. We're not the type of family where you have to call everyone every week, and fortunately we don't suffer from the sort of claustrophobia that afflicts some families where missing a birthday or Christmas is taken as a grave insult. But we're close enough that, when Mum and Dad celebrated their Golden Wedding anniversary a few years ago, we all got together, along with all our own children, which made for a very big turnout – thirty-four in total.

I am enormously grateful for the sacrifices my parents made for me and the rest of the family. Not just monetary, but those of time. I am also enormously grateful for all the understanding and love they showed me and my siblings. Though I fall short in many ways, I have their example to keep in mind, and for me to be able to aim for some of their ideals is a legacy that some children do not have the good fortune of inheriting.

# 2

## Schooldays

My first school was Whitehill Infants School. Though parents today may gasp at this fact, I used to walk to school on my own from the age of six or seven: about a mile, and crossing main roads. Nobody thought this odd and I never came to any harm. Today, I would be at risk from all the parents doing the school run in their 4x4s, afraid to let their children walk, for fear of them being run over by other parents also doing the school run in their 4x4s.

What about being abducted and molested? The plain fact is that, of all the types of crimes committed against children, being a victim of a complete stranger is the least likely and is fortunately rare. Much more likely is abuse by a family member or family friend.

I can't remember not being competitive. The race to finishing reading so that I could read one of the *Cat in the Hat* books was pursued absolutely, and early reports reflected my 'tendency to race'. A sulk of biblical proportions accompanied my casting as a shepherd in the Nativity play. Why wasn't I one of the Three Kings? And my fourth-year report from junior school was pretty prescient: 'Brian is determined to the point of obduracy when he thinks his point of view is correct.' I wonder if Eddie Butler's school reports read similarly.

They did not do progressive education at Whitehill. It was more Gradgrind than Guru Dev, but rote learning is effective for drumming in the essentials, and those who say this is not so are wrong. Before every assembly we did twenty minutes of mental arithmetic or spelling and I am now eternally grateful for this.

The school also had other somewhat Dickensian practices. In particular, that of forcing all children to eat *all* their school dinner before they were allowed to leave the dining room. I realise that some coercion is necessary to prevent kids becoming unduly fussy eaters, but I was a child who could not eat certain things without being sick. At the time, I could not eat anything rich and creamy, and in particular rice pudding. I used to howl each time it was on the menu, only to be told to get on with it. I tried, but one lunchtime I ate the wretched stuff, leaving the tinned peach slices until last to take away the taste, only to see the whole lot come straight back up into the dish, looking no different from when it was served. One of my mates used to put the school liver, which resembled an ice-hockey puck in form and taste, in his pockets. I often wondered what his mother said when he got home.

My first sport was football, both playing and watching. I used to play almost every break time and in the evenings on the local playing fields. Sometimes we all met on Saturdays and Sundays to play on the school fields, having scaled the surrounding fence.

From about the age of six, I was taken to watch Halifax Town FC play at the Shay Stadium, not to be confused with the Shea Stadium in New York. My uncle, Gladney Robinson, and his son, Keith, took me in their ancient motor. Uncle Gladney had played for Town in the distant past. In 1971, Halifax were promoted to the old Third Division and I attended religiously and was to witness both of Halifax Town's most famous victories.

On 31 March 1971, in front of a crowd of 19,765, they played Manchester United in the Watney Cup, a short-lived tournament held before the start of the season. A United team containing, *inter alia*, Best, Law and Stepney, were conquered by the Shaymen. Goals by Atkin after just three minutes, and Wallace, one minute after the Halifax keeper Alex Smith had saved a Willie Morgan penalty, gave the orange-shirted underdogs a 2–0 lead that they kept until ten minutes before the end. George Best gave United a consolation goal with a penalty to give them some credibility. Later, in a shocking series of events, the full magnitude of First Division hooliganism was visited on Halifax town centre by bitter United thugs. Their knocking-over of the few shoe racks outside Freeman, Hardy and Willis and Dolcis were headlines in that night's *Evening Courier*, along with the magnificent victory.

By 1980, Halifax were back in the Fourth Division. It was the turn of United's neighbours, Manchester City, to feel the wrath of the Shaymen in the FA Cup third round. Only 16,500 people this time, but they saw what can only be described as a brilliant performance on a pitch that was a quagmire to start with and got worse throughout the game. Paul Hendrie's goal was enough to beat Malcolm Allison's Blues, but Halifax had been given a secret advantage before the kickoff. The team had been hypnotised by the magician Romark, whose legendary powers appeared to have deserted him when he did the same to local fighter Richard Dunn when he fought Muhammad Ali for the world heavyweight title in 1976. Allison later complained that he had been spat at by one of the Halifax fans, but what did he expect coming to 'Fax with that bloody stupid great fedora on his head?

Those footballing memories have stayed with me; rushing for the *Green Final*, listening to *Sports Report* with its iconic theme tune, and never remotely coming near to winning the Golden Goal. I also did not understand until much later why the man in the white coat who sold 'mussels, whelks, prawns and kippers' used to attract ubiquitous shouts of ''Ave yer got crabs?' followed by general guffawing.

Town could not match the hooligans of legend. They never had a Firm or Crew; they had Mad Bob who ruled supreme at the back of the Skircoat Shed. Mad Bob was in fact a postman who lived in quite an upmarket part of town and was referred to by his mother as 'our Robert', but for years he kept the Halifax hooligan tradition alive on his own.

It was in football that I had my first sporting representative game. As number nine for the Halifax Town under-eleven team, I played alongside a few boys who later signed forms. With what was to become an obsessive drive to win, I honestly think I might have played lower-league football, but this path closed when I moved to senior school.

It was as simple as this: at that time in Calderdale you took your 11-plus and, depending on the result, you went to a grammar or a secondary modern school. In my unsympathetic way, I could never fathom how anyone failed this exam, which to me seemed incredibly easy. This was the start of an unfortunate lifelong attitude of intellectual snobbery. Try as I do, I just cannot shake it.

Going to Crossley and Porter grammar school meant parting with my junior schoolmates, nearly all of whom went to the only grammar school that played football, Highlands. A couple of them later played for lower-division teams. Crossley's played rugby, and that was that. It was therefore an accident that I played. Had I not had a family connection, I would have chosen Highlands, which was only a mile and a half from home, rather than six miles and two bus rides across town. As I did not have an elder brother at the school I had no reputation to live up to. It was probably for the best that there were no expectations, as I doubt I would have fitted many of the predictions.

Crossley and Porter grammar school was, if it is possible, a non-posh grammar school: all classes of Halifax society were represented. Two pupils in my year got put away for dwelling-house burglaries. I might have joined them on that path were it not for two things. First, I had the knack of passing exams. Second, I loved sport. It was the latter that would eventually lead me away from the negative traits that I flirted with.

I remember my first day, as it was the first time I wore a uniform.

I felt proud. I didn't know that my pressed tie would be used to tie me to the tennis-court wire netting for the whole of lunchtime as a manifestation of the ritual bullying of the 'bills', which was the ubiquitous term applied to all first-form boys.

I was at Crossley's between 1973 and 1980, and those years coincided with the last days of 'old school' practices. By way of example, it was only two years prior to my first year that prefects were stopped from caning.

Another practice lasted only my first year: the serving of school dinner by a sixth-former who was head of a table that had a member of each year on it. It was the job of the 'bills' to collect the plates and cutlery, the second-formers' job to clear. Depending on how much you were liked by the head of your table, or more often depending on whether he liked what was being served, you could get a full plate or virtually nothing. One boy in my year spent the entire second term eating under the table, having been banished by its head. He was thrown the occasional roastie, but in compensation he always got nearly all the liver whenever it was dished up. We moved to a refectory system thereafter, with dinner ladies serving.

Crossley's had also been a co-ed school, only in the sense that both boys and girls attended, but at break and mealtimes the sexes were segregated into their own playgrounds, gymnasia and dinner sittings. Sittings were now no longer divided, but boys and girls still queued at different doors and were served from different ends of the food hall.

To start with, I was an industrious, almost model, pupil. My first-year report contrasted sharply with every other I would receive. My second-year report actually attracted a comment from the headmaster as well as my form teacher: 'This is a most alarming decline. In Brian's first report there were no marks below 'B'; there are six in this one. Brian clearly is not trying in subjects which he does not like. He is also a disruptive influence in class on many occasions.' In fact, I must have been the nightmare that teachers hope is visited on them only once in their careers: a pupil who is inventively subversive; worse, one who is able to get others to follow his misguided lead.

Looking back, the comments are as valid now as then. In subjects I didn't like – basically anything remotely science-based and languages – I simply did not try. I didn't want to. This provoked the comment, endlessly repeated, 'Could do better; he could, if bothered, do well in this subject, but shows no inclination to do so'.

The first time I played rugby, I knew that I liked contact. This is something that you cannot instil into any player and it has nothing to do with size. I was always smaller than most of my opponents, but I flung myself anywhere without much thought of the consequences. I was as gung-ho about rugby as I had been with football. The major difference was that rugby was a full-contact sport; and I liked contact.

It will come as a surprise to those who follow rugby that at school, apart from in the first year, when I played flanker, for the next six years I played in every position in the backs, bar winger. After the first few practice games, they divided the boys in each year into three grades. I was walking back to the changing rooms when I heard one of the first XV say to his teammate, whilst pointing me out, 'That lad will be a hooker.' He was wrong for many years, but extraordinarily prescient in the long run.

When I now pontificate for the BBC, I am often criticised for attempting to offer a view on back play. In response, I would point out that, as well as the above, I also played in a Yorkshire under-nineteen schoolboy final trials at centre. Anyhow, there is so much bollocks talked about the alleged subtleties of back play that you would think it were a science akin to cosmology.

Crossley's had a well-developed house system, with each of the four houses named after a prominent Halifax family. On Thursdays, the school had house assemblies in the mornings, run by the house captains, with the teachers, also allotted to a house, playing a bystanding role. Throughout the year, house competitions took place in all sports, but also in music, art and drama. As

I couldn't draw, I never featured in art. However, in the sixth-form singing competition I came a very distant second to a boy called Graham Broadbent, who went on to sing at the London Coliseum as a main cast member of the English National Opera.

Of all the house competitions, I most enjoyed house drama. Each house had to put on a play that lasted an hour. No assistance was allowed in any respect from the staff. Acting, directing, music, lighting and so on were organised by the sixth-formers. The play was performed in front of the junior school and then the seniors. The two winners were then performed in the evening in front of all the staff and parents. My year in charge saw a winning performance of the N. F. Berry play *The Hole*, in which I played a bemused Cerebro – largely because I had no real clue about what the play meant. It shows that if you are sufficiently earnest and technical you can fool people into thinking they see more than they do: the emperor's new clothes.

Within the house system, apart from sport, I enjoyed all things that involved public performing. I think that part of the reason I wanted to follow a career as a barrister, rather than a solicitor, was the element of 'acting' required when addressing the court. Had I thought deeply about what really interested me and from what I got most satisfaction, apart from sport, I may well have gone into the theatre in some capacity.

Though my academic output rapidly stalled in any subject I did not fancy, my sporting endeavours flourished. I represented the school in the first teams at rugby, cricket, basketball and athletics. At some point I captained every team I played for, be it rugby, cricket or basketball.

One game, and its aftermath, is an example of the almost unnatural attitude I had to winning and losing, even way back then. I was part of the school's under-fourteen cricket team that reached the final of the Calderdale twenty-overs-a-side competition. Despite hitting thirty-seven and contributing with the ball, I had what I thought was a plumb lbw shout turned down by their team's umpire; the boy given not out went on to hit the winning run. Looking back, this was one of the first times I can positively remember Gollum (although he/it was not given that name until much later) appearing. 'Loser. Loser. Who cares if you top-scored? You couldn't bowl the real batsman out, could you? He hit the winning run – that was your fault. Pathetic. Loser, loser.' I walked out of the ground and I hurled my runners-up trophy over a nearby wall. I didn't want a reminder of my failure. When my mother asked if I had received anything for reaching the final I lied and told her that only the winners got a trophy; I was too ashamed to tell her the truth. This was a victory for Gollum and an episode that would be re-run in my head many times in years to come.

Even in my early schooldays, I played and trained with an intensity that was exemplary, and only later did I question the ultra-competitiveness that was evident from about seven years of age. It was this obsession that was to save me from what could easily have become a much darker path.

As I lived across the other side of the town, I did not have any of my schoolfriends around in the evenings. As such, I gravitated to the kids who were about and had a spark about them. I linked up with a group of lads from the local council estate who had, or thought they had, no prospects other than those of their parents, many of whom did not work, or did so whilst cheating the dole. They were the antithesis of my then churchgoing life, so seemed edgy and exciting. We did things that I cannot be proud of. Breaking into the Mackintosh's factory and nicking sweets seemed like a laugh, as did the trips around town shoplifting. Burglary and theft were not labels I would have attached to what seemed like fun; but had I been caught, as many of them were in later years, that is how the charges would have been framed.

Fortunately, after-school sport and evening karate lessons limited the time spent on nefarious activities, and I eventually became so absorbed in sport that I did not have the time to hang around with my former mates. I took up karate at eleven and by the age of fourteen was a brown belt in Shotokan karate, one below a black belt. At the tender age of fourteen, I fought in the open-age British All Styles championships at Crystal Palace for the Halifax Shotokan club. I got the shit kicked out of me, even though it was notionally non-contact. As with nearly all things I took to, I became something of a fanatic. I soaked my hands in brine to make them tougher. Later, I regretted not continuing with martial arts. The flexibility and wider combat would have helped on the field, especially against the French, but rugby just took over. In addition, I would forever have had the oft-quoted phrase 'He's a black belt in karate' mentioned when referring to me – much like Danny Grewcock.

I did not appreciate how powerful an influence were my school-days in shaping my later personality until I was much older; nor how much I owed to my teachers. I now find myself repeating phrases, or putting to use things that teachers said over thirty years ago. Mr Hoyle, my English teacher, was a case in point. At the time, I didn't think he was much cop as a teacher, but I now realise that he, more than anyone, said things that I find myself remembering and using all the time.

It was he who taught two writing exercises that are invaluable. In the first, he challenged us to pick any passage of Shakespeare we wanted and then to rewrite the passage using fewer words. It is nearly impossible, and gave me a lifelong admiration of the Bard. The second exercise, one that helps me every time I write, was to look at our most recent essays and cross out every word that did not alter the meaning of what had been written. The first time you try this there is a probability that you will delete nearly half the text. Gradually this amount will lessen, but there is almost never a piece that cannot be distilled. On a good day, I can reduce the verbiage by around 15 per cent; on bad days, it is back up to nearly a third.

It was also Mr Hoyle who shot me down, deservedly, for mock-ing a classmate's attempt to act a role in a play. 'Moore, there are those in life who do, and those who sit on the side laughing. Do I need to tell you which one has my respect?' This is a homily which ought to be rammed down the throat of every non-performing critic in whatever field.

I don't think the distinction between teacher and pupil ever really goes away, even though we may develop into successful adults. After I had toured with the British Lions in 1989, I was invited back to school to present the sixth-form prizes. I remember that, when I was at school, this event had a reputation for being dull. Usually, some former pupil would speak about his 25-year career in the Civil Service and then hand out prizes to pupils who knew not who he was and didn't care anyway.

I had two advantages: I was a relatively recent school leaver and at least some of the pupils, and certainly their accompanying parents, had watched me play international rugby. As I sat on the stage, waiting for my turn, I felt panic rising within. I get this feeling before any after-dinner speech I make, even now. The first three rows of the audience were all teachers, some of whom had taught me. I had no real idea about what I was to say. I didn't want to go into a litany of my rugby achievements and didn't want to be boring.

When I stood up, an idea came to me and I started by asking a question. 'Does anyone remember the fire in the cellars in 1976?' There were a few nods and much puzzlement. 'Well,' I continued, 'that was me.' Cue general cheering from the pupils, some laughs from the parents and thunderous looks from the staff. I explained how I and two friends had crawled through a hole in the wall that bricked off a labyrinth which went under every part of the ground floor of the school. Crossley's had begun as an orphanage and the cellars were where the orphans kept their possessions. Not having a torch, we had lit some rags to light our way and things had got out of hand. As smoke started to billow up the steps from the cellars, the three of us crept, unseen, out of the corridor and into the toilets to wash off the accumulated grime. We emerged to find everyone evacuating the building and the fire brigade in attendance. As this approach to my speech proved so popular, I went on to confess to other unsolved crimes, like the end-of-year assembly when someone glued down the keys of the hall piano, forcing 'All Things Bright and Beautiful' to be sung unaccompanied.

Afterwards, I was invited into the staff room but after five uncomfortable minutes I said that I had to leave. When asked why, I told them that sitting in a room, outside which I had often stood all lunch-break as a punishment, just did not seem natural. To them this was a natural environment and they thought it odd that at my age I had not overcome such feelings.

This inferiority in the face of my former teachers resurfaced when I went to do a book signing in Halifax for the release of my earlier book. Four former teachers, including Mr Hoyle, queued along with the rest of a small Halifax fan club, and each time I came to sign and to chat with my former teachers, I could only gibber. It felt so wrong that they had waited for me and were asking me to sign something for them; hitherto, it had always been the reverse.

I enjoyed my schooldays and am grateful to my teachers, especially the ones who bore with me when I didn't deserve it. The often petulant teenager that I was must have been sorely trying, yet they were professional enough to persevere and do their job. I think Emo Philips, the comedian, sums up my sentiment rather well with a typically surreal and magnificent twist to his gag. 'You know, there are little things that you get at school that you just don't appreciate until you're older. Like being beaten once a week by a severely dressed middle-aged woman; something for which in later life you pay a lot of money.'

# 3

## Old Crossleyans, Roundhay and My Year Off

In my final year at school, I did something for a season that is now not allowed. On Saturday mornings, I captained the school first rugby team, whilst playing at centre. In the afternoons, I played hooker for the Old Crossleyans first rugby team in the then Yorkshire Merit Table. This is not permissible today because, with good reason, you cannot play two games in a day; and, with less reason, you cannot play in open-age rugby whilst at school.

Saturday lunchtime involved a frantic dash from school to the meeting point in Halifax town centre, grabbing fish and chips on the way – genuine Alf Tupper stuff. I had left Halifax RFC, where I had played second-team rugby since the age of sixteen, principally because of the fantastic times I had had playing for the Old Crossleyans cricket team. Often, a group of us would still be singing along to the fantastic jukebox the old boys then had; waiting to make up the 'Dawn Patrol' dedicated to seeing the sun rise, before wending and, more often than not, staggering our way to bed. It seemed such a great club and indeed it was. I don't think many of the England team in which I played ever played at a junior club; certainly very few of the present England team will have done so. The lifelong friends I made and the camaraderie I experienced in my season at the Old Crocs will stay with me as long as I still have a memory. It was, they are, special.

For this reason, amongst others, I sometimes rail against changes proposed in the laws of rugby by the IRB that would affect the Crocs. The fact that law changes apply throughout the game is often not given the weight it deserves, especially bearing in mind that the top echelon of the game is small in number. Though the IRB appears to think otherwise, rugby belongs to clubs such as the Old Crocs as much as it does to any Super 14 player or fan. Indeed, the soul of rugby, the unique atmosphere, resides in such clubs and not in the professional game. Moreover, I hear more common sense talked at some junior clubs than by a good number of committeemen both at the RFU and the IRB.

The Old Crossleyans, as the name suggests, was originally a closed club: you had to have been to the school to be a member. As with most clubs, this rule was changed to widen the membership and funding. It now has rugby, cricket and squash sections that all share its fantastic wood-panelled clubhouse. I am proud to say that the club was good enough to frame a full set of my shirts from all the international main-board countries. These are augmented by shirts from James Naylor and Jim Mallinder, two England backs.

Each club has its peculiar atmosphere, but the humour at the Old Crocs was intelligent, and not based on excess and breaking things. One evening, we were fined if we did not say everything in an operatic falsetto; another time it was in a Dame Edna Everage voice. Much of the banter, I later discovered, came from early Monty Python and Peter Cook & Dudley Moore sketches. I loved it.

Crossleyans was one of five rugby union clubs in what was really a rugby league town. League had many junior clubs, and Halifax RLFC had a proud history. Illingworth, where I grew up, had a strong amateur team. For a couple of years, I played in the 'Workshops', an amateur competition that was for the employees of local businesses plus a few outside players brought in to make up the teams. The summer before joining the Crossleyans, I trained regularly with Mick Scott, the long-serving loose forward for Halifax and Wigan. He tentatively raised the possibility of having a trial at Halifax, but I told him that I was set on going to university, which would mean I could not play professionally. I sometimes wonder whether I would have made it in that code as well.

There was no animosity between union and league players; that was the province of both supporters and committeemen. Many a time, I watched Halifax RLFC beat better teams, using the outrageous slope on their then home ground at Thrum Hall. I am proud of the photograph I had taken with Chris Anderson holding the Rugby League Challenge Cup won by Halifax when they beat St Helens in 1987. I actually saw their loss to a great Wigan team the following year and was honoured to be allowed to join the Halifax players' dinner after the game.

The season I played with the Old Crocs, they had a good first-team squad, augmented by a couple of recruits who were dropping down from senior rugby. In particular, Brian Campsall, formerly of Morley, later to become an international referee, joined as scrum half.

Yorkshire Merit Table rugby was a hard proving ground. Teams like Selby, Goole and Castleford had forwards who were miners from local pits that were then still open. They were strong and played direct, no-nonsense rugby. I could not have had a better introduction into the arts of the front row.

Throughout my senior career, I was lucky to have had good props to support me. Graham Thomas, Paul Jackson and Derek Ainley were very good junior props and had played for the Crocs for many years. They had to use all their experience to help me through the rough times, and never failed when I needed them most. Actually, they most often had to save me from myself as at that age I was too often an undisciplined idiot who would fight anyone. I was lucky that I didn't get the severe hiding I deserved.

We won the 1979/80 Merit Table with a 100 per cent record and I played in every game, escaping many sending-offs that I also probably deserved. Campsall, in an interview in 1994, recalled the problems I caused: 'I told him when we played together that he had a great future, but the most difficult job was keeping him on the field. He was a wild lad and in those days, when you played against clubs like Bramley, it was like street fighting. For me it was a case of getting in quickly and holding Brian back. He was hellishly competitive. The red mist would come down and he'd go wild. I was the scrum half so I was round the back of him ready to dive in.'

The picture of the squad that won the league is one of my favourites out of the hundreds of team photographs gathering dust in my attic.

My transformation from silky back to rough hooker was very much a case of serendipity. In a provisional under-sixteen Yorkshire Schools trial, I had played as a scrum half, but not shone. During one of the sessions, there was an injury to one of the hookers, and to foreshadow the inevitable 'Thanks for coming', I was asked if I would fill in. I knew I hadn't played well so I accepted. I don't know how this happened, but without ever having played hooker before, I took three strikes against the head and then, being a back, showed well about the pitch. So impressed were the selectors that I got selected for the next trial, and the next, and ultimately the final trial. In that trial, I also did well and I thought I had edged it, but I was not picked. Afterwards, the selectors were remarkably candid about the reason for this, saying that they were astonished to find out that was only my fourth ever game at hooker, but they just could not take the chance of selecting me with so little experience. I wasn't happy, but they were probably correct. In any event, I had been introduced to the position at which whatever natural talent I did have would be ideally suited. I was member of the Dark Arts Club.

Playing twice in a day was very tiring. Some nights I would wake with terrible cramps in my legs, and often the late Saturday nights would still be apparent on Monday mornings when I dragged myself off to school. My parents never complained about the late hours I returned home, though they weren't pleased the time I vomited on the landing. They were remarkably tolerant and my dad would sometimes kindly massage my neck and back, which were always sore on the Sunday morning after games.

Unfortunately, though it toughened me up, another consequence of playing open-age rugby, which was often very rough rugby, was that the cynical aspects of play went back with me into school matches, where again I might have been dismissed many times had the referees known what was going on. In fact, I was only sent off once at school, not for foul play as you might imagine, but for insolence. In an under-fifteen game, against St Michael's School, Leeds, I complained bitterly about a decision and the referee asked me to repeat what I had said and then told me to keep quiet. In the most sarcastic tone I could muster, I said, 'Yes – *Sir*'. The referee was right: you cannot have cocky little fifteen-year-old know-all-know-nothings speaking to referees like that.

After another game had ended in a free-for-all, my PE teacher Mike Capelin told me that, though I had talent, I was going to get into serious trouble if I carried on like this and somebody would get hurt. He went on to tell me about his friend Steve Fenwick, who had been a similar character in his earlier years, but had later reformed. At the time, I thought this was a stupid example: Fenwick was an international and a British Lion. How would this ever apply to me?

I never played for any England schools' team, at any age group, but I did get selected for Yorkshire under-nineteen schools as a hooker, along with Martin Whitcombe, later an England B and Leicester player. That season I played against a Wales under-nineteen team containing a useful number 10 called Stuart Barnes. I was dropped after that game because the Welsh forwards, who were much stronger, gave the Yorkshire pack a real pasting. Unable to see any put-in and driven backwards continually, I managed to get most of my own ball. As I was the only forward dropped, I felt like a scapegoat, particularly when the next game was against the Yorkshire Colts, a notoriously rough match, to which I thought my streetwise knowledge would be suited. I have never been able to rid myself of the perceived injustice of this decision – not that I hold grudges or anything.

I had planned to take a year off before going to university, but my gap year was not the usual sojourn to exotic, distant places; not unless you count Broughton Park, Manchester, as such. Because my hooking was improving and I retained the speed and handling ability of a back, interest from local senior clubs had been aroused.

I received a letter of invitation from the then England centre, Richard Cardus, later of Wasps, to join the Roundhay club in Leeds. They were at that time the less fashionable of the Leeds clubs. Headingley, where played one Peter Winterbottom, had the better reputation. I was sad to leave the Crossleyans, but both parties had known this would only be a one-year affair and that I would try to move up the rugby ladder. They were thrilled that I had been invited to Roundhay and I went with their best wishes – as I did in every future move I made. To commemorate my first cap, they bought me a beautiful watch on which was inscribed 'We are proud'.

Though Roundhay was not, and never became, a nationally famous club, when I joined they had a number of very good players. Along with Cardus were Andy Mason and Andy Staniland, who were outstanding backs and who both later turned professional. The forwards were bolstered by the arrival of Roger Burman, a prop as wide as he was tall, but an immense scrummager. My first training session with them was a leap to a level never experienced before, and I was nervous, but determined. Their hooker for a number of previous seasons was John Gill, who turned out to be a great bloke, though it took me almost the whole season to recognise and acknowledge this. As an established first-team player, he must have had regular challenges from hookers from other clubs. When one of his teammates, Chris Holly, nodded towards me during the opening warm-up run and said, 'Gilly, he's here to take your place,' Gill replied by saying, 'I've seen 'em come; I've seen 'em go.' 'Right, you bastard,' I thought, 'you'll be seeing a lot of this one.'

After about five games I got my chance against Huddersfield and, when handed the first-team shirt, I was told 'Gilly said to look after this for him'. 'I will, I'll look after it all season' was my cocky response, partly caused by acute embarrassment at being singled out, but partly betraying what had by then become fierce lust to possess the place and retain it.

I learned a lot in that season. The jump from junior to senior club was huge, not just for the size and strength of the players, but technically it was much more difficult. One of the things about playing in the front row was that I never stopped learning. Every now and again, somebody would pose an unexpected problem, something that I had not come across before. It was then a question of finding the solution as quickly as possible.

One floodlit Wednesday evening, Roundhay played away at Headingley. This was the first time I played against Peter Winterbottom. Some years later, during a discussion after I had moved to join him at Harlequins, he told me he had thought after that game that I was a complete lunatic. He couldn't be blamed for this assessment, as the game turned into a war between the two front rows: Ray Rowett, me and Roger Burman against Adam Machel, a friend of Wints' who drove a yellow Rolls-Royce, Tim Sinclair, ex-army, and Paul Huntsman, who later played for England. Sinclair saw me as an upstart, which I was. I saw him as a snobby army boy and we and the others slugged it out for the whole game. Afterwards, in the bar, an ageing Yorkshire Committeeman came up to me and said, 'As long as I live, you will never play for Yorkshire.' My diplomacy skills were less well honed in those days, so I replied by saying, 'Fuck off, by the time I'm eligible to play for Yorkshire you'll be dead anyway.' We were both right: he died shortly after, and I never played for Yorkshire.

In the north of England, the mention of Pacey, O'Hara and

Harris brings out cold sweats in former front-row players. This was the Broughton Park front row and they were the best unit around. The first time I played against Keith Pacey, the hooker, I couldn't move my feet. No matter which way I twisted and turned, he pinned me to the floor and I had to try and nod the ball back, or claw it back when it had passed my foot and it was nearly out of the other side of the tunnel. In the bar, I asked him how he did this, and he wisely told me that if he divulged the secret, it wouldn't work any more. I never did work out Pacey's secret, but as I developed as a hooker I picked up a few of my own.

Two years later, Nottingham played Broughton Park towards the end of the season and this time, whilst still very uncomfortable, I managed to get my own ball. This told me how much progress I had made in the intervening years, even though I was still not the complete article. Some years later, I met Keith in Edinburgh before a Calcutta Cup game and he introduced himself. I have to admit I didn't recognise him but then again he did look totally different. He is now an IT multimillionaire and good luck to him; he was one of the best.

That season, we progressed into the third round of the John Player Cup and drew Leicester at home. For Roundhay, this was a significant step up. We were very much in the second tier of national rugby, and a home tie against the famous Midlands club was special. For me, it was more so because I was to play against one of my schoolboy heroes, Peter Wheeler, the then England hooker.

In the end, it was a comfortable victory for Leicester, and as a front row we never really challenged, as our loose head, Stephen Lumb, went off with an eye injury early on. That left me striking at every ball on Wheeler's put-in. In the bar after the game, he – jokingly, I think – told me I should have had more respect.

Tony Biscombe was the Roundhay coach and I liked and learned from him. He later became technical director at the RFU, sharing in the World Cup 2003 win. It was Biscombe who first alluded to my potential representative career. He reminded me that although I was playing first-XV rugby, I was still young enough to play Colts rugby. At the time, the schools and Colts teams ran under-nineteen teams, the latter for those players who were no longer at school. The trialists would be a mixture of seventeen- and eighteen-year-olds, and at that level an extra year made a big difference in terms of physique and experience. I had the distinct benefit of a season in open-age rugby. Many Colts did not play in senior teams, and playing in the Roundhay first XV meant I was playing at a higher level than most.

I did not have a trial before attending my first Yorkshire Colts session as I had been watched whilst playing for Roundhay and I later found out I had been considered for the Yorkshire full squad. A number of players were asked to act as defenders after a couple of periods so that other players could run through drills. When it came to practising tap-penalty moves, the 'opposition' lined up a move that I had seen twice before that season. The scrum half stood over the ball and the hooker stood almost parallel to him and about seven yards away, with his back to us. The remaining forwards stood fifteen yards back from the ball in a line. The idea was that the scrum half tapped the ball, passed it to the hooker and then looped around the hooker feigning receipt of the ball. Immediately after, one of two designated forwards would run diagonally past the hooker, the first also feigning, and the second receiving the ball from the hooker.

When this move worked, it was effective because the defence did not know which of three runners would get the ball, and if they got pulled out of position by a runner who did not receive the ball, a gap appeared that could be exploited. However, its success rested squarely on the runners timing their charges so that they each passed the hooker within a matter of moments. If they got this wrong, the defence had time to look at a runner and spot whether he had the ball, and if not, they remained in position.

I asked the coaches whether it was 'full on' defence, because often players need to run through a move with token opposition to get some familiarity with it. They told me that it was as you would do in a game. As soon as the scrum half touched the ball with his foot, I sprinted at the hooker. When I smashed into his back he collided with the scrum half who was then knocked into the path of the first running forward, and that collision resulted in both forward runners hitting each other. As a bewildered set of coaches eyed the four prone players and then looked at me in astonishment, I said, 'Well, you did say as in a game.' I came away believing that I had a good chance of wearing an England shirt.

After one training session at Roundhay, I was chatting with Biscombe and he told me he had some bad news: the RFU had decided to alter the age limit for Colts rugby and reduce it by a year to under eighteen. I was mortified and felt that my chance to wear the rose had gone and had been taken away by an administrative decision. However, whilst sympathising with me, Biscombe casually remarked that he was also disappointed that the England Under 23s had not taken up his recommendation for me to be included in their training squad.

I was genuinely shocked to be considered as a potential Under 23 player. At the time, I was concerned with first-team rugby at Roundhay and possibly getting into the Yorkshire County squad, if for no other reason than to ram the words of that Headingley Committeeman firmly down his posh throat. Until that conversation, I genuinely had never thought I could or would play for England at any level other than youth rugby.

To finance my year off, I did a number of jobs: some were beneficial because they were hard physical jobs; others mundane, but had the benefit of reminding me that for many people work is a desolate experience used only to acquire enough money to get by. I was a storeman at Webster's Brewery in Halifax; a plumber's mate; a painter and decorator; and a hospital cleaner and porter. All these helped me get by. The job that I remember most was as a labourer, helping with the renovation of an old barn in Luddenden Foot, near Halifax. The village is splendid and the scenery likewise. For a couple of months, I fetched and carried, getting fitter by augmenting a full day's labouring with punishing runs in the evening. This regime was invaluable when I began playing at Roundhay and was one of the reasons I retained very high levels of fitness throughout that season.

There were, however, a couple of occasions on which I had painful reminders that I was on a serious job. Whilst carrying a load of bricks across a floor joist, I slipped, landing one leg either side of the joist. Any man who has done something similar will now be squirming at the memory and will fully appreciate my reaction to this, which was to gasp open-mouthed, unable to utter a sound for a good minute. The following day, the whole of my groin and upper thighs were black, but as I have gone on to have two children, I escaped the most extreme consequence of the slip, though you could not have convinced me thus in the immediate aftermath.

Halfway through the job, a lorry dumped a load of Yorkshire stone into the next field and I set about a week of stone dressing. This is basically using a hammer and chisel to break off the edges of the roughly hewn stone, making each one a relatively uniform size and shape that could then be used for building. Smacking a large chisel with a lump hammer is dull repetitive work, but it does give the satisfaction of hitting something hard, which appealed to my primitive urges. Unless you are an experienced dresser, it is also impossible not to suffer regular cramps in your hands and forearms. Due to the lactic acid build-up, at times my hands locked, or my forearms seized and I could not even pick up a much-needed cup of coffee.

The week I did this turned out to be one of the most glorious seen that summer. I, being English and thinking sun cream was for poofs (as they say in Yorkshire), took off my shirt and went about my business. By about ten o'clock that evening, my back was badly sunburned and had blistered all over. My sister Gwen, then a nurse, said they were akin to third-degree burns, but had no sympathy for me, rightly pointing out that it was my own stupid fault. Unfortunately for me, this coincided with what were then important training sessions and one game when I was trying to force my way into the Roundhay first team. The pain whilst scrummaging fortunately went after the blisters had rubbed raw, which took about twenty minutes. Prior to that, it was indescribable.

When the rugby season finished, I went to the most enjoyable job I had during my gap year. Well, not exactly the job, but the location, which was London, where I spent six weeks at the King Edward VII Hospital. My sister, Ai-Lien, was in charge of all the hospital support staff and wangled a job for me cleaning and doing general portering jobs. She also insisted that at work I call her Miss Moore, which went down really well with me.

At the same time a schoolfriend of mine, Tony Phillips, was working as general dogsbody at the Regent's Park Open Air Theatre, and living a bohemian life in Finsbury Park. The season's plays were *Androcles and the Lion* and the perennial and now seemingly compulsory *Midsummer Night's Dream*. That year, the principal actors were Kate O'Mara, the sultry siren of BBC's *Triangle*, and Gabrielle Drake, who inexplicably went on to do *Crossroads*, where she stood out as the only character who could act. They were gorgeous, and whenever we had any opportunity to hang about after performances where they too were lingering, we sat there and drooled from afar.

Many years later, I saw O'Mara in a play where she wore the most unfeasibly low-cut dress. In the row in front of me were about thirty French students who cheered wildly the first time she curtsied and, as she took her final curtain call and slyly looked up and then bent further forward, they stood to a man and whooped and whistled. Only my semi-erection prevented me joining them.

Tony later went on to study at the Bristol Old Vic, and went into repertory theatre. He is now head of commissioning for the BBC World Service and has won a number of awards for his radio programmes. One evening, he locked up the theatre and, as we were leaving, we were surrounded by police. We protested our innocence, and even though Tony had the number of the theatre manager and asked the police officers to call him to verify that he worked there and that I was his mate from up north, we were arrested and taken to Paddington Green Station. Over the next four hours, we were questioned separately. I was quoted the Queen's Rules, which preceded the Police and Criminal Evidence Act, and when I was manhandled I became stroppy. It was put to me that they had found the bar till jemmied open, which was a complete lie. I was asked sarcastically what a northern monkey was doing in a theatre, of all places. I replied that I was studying Shakespeare. 'He was a playwright, in case you haven't heard of him.' Not the best comment, but by this stage I was royally 'fucked off'. We were eventually released without charge. Why were we arrested? Tony is black, there could be no other reason. Racism for most people is something they read about and debate. When I was directly confronted with it, it was maddening; and for a long time this incident left me with a deep antipathy to the Met. This only changed years later when, as a solicitor, I worked closely with many officers on civil and malfeasance cases.

# 4

## Nottingham University

My school, having little Oxbridge experience, did not understand that advising me to apply to St John's College, Oxford, to do Politics, Philosophy and Economics (PPE) was not a good idea. As an academic college, any sporting prowess I might have had would probably be an impediment rather than a positive.

Though I passed the written exam without too much trouble, I knew after the first two questions of my interview that I was not going to do PPE at St John's.

The first conundrum was this: 'If God is omnipotent, can he create a rock that he cannot lift?' If asked this now, I might have a stab at talking about the paradox of omnipotence and logical absurdity. Back then, I was simply bemused. Whilst gibbering out something about double negatives I was thinking, 'I'm from Halifax and I play in the front row and, anyway, what would He want to be messing about with rocks for?'

The second question came in the form of this dilemma: 'Imagine you and two friends have been arrested. You are in the middle of three cells. The friend to your left, when questioned, will always lie. The friend in the cell to your right will always tell the truth. What do you do?'

For what seemed like an age to me, though was probably no more than an uncomfortable thirty seconds, I tried to think of anything that might sound sensible, and in the end I said, 'Can you ask me another question please because I feel I have an unfair advantage in answering this, as this has actually happened to me.'

They were sufficiently polite to carry out the rest of the interview, but I was not going to follow ex-alumnus Archbishop Laud and stalk the venerable cloisters of St John's.

My second choice had been Nottingham University to read law. The reason for choosing a 'proper' subject was based on nothing more than the fact that I used to watch the TV show *Crown Court*. I imagined that if I could not be a philosopher, I could hold forth in court. My mother also told me that, if I didn't get into Oxford, I should do a proper degree. Actually, I wish I had done history, which I really enjoyed and in which I am now taking a BA (Hons) with the Open University.

Candidates who put a university as their second choice are not usually successful in their application, especially when the university is one as highly regarded as Nottingham. In addition, it is unusual for applicants to be offered a place without interview, unless they are outstanding – which I wasn't. On top of this, the Nottingham law faculty is one of the best in the country and competition for places is keen.

I have no idea how this happened, but I was given an unconditional offer, without interview. At the time, I shrugged my shoulders and thought 'Great'. It was not until much later that I began to have an idea of how unusually lucky I had been. When the first-year law students assembled in the magnificent Trent Building, they were discussing their interviews and how difficult they had been. It seems that some of them had had to take a mock law paper that took an hour. The first time I told somebody that I had not even been interviewed and told them what A' levels I had, they looked so offended that I decided I wouldn't tell anyone else.

Nottingham has a fantastic campus, with fourteen halls of residence as well as the main student-union buildings. Each had its own bar and over the next three years I would become intimately acquainted with most of them.

The allocation to a particular hall is random, and I imagine that everybody claims they had the best deal. Sherwood Hall was a mixed hall and the intake over the three years prior to mine had earned the hall a reputation for, shall we say, eccentricity. I always find situations where I am thrown into the midst of strangers quite stressful and this was no exception. It did not help that I seemed to be in the quietest part of the hall, whilst the noise came from elsewhere. I later discovered this was a positive boon: you could create mayhem elsewhere and then disappear into relative obscurity.

The first week at university is a hive of activity. Nottingham's fresher's week is called Karnival, and stalls are set up in the union building to entice students to join various clubs and societies. If there is anything that interests you, the chances are there will be some sort of society to cater for you. I would go so far as to say that if you do not enjoy your days at university and make lifelong friends, then the fault is yours.

I was to spend little time in the Trent Building and even less in its magnificent law library, save for a frantic few weeks before each set of exams at the end of the year. It wasn't that I didn't get on with the other law students; rather, I never got to know them as I was there so little. My mates in hall seemed more fun. The law faculty had a competition for the best slogan for their faculty sweatshirts: the chosen words were 'Loitering within Trent'. My entry was 'Equity lawyers come with clean hands', which I thought was much more amusing.

Hard to believe, but there was someone more workshy than me: one of my friends, Andrew Denton, who went on to become a top construction lawyer. Nearly thrown out twice, he fell asleep in one of his exams and got bollocked for making up the case of Bilge v Corrigan [1977 1QB] that had the tutors spending hours trying to find the precedent.

The real benefit of being in a hall of residence was that your immediate social circle did not consist of only those on the same course. This meant my friends were from widely differing courses, from all ends of the country and of all social strata. There are too many stories to tell and most of them lose a lot in translation. You had to be there. However, there are a few that I remember fondly.

Over the years I had a number of mates who came to visit, including two notable visits by contemporary rugby players. Dylan Davis, a Loughborough prop mentioned later, came for a weekend. He turned up in a yellow TR7 on the evening of the university rugby-club annual dinner, to which he had invited himself. The meal was held at the Albany Hotel Carvery – 'all you can eat £9.99'. Davis signalled his, indeed our, intention to take full advantage of the stated terms under which we dined when, on his first visit to the meat counter, he picked up a whole roast chicken. In reasonably smart time, we proceeded to eat everything on offer but, typifying students, decided we must eat on. I asked the *maître d'* for more beef and he said he was sorry but we had eaten them out of house and home and they could not bring anything more. Although close to bursting, I countered with my vast first-hand knowledge of law, telling him that they were in breach of contract, having advertised 'all you can eat' and that we could indeed eat more. At this point, one of the second-team props vomited all over the serving station and I thought my argument lost a little weight, so I sat down.

I mention our following night's finale only because there is photographic evidence of our pointless behaviour and it reminds me that at some point I looked young. The 'who is hardest by eating the hottest curry' competition found three of us trying to ingest a curry that was bubbling crimson in colour and virtually impossible to eat. Neither Davis nor I would quit; the honour of our universities was at stake. We thus continued, each taking a mouthful so hot that even though we knew water would not help long-term, we had to almost shove our faces into the jug after each turn.

A similarly, if not more chaotic visit came from the then Leicester and RAF prop Martin Whitcombe, with whom I had played in the Yorkshire Schools under-nineteen team. Whitcombe, whose nickname was improbably 'Wimp', was basically an engaging madman. The stories about him are legion and not exaggerated.

On one Saturday evening in Nottingham, he managed to get me barred from my local pub and then my favourite curry house. As we looked for a taxi to get back to the hall, we managed to flag down a driver who kindly agreed to carry five of us, one more than the limit. As we approached Sherwood, one of our company started humming the Lindisfarne song 'Run for Home', a signal that a 'runner' was on. For the first time, I wasn't in agreement with this, principally because I was in the worst position: in the middle of the back seat and therefore last to get out. Nevertheless, I knew when the car stopped that they would be off in all directions.

Sure enough, everyone scattered, with me and Whitcombe ending up together. For some unknown reason the driver, justifiably angry, decided to chase us two rather than the smaller members of the group. More than once, Whitcombe said, 'Let's stop and chin him.' I disagreed and followed Whitcombe into one of the quads of the hall.

Locking ourselves in one of the bathrooms, we could hear the driver continuing his search of the hall and decided to exit via the small window in the bathroom. Whitcombe went first, and just after he got through the window, I heard a crash and a shout from below. I looked out and saw that beneath the window was a large bush and an eight-foot drop. I ignored Whitcombe's urges to follow him, not wanting to be possibly tipped on to my head into the bush. I said I would wait until the driver had left and go out by the conventional route.

I waited a couple of minutes and heard nothing, so I slowly opened the door, only to see the driver standing down the corridor. I went back in, thought I had locked the door, and made to climb through the small window. Unfortunately, the small bobble of the window bar that kept the window open caught on my jumper and stopped me from going through.

The door then burst open and the driver grabbed my legs and tried to pull me back. At the same time, Whitcombe grabbed my wrists and tried to pull me through. Seeing that I would fall head-first into the bush, I shouted at Martin to let me go and that I would pay the fare. He wasn't having any of this and yanked powerfully, propelling me into the bush. Fortunately I received nothing more than a few cuts and bruises.

In my final year I was elected hall president and went on to make little or no difference to the lot of the Sherwood student, but enjoyed myself hugely at the hall parties of the thirteen other halls on campus. Free tickets were obligatory for all hall presidents and I managed to embarrass myself spectacularly at one event by walking through the dining hall without pants and falling semi-conscious into some nearby bushes.

The real benefit of university is not the education, though that helps; it is the widening of your horizons. Meeting people from all over the country, from all classes and with widely differing views, takes you out of the smaller world that is school. When you hear and see what others have done or plan to do, things that you never thought possible suddenly seem routine.

I never complained about the cocoon of living in hall. Some hated the 'goldfish bowl' that allowed everyone to know your business, but having your meals cooked, no washing up, your room cleaned and bed made, were things I happily accepted. These luxuries were missed every time we broke up.

Unlike most students, I didn't go home to be looked after. Every vacation, as I had done before I started my law course, I worked shearing sheet metal at Exstock Ltd, owned by Nottingham supporter, Jim Helps. Starting at six in the morning and grafting until five-thirty put student life into sharp perspective. It was heavy work, but did my fitness no harm at all. After two weeks of shearing tons of steel, my belt could be fastened two notches further in and my overdraft had also been sizeably reduced.

It provided regular repeats of the lesson that, however dull I could pretend the lot of a student was, it was light years away from the genuinely debilitating boredom of hard manual labour; so stop feeling so bloody sorry for yourself. Doing factory work also made me realise what most people have to do to get by. There wasn't one person there who did not express a desire to leave, to do something less demanding, or something they had always dreamed of. Hardly anyone did leave. When I went back several years later, the same faces clocked in and out.

The story of one guy illustrates the point I made earlier about further education expanding your horizons. Steve worked as the delivery-lorry driver. He had been in the army, where he had gained his HGV qualification and, though not academic, was no fool. Unlike most of his co-workers, he did not endlessly speculate about what he would do if he won the pools (pre-Lottery). He used to engage me in discussions about current affairs, sport, in fact anything that came to mind.

I lent him A. J. P. Taylor's *Origins of the Second World War*, which he read quickly and remembered more accurately than some of my friends who were doing history degrees. I urged him to do a degree. He was single, lived at home, and only his lack of formal qualifications stood in his way. I explained that, given the right approach, many colleges would overlook his lack of paperwork if he demonstrated life skills and eagerness. He said he would think about it.

When we talked about travel, he spoke fondly of his time in Germany with his regiment. However, he didn't dwell on the piss-ups, the fights and so on; he talked about his views on Germany as a country, the people, and in particular their struggles with the legacies of defeat in 1945. I said he should go on a gap year and see where it took him. He said he would think about it.

I worked there, on and off, for four years and all the while he thought about it. He said he was worried about whether he would have a job when he got back, what about all his mates, how would he organise it? I told him he had an HGV Class 1 licence, he would never be out of work; his mates would still all be here when he got back and I knew people who would help him whatever path he chose.

When I revisited for the last time, he was still there. Had he gone to college, he would have mixed with students who had travelled. He would have seen that, whilst there were very bright people around, there were some dullards as well; and none with a right to judge themselves better than him.

The university had a well-organised programme of inter-hall competitive sport on Wednesday afternoons. This was important for the many that were not good enough to play for university teams in their sport, but wanted to play meaningful games. Meanwhile, I started playing for the university first XV on Wednesdays, as well as for Nottingham on Saturdays. I had to stop this because it was too much and I seemed to get injured in student games. One of the more embarrassing injuries, which kept me out for three weeks, was when I badly twisted my ankle when landing on the supporting base of a netball goal in a 'boys v girls' charity game. Looking back, the injuries could have been caused by the accumulation of games. Alternatively, it could have been over-training, in particular, attending the early Friday evening, 200-strong, mixed aerobic class, containing what can only be described as an unfeasible number of stunning women in tight, short, Lycra gym kit. In summer they wore even less.

I played football for Sherwood Hall and in my first year played in the five-a-side team that won the university's open competition. All the other players had once played, or did at the time play, semi-professionally.

I believe Nottingham now has a better record in UAU (Universities Athletics Union) national competitions, but when I was there it was not a powerful force, though it did produce the odd notable sportsperson. However, my time at university coincided with a number of other student rugby players who were above average for a Nottingham intake. John Ward played prop for the England Under 23s; Nick George had played for Yorkshire Schools; two of the other forwards had played for Wales at schoolboy level.

In my final year, the university team won the Notts, Lincs and Derby Three Counties Cup. This competition was satisfying, not just for the win, but for the blow we struck for student rugby, which regularly has to endure student-bashing when the opponents are local junior clubs. A cup game against Mellish RFC, situated in a mining part of Nottinghamshire, began with the usual pasting being handed out to student players on the floor, whether they were near the ball or not. Having been a past recipient, this time I called together what was quite a streetwise pack by student standards. I made it plain I was not going to take this and demanded we fought our ground. For the rest of the game we actually bullied an open-age pack, at one point pushing them over from a five-yard scrum, whilst I commented, saying something approximating (and I paraphrase), 'Are you finding this instant pleasurable, you anthology of procreating illegitimates?' After the game, Mellish complained to the Three Counties Committee about our rough play. Oh, the irony.

That same year, the university team also reached the UAU final at Twickenham, losing to Loughborough. After beating a Durham University team containing Mark Bailey and Francis Clough in the semi-final, we did what most people dream of, if in slightly different circumstances: we played at HQ, Twickenham. That the RFU allow many levels of the game to play their respective final games on the same pitch as their heroes is laudable. It means a great deal to anyone who has had the experience, and for nearly all it is the only occasion on which they will ever do this. This does not happen in many other sports, but for the stated reason it should be allowed where possible.

The Loughborough team contained some names that are familiar to all rugby fans: Andy Robinson, Dave Egerton, Steve

Burnhill and others who played at lower England levels. They were better than us and, although it was a good enough effort, we were never really in a position to win. This was not the point for many of the supporters from Nottingham, many of whom were football followers and our supporters for that one occasion. For this reason some of the singing – well, chanting, really – was different from 'Swing Low, Sweet Chariot', though it betrayed its educational element throughout. Particular favourites seemed to be 'We've got more A' levels than you'; 'You can't join your letters up', and 'You can stick your fucking purple [the colour of every piece of clothing worn by a Loughborough sports jock] up your arse'.

One of my friend Andrew Holmes's proudest sporting moments was mooning at the RFU Committee box from the halfway line, whilst inside it a flustered Athletic Union Secretary tried to make distracting small talk. It didn't cause as much controversy as I thought it might; then again, what was seeing another arse to most of the Committee?

To be honest, the amount of work I did to obtain a 2:2 degree was disgracefully little. I joke about majoring in plagiarism and photocopying, but it is not far from being accurate. What this idleness proved is that you actually don't have to be super-bright to be a lawyer; all that is needed is being thorough.

Just a few weeks before my final exams, I received a letter from the RFU telling me that I was first-reserve hooker for the England tour to South Africa. This was a total shock to me – though obviously thrilling – as I had not even played at England B level at the time (although, as I explain in a later chapter, I was already playing for the Under 23s). The problem was that, if I was called up, it would be at the same time as I was meant to sit my final exams.

The political situation was also a concern, although the intense pressure to exclude South Africa from international sport was to get far greater over the next ten years. There was vocal opposition to any touring team, but then, as now, I did not believe that sport should be singled out as a convenient scapegoat for politicians to pretend they were taking action. I therefore went to the head of the law faculty, Professor J. C. Smith, a brilliant academic who almost single-handedly wrote the 1968 law-of-theft statutes. I explained my dilemma to him and asked him if I could delay my exams in the event of a call-up. I did not ask to miss them, just to take them later. Without much consideration he said no. He told me that law was what I was at the university to study and it must come first. I told him that I was disappointed and that I thought he was being very shortsighted, but he did not alter his stance.

He asked me what I would do if I got the call-up. I told him that I would go, saying that anybody could study law and in fact you didn't even have to be that clever to be a lawyer, but to play for your country was something very few achieved. His reaction was not one of anger at what some might have deemed an arrogant rant; it was something I did not expect – indifference. He was not uncaring. Rather, I believe, sport was so far from his academic world that he could not see that what I sought was the equal of what I studied.

Luckily I did not get the call, because that tour was a disaster, with England losing all the Tests badly. Many of the players never played representative rugby again. Another slice of luck: when not playing in a team was better than playing.

Years later, after and because I had played for England, the law faculty asked me to go back and speak at a fundraising event. Naturally, they did not invite me for my standing in the legal world, and thus I felt my comments to Professor Smith had been vindicated.

At that time I also made decisions about my legal future that were dictated by rugby. I wanted to stay playing for Nottingham but I had also intended to become a barrister. Not because I knew anything about being one, but because I pictured myself as a great advocate, winning cases that were seemingly unwinnable. Fortunately, I was the recipient of sound career advice from the clerk of a set of local chambers, Michael Churm of Ropewalk Chambers. This was the set to which I would have applied for pupilage (traineeship).

He invited me to lunch and began by saying that, from what he had heard from barristers in his set, I was reasonably tenacious and might have the makings of a counsel. He said that he would be prepared to offer me a pupilage with the sole caveat that I agreed not to try and play any rugby above the level of the Nottingham first XV. He waited for my response, already knowing my answer, but nevertheless wanting me to articulate it. I told him that he knew that I could not promise that, to which he replied, 'Do you know what you will have to do to become a successful barrister?'

He then asked whether my family had money or a legal background. When I replied they had neither, he told me what his pupils and juniors who were in a similar position had to do to be successful. As barristers are self-employed, they only earn when they work; they cannot offload work on to colleagues. Furthermore, many barristers wait years, yes years, for their fees to be paid by instructing solicitors. Even when they become more senior, their workload increases without them being able to use a team to do the mundane work. For the first five years they work without holidays, trying to build a practice, travelling wherever their briefs dictate. They are self-reliant and it is attritional.

He finished by asking me what I would do if I received a brief to appear in Cardiff Crown Court tomorrow and I was also asked to go to an England Under 23 training session. I didn't need to answer and he went on to explain that, having turned down that brief, I would be unlikely to receive any further instructions from that firm, and once word got round, even unfairly, that I was more concerned with my rugby career than the law, others would not instruct me. I decided to become a solicitor.

This left the problem of where to do my law Part II exams. I had already secured a place at Gray's Inn, where I would have taken the barrister's equivalent exams (which are considerably easier), but I now wanted to go to Trent Polytechnic in Nottingham, which had a very good reputation for teaching this solicitor's course. This was because, unlike the colleges of law, they were selective about their intake and admitted far fewer applicants. I found out later that I had been 500th on the waiting list for a place but rugby connections twisted enough arms to secure me one.

Only halfway into the course, the worst fears of the tutors appeared to be confirmed by my poor attendance record and test results. I expected the course to be an extension of what I had gone through at university. When they had a roll call for my first lecture, I looked round to see if anyone else found this odd. They didn't. When I learned that they had compulsory tests every two weeks, I was staggered. I had always got by with last-minute cramming of information and an ability to regurgitate this on to an exam paper in reasonably cogent form and then forget it as quickly as it had been learned. I was utterly unfamiliar with continual assessment and didn't take to it at all.

Nearly every other person on the course worked very hard and some for good reason: whilst I saw the course as just another step on a programmed course to becoming a lawyer, there were some people who had given up jobs to change their career; some had families that were supporting them through this process. For these people it wasn't even a semi-joke.

One of the things I found tedious was the endless learning of time limits, formats and other administrative facts. When I later got into practice, these were available in a book and could be looked up quickly. The ignorance of a particular fact was then easily rectified. Of far more use would have been the things we were not taught, like tactical approaches to cases and how to deal with other solicitors in correspondence so that you did not inadvertently concede something. They later revised the course substantially and eliminated a lot of the rote learning.

Although my attendance was uniformly poor across the subjects, there was one lecture that I missed more than any other. The Friday 2 p.m. lecture on criminal law by Michael O'Connell coincided with the time when I and my contemporaries all went for a drink and usually stayed until a bit later. O'Connell was an entertaining lecturer and a rugby fan. When he clocked one of my rare visits to his lecture, he looked up and said, 'Ah, Brian Moore. Do you know, I have paid more times to watch you than you have watched me for free?'

My course tutor, Bob White, was obviously one of those who had had his ear bent to admit me and also one who disagreed with the decision. I couldn't blame him. Halfway through the year, he pulled me to one side and asked me to consider leaving the course: I was obviously not committed to it and was almost certainly going to fail; by which he meant I would not pass at least six of the seven exam heads first time. If you did not do this, you had to retake all seven; if you got six, they allowed you to re-sit the paper you failed.

He reinforced his view by saying that their department statistics proved conclusively that students who regularly came in the top 50 per cent in their regular tests went on to pass first time. Those in the other half, especially those near the bottom 25 per cent, almost always failed at least two heads. I was wasting my own time and theirs. I protested, like a smartarse, by saying that every student couldn't come in the top half and what if it happened that one year all students were good enough to pass; there would still be a bottom 50 per cent because it was relative to the other results, whereas the exam pass mark was fixed. This was actually true, but we both knew the point he was making and that he was right.

I refused to leave and did the usual cramming.

When it came to the exams I approached them with a relaxed attitude. Unfortunately, those to whom they meant the most often turned out to be students who tried to learn absolutely everything mentioned at any point in all the lectures and tutorials and who fretted inordinately before each test. Having done so, you can imagine their mental state immediately before the actual exams. In some cases, this hyper-tense environment affected them so badly that they did not do themselves justice and failed.

In retrospect, it was probably cruel of me to have emulated Andy Denton by inventing what I claimed to be an important civil-law case and letting my tutorial group fret further still when they couldn't find it.

I passed all seven heads first time. I found out about this in a call I received from my university friend David Bradley, now the managing partner of a huge global firm, who had gone to his local train station to get the earliest edition of the paper that carried the results. He said that he had some good news: he had passed all heads. He asked if I wanted some more good news. I said I did, and he told me I had done likewise. He then asked if I wanted some unbelievable news and, when I agreed, he told me our mutual friend, Chris Stansfield, now a partner in a national firm, had done the same. This last fact amazed both of us because 'Rooster' had been even lazier than me and had actually fallen asleep in his company-law exam.

The next day, as I smugly strolled down the corridor, my course tutor Bob White passed me and, without stopping, he whispered out of the corner of his mouth, 'You lucky, lucky bastard.' Once again, he was right.

# 5

## A Legal Career

I never gave much consideration to my law career. The fact that I had chosen to study the subject at university was based on the flimsiest of grounds. Nevertheless, a law degree is a useful degree in many ways, applicable tangentially to all manner of careers in addition to a career as a lawyer; to that extent, it was an inadvertently sound choice.

Having been set on a legal road, it is no exaggeration to say that my subsequent career came from a combination of two things. Firstly, at a time when important decisions had to be made about my employment, I was so focused on furthering my rugby career that I did not consider alternatives seriously. Secondly, when I got on to the legal conveyer belt, the next steps were so clearly laid out that they subsumed me and I ended up blithely reaching for the next step, without actually thinking about whether I really wanted to go in that direction.

After passing my Part II solicitors' exams in 1985, I was taken into articles, now called traineeship, with a local Nottingham firm, Messrs Huntsmans. It was a small firm specialising in plaintiff civil litigation, much of it for large trade unions. My Principal was

Mike France and I will always be grateful for his kindness, but in truth he gave me far too much latitude and too little supervision for someone of my limited/non-existent experience.

In articles, I had to do a number of disparate areas of law (called 'seats'), the aim being that I would gain some all-round experience and have some indication of what area I might choose when I qualified. Most students rightly take as much trouble in selecting the firms to which they apply as do the firms in interviewing and choosing them. I simply took the first offer to come my way, it being an offer that came through rugby.

In the end, my subsequent career in litigation was one that was always going to suit me, but it came about by accident and should not have done so had I shown proper care in what I was doing.

I did my conveyancing seat and nothing about it remotely interested me. The only modicum of mirth that ever came out of the subject was when ex-law student John Brain, the former Gloucester lock and later successful coach, was training with me at an Under 23 session. Having caught one in the balls, he rolled around shouting, 'Oh, my fee simples.' See what hilarity you can have through law.

I did my other seats in family law, crime and then civil litigation. The areas of family and crime are ones that are immediately attractive but only because they are naturally comprehensible: the issues and facts are real, not abstract. This is not the case with company law or other more esoteric areas like property, tax and, God forbid, pensions and the like. I duly sat in on interviews in the office, in the cells, outside court, and sometimes attended the police stations and nearby prisons on my own to take statements. It felt like worthwhile work and at the time I did not see it for the circus it was. That would come soon enough.

With civil litigation, I visited factories and attended 'surgeries' at various union branches dotted throughout Nottinghamshire and Lincolnshire. I suppose it's the case with any food that is mass-produced, but seeing chickens and biscuits under mass production was so vile that it has given me a distaste for anything other than properly organic meat as well as a dread of Garibaldi biscuits.

Whilst sitting behind counsel in a criminal trial, I experienced the most extraordinary behaviour from an advocate. My client was a middle-aged black woman, charged with drug-dealing. It was obvious to me and ultimately to the court that, whilst her house had been used for dealing and she had been caught in possession of drugs, she was not the dealer, but was too frightened to name the person who was. I had instructed a good criminal barrister from local chambers, but was told by the client, who had in turn had it suggested to her, that I should instruct a black counsel from London. Over the next five days, this new counsel was theatrical, denouncing racism, tearing up exhibits, and during breaks lecturing me about Afro–Caribbean culture. In my view he should have paid more attention to the presentation of the case than his sermons.

When I qualified, I wanted to stay with the firm, but for some reason they prevaricated, and I accepted a job in a small Newark firm, which I should not have done; but the eventual offer from Huntsmans came late and I felt it would not be honourable to go back on my word. Thus, I started as a general practitioner and soon found myself out of my depth. In retrospect, the fault was partly mine: having vowed during articles never to touch land law, I found that in a small market town it was an inevitable part of my workload. Furthermore, I had to do probate and other tedious subjects and, in line with previous subjects that I did not take to, I did not take enough care.

On the other hand, it was ludicrous to expect a newly qualified solicitor to take on such a wide range of subjects and, in most firms, detailed supervision would be given for up to two or three years after qualification. Moreover, even then, law had become so complex that it was impossible for anyone to be sufficiently skilled in multiple areas of it. I believe that, today, a lawyer would be doing well to master properly two different and unconnected areas, never mind six or seven.

There is nothing remotely interesting to report from my year and a half in Newark, apart from the incident that brought to a halt any ideas I had about specialising in criminal law. I had appeared in the magistrates' courts and even conducted a couple of very low-key trials, which I thoroughly enjoyed, although I cannot vouch for the magistrates' bench that sat through them. I also enrolled, as did all the other Newark lawyers in this area, as part of the duty solicitor's scheme. For those unfamiliar with this social service, it is meant to afford all those in custody the ability to consult a lawyer about their detention and matters surrounding their arrest and possible charging; it is made available twenty-four hours a day.

One night, I was on call and was rudely awoken with a call from the Newark police station. It was 4 a.m. Not surprisingly, I was not full of the joys of spring, but I duly drove to the station. On speaking to the custody sergeant, I was told that the person who asked for a lawyer was in custody with two others. They were suspected of doing a number of house burglaries near the A1 and they hailed from Merseyside.

I went down to the cell and introduced myself to the detainee. I then started to explain the offences of which he was suspected and that I was the duty solicitor. I was utterly taken aback when the youth simply said, 'Who the fuck are you?' Quelling the surge of anger that instantly leapt up inside me, I began again, only for him to say, 'Fuck off, I don't want you, I want my brief. My brief is on his way.'

I left the cell and returned to the custody sergeant and asked if the youth or any of his co-detainees had made any calls. He said no and that, when the youth I had seen had mentioned a lawyer, they had called me, thinking he was referring to the duty solicitor. I told him that the youth had just told me his brief was on the way. The sergeant told me that was impossible. Back I went to the cell and confronted the youth with this fact and asked him how his brief could be on his way. He just said, 'Fuck off, I don't want to speak to you.' Professionally, I should not have done this, but I am glad

I did, and actually as a normal citizen I now wish I had gone further: I grabbed the lad by the throat and pinned him against the cell wall, leaning forward to say, 'Don't you ever speak to me like that again, you little cunt.' He lost his swagger and simply blubbed, 'I don't mean to be rude, I just want my own brief.'

Sure enough a few hours later, his solicitor appeared. I asked him how he knew about the arrest and he claimed that his client had called him. I didn't use these precise words, but I told him I profoundly doubted his story, given that I had verified that his client had made no calls. He told me to mind my own business and I did wonder at the time whether or not to repeat the actions I had earlier visited on his client, but decided not to. In truth, this episode had left a sour taste for many reasons.

During the subsequent bail applications, it became clear that the three suspects were an organised team of burglars. It did not become clear how the solicitor turned up, but it certainly was not for the reason claimed. It may be that another member of the gang, unapprehended, had called and requested his presence; it could have been pre-arranged for him to set off if he hadn't got a call by a certain time. Whatever the truth was, none of it reflected well on that solicitor. For me, I realised that, to these people, it was simply a game. They did not have any remorse or care a jot about their victims, and whilst I would willingly help the vulnerable or those making a mistake that they regretted, I would not and could not be part of this charade.

I left Newark in 1988 and joined a much larger firm, then called Browne, Jacobson and Rouse, in Nottingham. This was the start of my civil-litigation career, which lasted more or less for the rest of my time in law, bar the final three years. Given the right supervision and then independence, I progressed to become comfortable with the work and enjoyed what was basically stylised arguing all day. That suited me fine.

During my time with the firm, I was to play for England and the British Lions. They were supportive and gave me the time I needed out of the office for training sessions, games and tours –

not insubstantial when it came to a Lions tour. People often said to me that I must have had very good employers to have got all that time off, and indeed they were. If it had not been for the munificence of such firms, none of the England team could have played to the level they did; a fact completely ignored by the RFU, who later refused me permission to wear a training top with the name of my firm on it. The RFU didn't even make provision for a couple of tickets to go to our employers as a thank-you. We were told that if we wanted to take care of them, we must do so out of our own ticket allocation.

However, in response to the question about time off, I always add this point: whilst I was given the time off, I was not given a discounted budget and had to earn the same fees as other people of similar qualification. Therefore, whilst I was given the time away, I never went to my employers and said that I was 25 per cent under budget but this was because of rugby and did they mind? I remember being in the lift at work and on the way to another international when someone made a remark along the lines of 'Off to play again?' I was keyed up for the coming weekend and for this reason didn't make light of the jibe. Turning round, I said, 'First of all, none of your business, but anyway, we have the same budgets so if I'm away for six extra weeks this year and still bill the same as you, what the fuck are you doing all day?' Blunt, but fair.

Although I liked the firm and made good progress as a lawyer, I decided to move from Nottingham to London for various reasons. When I moved, with the help of Roger Looker, the chairman of Harlequins, I joined Rea Brothers in their corporate-finance department. They were a good firm and I got plenty of time off to train and play, but my move was in the middle of what was then the worst post-war recession. Deals were not being done, and I and many others of junior rank were left with little to do. In any event, it became obvious to me fairly early on that the job was far more suited to those with an accountancy, rather than a legal, background.

I therefore set about going back to law, and through Edwin Glasgow QC joined a small firm called Edward Lewis and Co. When I joined, it had five partners and about twenty staff; when I left, it had twenty-six partners and over 200 staff. It was a firm poised to take off and I had accepted a seat at the right time. I enjoyed nearly all of my time at Edward Lewis. Within eighteen months, I was made a salaried partner. Within five years, I made equity, though it was ironic that on the day of my ascension I was thousands of miles away in South Africa, playing in the 1995 World Cup.

Edward Lewis specialised in defendant insurance litigation and, for a firm of its size, handled tremendously advanced cases, both in terms of their value and complexity. The three highest claims one year all came to the firm, although they were not handled by me personally. I had an interesting and challenging caseload, and eventually had a team of solicitors working under me. I moved through straight personal injury to professional negligence, policy wording and general insurance matters. A couple of my cases are still precedents from the Court of Appeal and I helped with a huge class of litigation that eventually had its lead case go to the House of Lords. It involved the everyday topics of champerty and maintenance (illegal financing of litigation by a non-participant), the details of which I will not bore you with.

I will take the time, however, to relate my experience of sitting behind counsel in what was then the highest court in the land, the House of Lords, because it was not at all what I, and probably many people, would imagine it to be. The first thing that struck me was the fact that the Law Lords did not appear gowned: they wore a suit and tie. Instead of the usual raised bench, which in the Court of Appeal presents a formidable platform from which the appellate judges look down on the advocates and all else, there was a horseshoe-shaped table around which sat five Law Lords, not three as in the Court of Appeal. The advocate stood in the middle of the horseshoe to deliver his submissions and they bombarded him with questions. Whatever is said about these men (for they were all men when we appeared) – how they are out of touch, how they are all Oxbridge, white and middle, nay, upper class – they are all incredibly intelligent. At times, it was clear they were playing with the advocates, asking questions to probe the intellect and to satisfy their own curiosity. I doubt whether many arguments are put to them that they have not anticipated.

For an advocate, it is a terrifying experience for many reasons. However, one reason must stand near the top of any list of terrors. In the House of Lords, there exists the very real possibility of an advocate presenting a case, only to find that one of the Law Lords they are facing was the architect of that particular piece of legislation. Normally, legal argument involves using the facts of a case, the relevant legislation and the relevant case law, wherein the statutory framework is interpreted. Advocates present a combination of these to try and persuade the court that their client has right on their side. Case law is voluminous and constantly shifting, as recent decisions clarify, confirm and even reverse earlier case precedents. There is also a pecking order with decisions: House of Lords; Court of Appeal; high court; county court; a bit like ace, king, queen, jack. The advocate usually refers to a case and then goes on to state what the decision meant and how it is relevant to his case. Although this sounds straightforward, it is not, because judgements often lack precision, sometimes purposely so. Usually when advocates cite a case in support, they do so knowing that the judges can disagree with their interpretation. But in the House of Lords, they face the prospect – precisely as happened with us – of one of their interlocutors saying, 'Ah yes, that was one of mine and I didn't intend that construction at all,' which is fairly difficult to argue against.

To face this brick wall must be terrifying, yet all the advocates in our case – Edwin Glasgow QC in particular – were sufficiently skilled to continue their address whilst frantically thinking of a way to restart their direction of attack. This was also done in the face of the Law Lords continuing to press them for clarification or explanation of their reasons for asserting the erroneous interpretation of the case in the first place.

We lost, by the way. But as with all lawyers, we won where it counts: in the pocket.

Towards the end of my time at Edward Lewis, I won a tender to work for the Commissioner of Police of the Metropolis, or the 'Met' as it's commonly known. Initially, I defended claims made by the police force against the Commissioner as an employer, but later I also defended officers in cases of malfeasance.

These jobs were very interesting, as they involved learning about police structures, training, procedures, riot control and the like. It also brought me into contact with many officers, and I have to say that my attitude towards them and the police force in general, which prior to this had been fairly jaundiced, changed markedly. The subsequent finding of the Macpherson Report that they were institutionally racist was a travesty and politically motivated. Yes, there were racists in the police. I came across some of them. There were unpleasant officers, but no more than if you took any random cross-section of any large organisation. You can argue that even the presence of a normal percentage of 'bad apples' cannot be tolerated in the police force, but that is a different argument, and certainly not one that supports the finding of institutional racism and wider bad behaviour.

What became apparent to me was the reality of what the police force is asked to do and the constraints within which it works. At the age of eighteen, officers are sent out on to the streets to face anything that is thrown at them. Their conduct is expected to be of the highest standard, and behaviour that many people would claim was justified if they were under similar scrutiny can suddenly become the subject of a complaint, sometimes maliciously so. Yet, at eighteen, can you honestly say you were sufficiently mature to deal with assault, death, rape and the like? I certainly was not.

I once got into an argument at a dinner party – surprising, I know – with a left-wing woman who spewed anti-police bile without qualification. I asked her if she minded me asking her a few candid questions, and she said that, being open-minded, she had no problem with that. It turned out she mistook open-mindedness for an ability to debate eclectically, and in fact she very much had a problem with questions that challenged what she believed to be ineluctable truths.

She had been banging on about police brutality at an arrest that had been in the news, and the fact that it appeared one officer had struck a person who was on the floor. This, she said, was indefensible: even if that person had been a threat, they were no longer so when down. I asked her if, when she set out for work, she had ever thought that she might be assaulted that day in the course of her job, or had ever entertained the possibility that she might die. 'Don't be ridiculous.' I went on to ask whether she had ever been in a public fight. I meant a proper all-out battle. She had not. I told her that I had, and it was a terrifying experience and one where my overriding instinct was to finish it as soon as I could, so that the threat, which was real and potentially injurious, was removed as quickly as possible.

When a person goes to ground, the first thing is to make sure they do not get up. And police officers have no way of knowing whether that person is going to draw a knife or, worse, a firearm and use it on them. I reminded her that it only took one miscalculation and the officer could be killed; a family destroyed, a widow left without a husband, and children without a father. At this, she simply snorted in derision, at which point I admit I became angry because the reality was that however much she tried to dehumanise the police, most of them are ordinary family men and women, doing a job – I pointed out – that she could certainly never do. At this, she exploded, accusing me of belittling her and of saying that she wasn't intelligent enough to do the job; neither of which I had said or done. I then pointed out that her reaction to simple questions round a dinner table had driven her to a state of rage. Given the pressures faced every day by every officer, she would never be able to remain calm. She then tried her best to be gentleness itself, but the point had been made and we both knew it.

As well as doing work for the Met, I also began to handle cases in an area now called sports law, although strictly speaking there is no such thing; it is merely conventional disciplines with a sporting context. Over time, I managed to get a sufficiently good reputation to be mentioned in the 'recommended' category for sports lawyers in *Chambers Legal*, the *Egon Ronay Guide* of law.

I eventually left Edward Lewis a matter of months before it dissolved. Normally, dissolution of a law firm is caused by a lack of work and profitability. Edward Lewis must be one of the few firms to dissolve when it was making very good money. In the end, the firm had grown haphazardly and was badly managed by a man who was an unpleasant egomaniac and who had several sexual harassment suits brought against him, many of which the general partnership were never told about. A band of sole practitioners finally refused to work together, even though it meant each partner losing a lot of money. I lost over £250,000 in retained capital. With better stewardship, the firm could have been a leading practice within its niche area of law. It could have been highly profitable, but inadequate management and a stubborn refusal by the partners to realise what was in their best interests made this impossible. A sad end.

# 6

## Nottingham RFC

Before I went up to Nottingham to read law, back in 1982, Tony Biscombe, the Roundhay coach, recommended me to the Nottingham coach, A. B. C. Davies (known as ABCD to all who knew him). Alan later told me that I came with the following glowing tribute: 'You've got a good 'un there – if you can just keep him on the pitch.' ABCD was to teach me much in my nine years at Nottingham, including how to channel my potentially ruinous aggression. For that, and so much else, I am irredeemably indebted to him.

I had gone up to Nottingham six weeks before the other students to take part in the Nottingham RFC pre-season training and trials. Arriving in a university town without its compliment of students is usually a ghostly experience. It should have been the same in 1982 because, between them, Nottingham University and Trent Polytechnic swelled the population by around 25,000 during termtime. However, because Nottingham deservedly had a reputation for great nightlife, it always attracted huge numbers of people from outlying districts and towns, and was never less than lively. Pitching into this atmosphere on my own was a little daunting, but I knew why I was there.

I knew none of the players when I attended the first training session. I was aware that John Elliott, one of the club's more successful hookers, had moved down the road to play for Leicester. John later went on to be involved in the RFU set-up in a number of roles, including the arduous role of England's sevens manager, which entailed spending weeks in Third World backwaters like Hong Kong, Fiji, Dubai, many of which carry the constant threat of kidnap and torture for England rugby managers. A tough job.

The hooking berth was to be contested between me and the other Nottingham regular Steve Varley, then and still a leading criminal-law solicitor in Nottingham. It was to be easier to oust him than John Gill at Roundhay. Whilst Steve was technically good, he would be the first to admit that he wasn't a killer; unlike some of his clients. Moreover, I was beginning to get much stronger and was very fit. These attributes, along with my far greater desire, saw me make the first team very quickly. He later confided that his first impression of my slightly psychotic approach to competition reminded him more of his clients than of a prospective law student.

In the early 1980s, Nottingham was starting to have more success against established sides. It had previously been a midweek or Friday night fixture for senior clubs. Though it took a few years to completely remove itself from that tier of rugby, Nottingham was to develop over the next ten years into a team that could, on its day, match any club, though it would never permanently break into the top tier of English club rugby.

My arrival at the club coincided with, or was shortly augmented by, a number of other young and talented players. The first few training sessions were indications of what was apparent to some, that Nottingham would not remain in the backwaters of Midlands rugby for much longer. The list of international players who played at Nottingham around the same time as me will surprise most people. In addition to me, Simon Hodgkinson, Gary Rees, Chris Gray, Chris Oti, Rob Andrew, Neil Back and Neil Mantell won caps, and Steve Holdstock, Peter Cook, Gary Hartley,

Richard Moon, Simon Hughes and Harvey Thorneycroft were all on the fringes of full international honours.

Before recounting rugby matters, I have to mention the special atmosphere that developed during my time at the club. I am certain that other players will have similar claims for the club at which they played, but I remain convinced that Nottingham was different. As a lot of the squad had arrived when young and had grown together, coupled with the fact that many were students or former students, a mixture of sarcasm, satire, cruelty and intelligence ran through the club's sense of humour. To tolerate that level of personal maliciousness, any group has to be intimate. It is not possible to be casually and humorously spiteful to somebody to whom you are either hostile or indifferent.

So merciless was the pursuit of any gaffe that sometimes nobody would speak for fear of saying something that would attract a barrage of ridicule. To step into this sort of environment must have been daunting for a new player, but they either sank or swam. Harvey Thorneycroft, in particular, found the adjustment an ordeal. Mind you, he didn't help himself with some of the incidents that occurred within a short time of his arrival. Turning up for a game, only to discover that he had brought his book bag but no kit, was bound to provoke mild derision. It got so bad at one point that he unwisely confided in one of the more poisonous of our number, confessing that he thought everyone at the club hated him. He was assured that this was not the case, only to find his confession the source of further good-natured mocking when he returned to the bar.

Though there was talent at the club, experience could, necessarily, not be obtained by any short cut. The first few years I played in the Nottingham pack, we had a mixture of honest junior club players and students; we struggled against mature packs. Often in retreat and without seeing the ball before the put-in, the early years taught me a great deal about how to manufacture a way, any way, to scrape back my own ball when under the severest pressure. This proving ground no longer exists because of the way the game has allowed itself to develop and, as anyone who went through it will agree, it was simultaneously hellishly difficult, but very satisfying.

One Friday night fixture was at Kingsholm, the home of Gloucester RFC. It was the first time I had played against the 'Cherry and Whites', and playing in their front five that night were Gordon Sergeant, Steve Mills, Phil Blakeway, John Fiddler and Steve Boyle. Those people from Gloucester who can read and are reading this will now have an evil grin spreading across their face. For those of you who have little familiarity with rugby, the footballing equivalent would be a back four of Tommy Smith, Jack Charlton, Ron 'Chopper' Harris and Stuart 'Psycho' Pearce.

Everybody has a selection of utterances that belong in the column headed 'Things I wish I had not said'. In the second scrum of the game, Fiddler sent a punch through that landed right on the middle of my nose. There is a point on your nose that, if struck soundly, makes your eyes involuntarily pour with water and he, purposely or by fortune, connected perfectly. I know not to this day why the following words came forth. I can only conclude they were the result of a dangerous combination of student arrogance and mental illness, but I said, 'Is that the best you can fucking do?' As the scrum broke up, he hit me again, twice, and I thought, 'My God, no, it isn't.'

This prefaced another embarrassing event, this time during a Saturday fixture at the same Gloucester ground. At the third line-out of the game, I found myself in front of the notorious Shed. This is a bank of standing supporters that runs the length of the far touchline. It is famous for its wit and appreciation of good, hard, honest rugby; indeed it is amazing how much noise 3,000 people and 7,000 hands can make.

As I prepared to throw the ball, a shout came from a man in the crowd. 'Moore, you're a wanker.' Not especially observant, I thought, but this was repeated whenever I came near the man and it went on for the whole game. On the coach journey back home this began to exercise me a great deal. I fumed quietly, thinking,

'I'm not having this. I'm a bloody law student. These people are all mutants.' I determined that if this was ever repeated, I would have an appropriate retort ready.

Sure enough, the following year it happened again, though it started at the second lineout. 'Moore, you're a wanker.' Turning round and affecting the most condescending voice I could muster, I replied, 'Yes, but at least I have to hold mine in both hands.' I turned back to get on with my task, whereupon, and within a split second, this response came, 'That's 'cos you're a fucking thalidomide, Moore.' Outwitted by a Gloucester mutant; I should have killed myself there and then.

Those early seasons also saw Nottingham invited to many of the Border Sevens tournaments held in Scotland at the start of the season. Having played all bar one year as a back at school, and being fit, I played a lot of sevens and enjoyed it. Although the tournaments were ludicrously tiring, Selkirk, Jedburgh and Kelso were charming small towns – though not Hawick, where later one of our props got his face slashed with a Stanley knife.

I cannot now be categorical, but I think it was at Selkirk where the other invited English team were Rosslyn Park. At the time, they were a famous London club and had produced many international and British Lions players. Their squad that weekend included Andy Ripley, Neil Mantell, Rad Montgomery and Chris Anderson. They were acknowledged sevens experts.

When we came down to the Friday evening dinner in the small hotel, we found ourselves sitting on adjacent tables. The only notable feature of the establishment was the collection of Chianti bottles that had been assembled by the owner and that proudly lined the side of the small bar. The distinguishing feature of these bottles was that they had progressively longer necks; from the usual stubby top, to one that was a good three feet to its tip.

Our squad included several young players who, like me, were students with hardly the cash to buy one bottle, let alone one of the extended variety. Many of the Park players had lucrative City jobs that were appropriately remunerated. A competition then began whereby we clubbed together to buy the first bottle to be drunk by all and it was passed round and finished. It was then the turn of the Park boys to buy the next and so on. I have always had a lot of time and admiration for Andy Ripley, for all sorts of reasons, but it is for incidents such as the following that I have the most admiration. He realised we had no more cash and, without making a big scene, he took away our embarrassment at not being able to carry on making reciprocal purchases by directing that all subsequent bills were to go to him.

In the next couple of hours we sank the whole of the owner's collection. Ripley's parting words, as we staggered to bed, were that we hadn't even been able to drink the neck of the last bottle; it was the one that was about a yard in length. They won the tournament without much trouble the following day.

One of a number of original questions that everyone asks when they sit next to me at a dinner is: Who was the best coach you ever played under? Undoubtedly my answer of A. B. C. Davies is one that draws nods of recognition only from the Welsh or those with a deeper knowledge of rugby. My views are also coloured by the fact that he coached me during my formative years and from student to British Lion. Although Alan had played rugby, a bad car accident left him unable to continue and he adapted his teaching qualification to become an innovative and meticulous coach. To me and many of the others who arrived as young players, he also became a friend and confidant.

ABCD was one of the first to use members of his coaching team to regularly watch the opposition before we faced them. A simple matter now, done by clubs in football and rugby even at a relatively low level. In the mid eighties, it was not like this: a lot of the analysis was done by team members who had knowledge of a particular team. Even then, much of it was anecdotal and not very objective.

Alan was also amongst the first coaches at club level, as far as I am aware, to hand out notes and game plans as individual documents. This was introduced by the England coaches a number of years later. Up to that point, the nearest most clubs got to technical analysis was the use of a blackboard.

Good coaches can approach their job in a variety of ways, but all have to be great communicators. It does not matter whether their focus is positive or negative, provided the essentials of what they want doing or practising is effectively transmitted. The very best instinctively know which approach will work with a specific player: when to shout; when to whisper; when to say nothing. The last of these is too often overlooked. Many coaches cannot refrain from that extra session, meeting or speech because they need to convince themselves that they have done everything in their power to help the team. When a coach has worked all week on something, it is extremely difficult to drop it.

Within a few minutes, Alan worked out that I was somebody who responded better to criticism and challenge, as opposed to praise and gentle persuasion. It is no surprise to me that it turned out this way, because the fierce voices of criticism that jump forward into my head whenever they can are merely extreme examples of the way I think and the way in which I analyse issues. I have often said that I am my own harshest critic, but I now think this is only partially correct. I do not doubt that I disparage myself in terms far harsher than does anyone else, but this is not the same as somebody giving considered, honest and occasionally brutal criticism.

The different ways in which Alan would motivate me were sometimes not even apparent until later. It is common to challenge players by telling them that they are not good enough, that everyone thinks they are not worthy of a place in the team, or that people are saying they have lost it. But in my experience this transparent ploy only works when the individual or the team is facing a 'backs to the wall' situation. It cannot be used repeatedly, because if it is necessary, there is probably a large measure of truth in the comments.

Only once did Alan give me a severe dressing-down, in the most basic way, in front of the whole team. The slating was before the

Midlands Division played the South and South West Division in 1986. We had lost the first two games, and in both I had lost a strike against the head. 'And if you lose another fucking strike against the head, you are history.' Embarrassed and humiliated, I fired back at him outside the changing room, as much to try and salvage some of my wounded pride. Have you noticed that when criticism has a kernel of truth, you rail against it more ferociously? It had the right effect and we won that game.

Occasionally, Alan would mention something about my opposite number in the middle of a chat in the bar after training. I once watched him leave open a page in one of the broadsheets that had an article on the rise of another hooker. Only then did I realise that the previous times I had inadvertently found papers on the breakfast or dinner table, which happened to be open at that page, this had been his doing too.

Another thing that also happens too often to players when they reach international level in team sports is that coaches stop coaching them. This is never correct. What is needed is a different form of coaching and both parties have to recognise this. Moreover, the basic skills of a sport are often never again addressed once a player reaches this level; this is also wrong because nobody, apart from John Eales, is perfect. In my experience it is as often the fault of the player who considers such elementary matters beneath him once he has played internationally, as it is the fault of the coach who thinks he can no longer impart anything useful.

Alan consistently offered advice on striking and throwing or lines of running and so on. Much of it came from observations he made of opponents or games he watched that did not involve his team. I cannot truthfully say that at all times I was open-minded about his advice, and infrequently we would have a row about a point he thought important and I thought trivial.

He was the first coach I came across who played specific music or speeches on the team bus before matches. He developed this into allowing music into the changing room, like 'Two Tribes', the seminal anthem of Frankie Goes to Hollywood. The latter caused dissension aplenty. I liked it, but others were firmly against. I gave way, unusually, because I had to agree that the marginal benefit I felt I gained from the music was insufficient when weighed against the severe distraction it represented for other players.

Once players from other clubs were on the receiving end of Alan's coaching talents, he rose through England's coaching ranks quickly. Always a player's man, his affability and inventiveness appealed to the feeling of change that was sensed in the late 1980s. After coaching the England B team for a couple of seasons, Alan took charge of the 1988 England tour to Australia. It didn't go well.

Although only three years before England would reach a World Cup final, the depth of talent was not yet sufficiently experienced to take on an Australian team that had been developing since their tour to the British Isles in 1982. Furthermore, England's touring record, even accounting for the successful teams captained by Will Carling and Martin Johnson, is woeful.

We were well beaten in both Tests and the only memorable incident was one that the player involved is not keen to have brought back into the public arena. The Yorkshire winger, John Bentley, played rugby league professionally and starred on the British Lions tour of South Africa in 1997. He is known as a rough lad. However, when he squared up to David Campese, in the first Test in 1988 at Ballymore, Brisbane, he came off second best, with Campese leaving him with a bloodied nose.

The assistant coach on that tour was even rougher, a Cumbrian farmer called Dave Robinson. Straight from the school of no nonsense, Robbo was rumoured to have used a shepherd's crook in rucking practices. Forwards had to hit the breakdown after passing under the crook and if they touched it they were dealt a salutary whack as they passed Robbo.

As a team, Davies and Robinson worked well, but both liked a drink. I did not find out until Alan had surgery many years later, that his accident had left him in a good deal of pain more or less every day, and he was fond of a nip to alleviate this. One night's revelries proved too much for them, and the squad had the unusual experience of the coaching team not making practice. It was noted by the RFU attending committeeman, as were a number of observations that both had made about the RFU. Neither career advanced thereafter. I cannot defend what happened, but frankly Alan was so far ahead of all but two or three English coaches that this incident could have been overlooked if the RFU had wanted to keep him.

Spurned by England, Alan took the job of head coach of Wales and turned them into a Championship-winning team. As with many others, he was to be the victim of one of the seemingly endless internal squabbles that rage through the WRU. The fact that Wales had been a dire team before Alan took over seemed to have been swiftly forgotten.

Unfortunately, though Nottingham forced their way into the first division of English clubs, we did not have a squad with enough talent to win things and turn the club into one that all players would consider joining for career advancement. The proximity and historic success of Leicester, just down the M1, and Northampton, that little bit further, meant the area was well served with senior clubs. All were better resourced and attracted bigger crowds.

Even though Nottingham is a city, it is actually quite small. That it has fantastic sporting facilities for a city of its size means many top-flight organisations chase a small pool of local money for sponsorship and investment. At the time when I played for the city's premier rugby club, or shortly thereafter, Nottingham had the following: a Test cricket ground at Trent Bridge; the European football champions in Nottingham Forest; Notts County FC; Nottingham RFC; the National Water Sports Centre at Holme Pierrepont; the Nottingham Panthers ice-hockey team; and later, the National Tennis Centre.

I know the club searched far and wide for funding, but to no avail. The harsh fact is that, even had we attracted such investment, it would have been a very difficult task to get enough people through the gate each week for the club to approach anything near self-sufficiency. Given the myriad of sporting alternatives, the well-publicised nightlife, bountiful shops, two theatres and a leading music venue at Rock City, the people of Nottingham do not spend their money on any sport in droves.

The first time I played against Bath at home was the start of the period in which they would dominate English rugby, winning leagues and cups aplenty. It was also the time that a man called Roger Spurrell played as their openside flanker. I don't think Spurrell will find my description of him as a lunatic the slightest bit offensive. Possibly apocryphal tales abound of him biting the heads of budgerigars, running raves and being generally outrageous, and during the game he committed all sorts of illegal acts. Though some would dispute this, when I ran in and toed him straight in the head, this was the only time I purposely kicked an opponent above the shoulders. The fulfilling dull thud I made on contact was satisfactory, for a few seconds only, as an act of vengeance for his various misdemeanours. When the ruck broke, Spurrell stood up and leaned towards me and said, 'Not on the head, son.' I bricked myself.

A non-frightening, but none the less unpalatable, experience was watching our then fly half, Rob Andrew, miss nine out of ten penalty attempts at goal in one fixture. It was bad enough being knocked out of the Cup by an average London Welsh side, but the misery was compounded, almost to despair, by the knowledge that we had Simon Hodgkinson, who kicked scores of difficult kicks when he played for England, as an alternative kicker that day.

With each miss I, as hooker, had to trudge to the middle of their 22-metre line to cover any attempt at a quick drop-out. Not much, you may say, but each time I had to endure the smirking mockery of the Welsh centre, Robert Ackerman. I bristled at the first few barbs, retorting in kind. By the time Rob had missed for the sixth time, I lost the will to respond, which made Ackerman worse. I would have done the same in his place.

If you ever enter a sevens tournament, it is far better to lose in the early rounds than to make the final and not win. This latter situation happened twice when we played in the Twickenham sevens. This was when the ground was full and the crowd allowed to be seditious. For one thing, you are exhausted after playing so many rounds. Moreover, the showers are cold and dirty, all the food has gone and they are invariably packing up the bar, so you cannot even get a consolation pint.

We lost first to Rosslyn Park and then Harlequins in successive years during the mid 1980s. The former final saw Martin Offiah flame his way to winning tries for the Park. Shortly thereafter, he signed to play rugby league. The latter witnessed a much closer tussle between Chris Oti for us and Andy Harriman for Quins. Poor Chris, being the only real speedster in our team, found that he was simply too tired to repeat his scorching performances in the earlier rounds and we lost narrowly.

The strongest memory of a game at Nottingham's home ground, Beeston, is of my final game against Gloucester. That day, I had all manner of emotions coursing through me. On the way to the ground I thought about the numerous good times I had had with my teammates: games, tours, training, just laughing. I had made my decision to go to London and play for the Quins the following season, and though I was excited about this, the loss of friends and nostalgia for times past almost made me announce, when I walked into the dressing room, that I had changed my mind.

For us, the game had no wider significance. For Gloucester, a win would mean they lifted the 1989/90 Courage Clubs' Championship. As I walked past the main stand on my way to get changed, I spotted that the organisers had brought the Championship trophy to the ground. The TV cameras were there and the assumption was clearly that Gloucester would win. Instead of saying that I had reversed my decision to depart, I launched into a long and loud stream of invective, centred on the basic premiss that all expected us to lose.

Immediately before we ran on to the pitch, and with a tremulous voice, I quietly said that I was proud of all we had done, but this was not about my last game, it was about each player's own pride. The ardour shown that day by my friends still produces a lump in my throat. On a hot day and hard ground, they flung themselves into tackles and rucks as if it was a relegation decider. I do not think Gloucester approached the game thinking their ascension was ineluctable, but they certainly had not expected this level of ferocity from a team with no incentive to wage war.

As I left the field after our win, I found myself walking next to Mike Teague who, out of the side of his mouth, said, 'You didn't have to do that, you bastards.' As he said this, a teammate jogged past me and said, 'That was for you. Good luck.' I looked at Teaguey who smiled and said, 'Fair play.'

A farewell presentation after the game found me struggling for words due to the fantastic gesture made by my friends in winning that game. I would – I do – miss them.

# 7

## The Road to My First Cap

The first shirt I donned for England was for England Universities, midway through 1982. It was a relatively comfortable final trial because by that point I had played three years of open-age rugby. The difference between those who had and had not was apparent straight away. My opposite hookers pushed straight, did not pressure me to the ground and never came anywhere close to getting rough; a bit disappointing. The team chosen had two fixtures, against Welsh Universities and French Universities. One was easy, the other far more testing.

The Welsh were not strong, because they had few universities. The Welsh game was held at Birmingham University and I took countless balls against the head. Watching the game was Derek Morgan, who at that time had considerable influence at all levels below full international. I did not know it at the time, but his recommendation would see me appointed captain of the England B team two years later.

We went to meet the French on their territory – just. Dunkirk wouldn't be top of most people's choice of venues, but I suppose it cut down on travel. In those days, there were no expenses paid.

Each student was reliant on his athletic union to help. Nottingham didn't help. We met in Dover on the morning of the day of travel, which meant anyone not south of London had to find their own accommodation overnight. I ended up in the cheapest B&B imaginable: it was so cold that I slept in my tracksuit.

The French, as in later years, were brutal and brilliant concurrently. Didier Camberabero played at number 10, scoring a scintillating try. (A few years later, in 1991, he was involved in probably the best try ever scored at Twickenham, the 105-yard score initiated by Serge Blanco and finished by Philippe Saint-André.) Up front, a foretaste of what it took to compete with the French was handed out as the packs fired into each other.

Being a student affair, the after-match dinner turned out to be one of the more memorable in a long series of such functions. I cannot deny that the propensity to misbehave was present in all the players, and it may be that things would have turned out equally badly in any event. However, whoever organised the dinner made a few schoolboy errors that contributed hugely to the near riot that ensued. After the game, all the players were desperate to rehydrate. Although in those days it would have been pints that were sought, we would have settled for water; anything to slake the thirst. Unfortunately, due to the sponsors for the game, the only liquid served at the pre-dinner function was Pernod, along with very small jugs of water to act as a mixer. What water was available went in a matter of seconds, followed by numerous bottles of the spirit. By the time the first course came, all the players were slaughtered. In addition, and I have no idea why, someone had placed on the tables entertainment bags containing things like streamers and hats, tubes and plastic balls. When one of us found that the little balls could be blown through the tubes, rather like the inside of a biro, all hell broke loose. In fact, if you blew hard enough, the balls would shoot anywhere in the hall at a decent velocity.

When the British ambassador got up to speak, he was met with a volley of projectiles that forced him to take cover by reseating himself. After several attempts to resume, he gave up. The French did not need to use weapons to quell their ambassador: they simply stood up with him and proceeded to sing until he sat down. All very childish; it was great.

With me in the England Universities front row that day was a Welsh prop, then of Loughborough University, Dylan Davis. He had a casual attitude to violence, which was fine by me when it was exploding all around, but off the field he kept me amused with dry observations. As we left for home the next day, Davis realised that he had lost his passport. He successfully re-entered the UK by camouflaging himself in a group of fifth-form school-girls, crawling through passport control on his knees.

The next step up the representative ladder was the England Students, a team that was selected from *all* further-education establishments, including Oxbridge, unlike the England Universities team. I felt that I had a good final trial and was very unhappy when told that I was on the bench.

The passing years have led me to conclude that timing is the most important variable in shaping fate. Although you can try to ensure you are in the best place at the best time, the majority of the time you are simply reactive. At several important junctures in my playing career and wider life, things happened that only later did I realise were seminal. In my playing career, this non-selection was one of two such incidents from which came the two best opportunities for the advancement of my representative career. Yet, had you told me at the time that every cloud has a silver lining, I would have tried to rip your head off.

The England Students played the Welsh Students at Gloucester towards the end of that season, and Julian Johnson of Cambridge University was picked ahead of me. The Welsh Students team (selected on the same basis as the England Students) included many players who were playing senior Welsh club rugby, and up front they hammered England, winning easily. Johnson did well to get as much ball as he did under so much pressure. I would have struggled similarly, but he was tainted by the losing performance and I replaced him for the next game. Had it been me and not him chosen to play that night, I might not have been writing this book on the back of an international rugby career.

When I am asked which was my favourite tour, I do not say the England Students tour to Japan and Hong Kong in 1982, which took place at the end of the season, but this would be the accurate reply. It holds that position for several reasons. As my first representative tour, it was bound to provide vivid memories because of its novelty. Also, it being a students' tour necessarily meant that everyone was roughly the same age and had similar perspectives. The sense of humour was wry, if not cynical, and it was applied without fear or favour to anything and anyone who happened to be conveniently in range at the time. We had a players' court every day, and none was less than very funny; occasionally they were inspired.

My opposing hooker in the party was a man who had kept me out of the Yorkshire Schools team a few years earlier, Paul Sidi. At the time, he was playing for the first XV at Harlequins and had been in a final England trial, which fed my insecurities but stiffened my resolve to claim the first-team place on tour – which I did.

Even though I was the contemporary of everyone on that tour, the confidence and assumed superiority of some people, mainly those from Oxbridge and public school, intimidated me. I compensated for this by being aggressive on the field and verbally combative off. Some would describe it as unnecessarily confrontational, but how many other players thought long into the night about whether they were right to have maintained this or that point of view in a discussion/argument over an otiose issue?

The tour started on the south island of Japan and worked up towards Tokyo to meet the New Zealand Universities, which had started in the north island of Hokkaido and were working their way south. The two teams then met with the full Japanese team for a tripartite tournament in Tokyo.

To demonstrate the dissimilarity of that to other tours on which

I went, my most significant memory was not of the bright neon of Tokyo but of the three days spent in a monastery in Tenri, just before we hit the capital. Rooming and living traditionally was an experience that would not be repeated – chain hotels would see to that. The atmosphere created by the surroundings gradually affected the whole party. We still laughed uproariously at times, but a feeling of spirituality also permeated, at first fleetingly, then palpably. After the hectic pace of Japanese suburban life, there was no better contrast or preparation for the tournament ahead. We developed into a very good team and our 43–0 win against Japan was, for many years, the only time their full side was whitewashed.

The game against the Kiwis came last and the build-up was also unique. For the seven days prior to the game, both sides used the same hotel; stared at each other over breakfast before training; shared the training ground with one or other taking first turn; then it was back to staring over dinner. You need not have much imagination to appreciate how each encounter incrementally increased the pressure in both squads. By the time the morning of the game arrived, both sets of forwards were taut, and inevitably the first exchanges were not for the timorous. What I remember from the game is that it was the first time I had played in a game where vicious rucking attracted nods of approval and not the referee's whistle. This recollection is strengthened because we out-rucked a New Zealand team. Difficult to forget moments like that.

The team photograph of that squad includes many who were to go on to be full internationals and senior club players, which shows what a special group of players came together: Chris Martin, Simon Smith, John Carr, Mark Bailey, Fran Clough, Steve Bates, Francis Emeruwa, John Ellison, Colin Pinnegar, me, Steve Peters, Pete Enevoldson; all went on to play at a very high level.

There followed, in successive years, three memorable tours with the England Under 23 team. At one meeting at Bisham Abbey, where later the England football team would reside, there was a part of an introduction that sticks in my mind to this day: 'Our research proves that over 40 per cent of players who play for the

England Under 23 team go on to get full caps.' I am often asked, 'At what point did you think you would play for England?' I never knew, certainly not with Cartesian certainty, that I would be a full international, but the second after that address I knew there was a chance of being in that 40 per cent, though I doubted I had the talent.

This doubt was fuelled by my then direct adversary for the hooking position, Mike Dixon of Lancashire. He had already played in a successful North of England team, was about six-feet-two and seventeen stone: a modern-day hooker. Actually, not so: he could also throw, and strike the ball when it was put in straight. I was faster, but even at that time the talk was of size meaning all. Dixon was not just big, he was big and good; the former of no use without the latter.

Our tour to Romania saw Ceauşescu's regime in all its appalling pomp. Central planning of the economy meant that in a five-floor department store roughly the size of Harrods, there was genuinely not one item that I wanted to buy, even though to Westerners it was all dirt cheap. Looking back, it was this experience that shaped my thoughts about pragmatism over principle both in politics and a great deal else.

There were bizarre highlights: the visit to see a Romanian come-dienne; the discovery that our bottled water was in fact being hosed from a rusty stand-pipe behind the restaurant kitchen; and coach Dick Greenwood's eccentric approach to fitness.

In my earlier book, I was unfair to Greenwood, describing him as little more than a flogger. He was in fact the first in the England hierarchy to understand and to try to achieve vastly increased fitness levels. His encounters with more senior players are now the subject of misty-eyed reminiscences; suffice to say he had little success. Whilst he managed to force players to do his sessions, he never got anywhere near changing their philosophy.

A younger, less cynical group were better suited to try this revolution in thinking, but he misapplied his knowledge. Greenwood determined that we had to experience the new level of session required. This would have been correct at the beginning of a season, as part of a carefully laid-out schedule. It did not, indeed could not, work the week before a Test match. The difficulty was that players realised this, and the fact that Greenwood imposed it at the wrong time made players disinclined to accept the principle behind the practice. One training session took place in temperatures of over 100° Fahrenheit and although at the start we had been promised a game of five-a-side, in the end it was only offered after nearly an hour of anaerobic sprinting/jogging. As we gasped on the floor, only three days before the Test match, football suddenly didn't seem so attractive.

Two further tours in 1983 and 1984 were to Italy and Spain. Neither merit recall for great rugby, but there were many things that happened that would have a wider significance years later.

The Spanish tour was led by Alan Black, the then Wasps coach. A Geordie personified, Blacky started the training sessions with laps of the field, during which we chanted like American GIs, 'I don't know, but I've been told.' He introduced us to the 'Dead Ants' call, from whence stemmed my first, but not last, severe bollocking from an England manager. This call could only be given at certain times and only a certain number of times during the day. On the call of 'Dead Ants' we all had to hit the deck on our backs with arms and legs waving like said ants. Puerile – yes; part of rugby tradition – yes. The problem was that it belonged to junior rugby tours, not when we were ambassadors for our country.

Normally, the sight of thirty players writhing about only caused mild bewilderment. In a restaurant in San Sebastian, however, this was not the reaction. At the call, we all dropped with commendable zeal, causing the chairs, tables, crockery and glassware to fly in all directions. Thinking this was an ETA attack, the other diners fled from the room in terror. Our security escort politely explained this should not be repeated. He also explained why the wearing of black berets, part of the ETA 'uniform', would not be especially welcome when we disembarked at Barcelona airport, our next leg on the tour.

It was after the game against provincial opposition that I was made captain of the midweek team. As we stood to applaud our opponents from the field, I made the Dead Ants call and, as ever, it was followed without demur. At this, the tour manager, Mike Weston, raced from the stand to yell at me, telling me that if I ever repeated this, I would never play for England again. I dared not tell him that I had seriously toyed with making the call after we had scored one of a number of tries in the second half.

I don't know why Mike Dixon didn't feature after this tour, but he just dropped off the scene. Maybe he just decided he didn't want it that much. Had he continued playing, it is likely that I would have spent many years on the England bench. I honestly do not know how I would have coped with that.

The Spain tour was in 1984. I had my LLB (Hons) degree in law; I had a place to do my law Part II exams; and Nottingham RFC was starting to emerge as a senior rugby club. Even taking into account my personal life or my professional career, from that year onwards, every decision I made in my life first took into consideration what effect it would have on my rugby career. This was to be my absolute priority. The single-mindedness I showed from that point on would help me achieve things in rugby that I previously never allowed myself to dream of, but it would also come at a price.

The next level on my trail for a full cap came in 1985, when I was selected as the captain of the England B team to play Italy at Twickenham. Each step towards a full cap provoked in me the fear that the newly achieved level would be the one at which I would be exposed. Here would be where my limitations, known well to me, would be laid bare. My selection for effectively the England second team was a step that certainly induced that feeling. This was just one bound away from the real deal. No longer was that aim fanciful: it could be focused upon and realistically targeted.

I was twenty-three when picked as the B-team captain. The aforementioned Derek Morgan approached me and told me the decision was the result of him being impressed by my performance and demeanour in the university game at Birmingham against Welsh Universities all those years before.

I didn't doubt that all players more senior than me were shocked by my announced captaincy. The forwards alone contained seasoned players, some final trialists, even some with full caps. I could see that they were not pleased with my appointment, and in their place I would not have differed from their view. In large measure, I thought someone else should have been given the armband, but I was nevertheless both thrilled and daunted to be appointed.

I decided to make myself face down any opposition, even though it was a difficult task. But I knew that, if unaddressed, it might lead to whispering and resentment. I got the team into the changing room before the first training session and said, 'Some of you are undoubtedly thinking, "Why the fuck is he captain?", that you have greater experience, have played at higher level and are older. You have a point. I didn't expect it and nor did I ask for it. If any of you declares openly that you want the job, I'll hand it over; but if you don't stand up now, I don't want anyone talking behind my back.' I waited for a few seconds, praying that nobody would test me because in reality I do not know if I would have done as I said. I was relying on – exploiting, in a way – the fraternity and respect that runs in rugby. There were no takers and we got on with it.

During the game, there was an important call on a penalty. We were leading but not by a great margin and I called for us to run a penalty. The kicker, David Johnson, a very experienced fly half from Gosforth, said, 'Are you sure? We're not many points ahead.' His offer of advice was an act of respect, giving me a different point of view from a senior man. Needless to say, I ignored his advice. Thank God we scored from the play.

I was twenty-three and captain of England B. I cannot deny that part of me looked over the fence and coveted both a full cap and the big job. I didn't even know who Will Carling was at that time.

# 8

# An English Revolution

In these days of ultra-professionalism, it is difficult for many to remember the state that English rugby was in as little as a couple of decades ago.

My first contact with the full national squad came in 1986 when a late-night call located me in the middle of a heated row in an Indian restaurant, where I was refusing to pay the 'discretionary' 12.5 per cent service charge. It appeared that nobody had done this before; then again, they had not come across the might of a young, know-all-know-nothing, law student.

I arrived at the Petersham Hotel, Richmond Hill, late on the Saturday evening, having left the curry house quickly, and knew only a few of the squad. It was intimidating to walk into a large group of players, all appearing to be tight-knit and familiar.

The first problem was to find some kit. Having only shorts, socks and boots I made a couple of unsuccessful pleas to players I knew and was then told by the management to try Steve Brain, the then incumbent hooker from Coventry. He and I did not dislike each other, but neither were we on good terms. I had previously been sent off with Brain in an earlier club match for fighting.

Actually, it was not a fight because that requires two people to attack each other. In fact, Brainy had leapt on top of me following a ruck and begun administering a beating that I managed to stop by grappling with him. I didn't even get to throw a punch. That he got banned for five weeks to my four enraged him. He seemed to forget that I had not thrown a punch.

As I entered his room, he looked up and in his very broad West Midlands accent said, 'Oh, all right, Mooro, be with you in a minute.' He appeared to be unscrewing a large standard lamp – though for what purpose I did not immediately twig. His next words gave me a vague inkling: 'This will look really nice in the front room.' On hearing of my need, he threw me tracksuit top and bottoms, adding, 'I'd better fucking get them back.'

Although I knew a couple of people from Nottingham, they had their own things to sort out, so I wandered about the bar with the knowledge that some players were saying, 'Who the fuck is he?' Players very soon forget the daunting experience of joining an established team. Some may say they had no such qualms, but not many, in truth.

I didn't realise that at Sunday morning sessions, the reserves were not there to compete, but to offer token resistance. As I got fully stuck in, I was told by several senior players, in no uncertain terms, that this was not how it was done. I was also not popular when I got all my lineout throws right. I didn't realise that others would think this uppity. All in all it was exciting, as it was the first time I had been near the squad, but it was also depressing that it was far from the competitive, high-level training I had imagined must take place in the full international team.

Something I learned, though only partially, was a lesson from the now sadly deceased Maurice Colclough. He had a reputation as a hard man, which he was, but also as a loud and uncultured madman, which he wasn't. After the session, he waited until there were just the two of us in the changing room to tell me how well he thought I had done. He had no need to take the time. For all he knew, that might have been the first and last appearance of yet another stand-in. But it meant everything to me at the time and showed the humanity of a man that few saw.

The truth was – and this is no exaggeration – practice sessions were planned only in the sense that instructions were given in a vague manner. The respective drills and exercises had no logical pattern and at times were counter-productive. I am not sure where the ultimate responsibility lay for this amateur approach. The coaching staff, headed by Martin Green, had some responsibility; the manager, Mike Weston, must have had some too. Thereafter, it was difficult to discern what influence people like Don Rutherford, the RFU Technical Director, had on team affairs. He seemed to duck in and out of the scene according to whether England had been a success or failure.

I listened to the tales of previous years from the older players. They were often hilarious, but were properly the province of an Old Boys vets' tour. Nobody would believe the tales of excess; they were too extreme. Stories of Maurice Colclough throwing TVs out of hotel windows; Chris Butcher swinging off the luggage racks on the coach before a game; management spending three days' worth of the players' tour allowance on personal items; all the sort of stories you expect from a vets' tour, not a national team. Paul Rendall, known to all as the Judge for his harsh but fair judgements in the players' court sessions, told me of a dinner on a South African tour of 1984 when they were informed that the evening function would have a busload of nurses attending. This is a regular rumour on tour. The difference here was that when they walked in, they did indeed find a gaggle of said nurses, all sitting waiting for their arrival; the stuff of fantasy.

Thus, the atmosphere that pervaded the England squad when I first became involved was quintessentially that of the amateur English. Anyone who approached his tasks with anything approaching dedication was viewed with suspicion. If you publicly avowed such dedication you were the object of ridicule. If you didn't drink vast quantities, you were almost certainly gay.

It has never been the English way to publicly show dedication.

Far better to embrace the cult of the amateur: try your hardest at the time, but never take a professional approach. Also, you must be self-effacing about your efforts and especially any success you achieve thereby. I never understood this, or accepted it at the time; possibly not being one of those naturally blessed with a surfeit of talent.

To say I was intimidated was a grossly inaccurate summary of my true feelings. I was terrified. It was not that I did not think I could play a bit, but like every jump in age group, or to a more senior team, I thought as I have said that this would be the level at which I would be exposed for the limited player that I was. More than that, I felt I would not fit in, not be respected and, even if I was picked, the feeling of the existing internationals would be that I did not deserve to be capped.

Faced with feelings that were familiar, but not understood, I retreated to my stock response, which was aggression, intellectual and physical. When comments were invited, I would frame my answer to try and give the impression of instinctive wisdom. In training sessions I would run for longer, seek extra work.

As mentioned earlier, Dick Greenwood had attempted to inculcate fitness as the main area of improvement, but by 1986 he was no longer involved in the RFU set-up. Rightly, the RFU had decided that they would utilise someone who had credentials from the sport of athletics, not only because he would have the requisite knowledge but because he could also point to his successes.

Tom McNab was brought in and he had worked with Daley Thompson, amongst others. McNab was astonished at what and how little was done to improve players' technique and fitness. He also did not understand the rugby culture of drinking: why would anyone want to drink alcohol to the point that they were physically sick? Yes, he had a lot to learn.

I vividly recall the first time we were introduced to the new athletic training drills and had a weights session with shot-putters Mike Winch and Judy Oakes. The cadence drills that individualised the different parts of sprinting caused all sorts of merriment.

The first is the high knee lift, which you do by driving each knee upwards alternately. After ten drives, you take ten long bouncing strides like those of the final phase of the triple jump; you then immediately go into pumping your legs as fast as you can but making only a few inches with each step. Some players could not even get these drills in the right order; others couldn't last the full thirty seconds.

Then we came to the concept of the 'jellyjaw'. If you watch any sprinter in slow motion you will see that although his body is straining to produce as much speed as possible, his jaw and cheek muscles will wobble because they are loose. This is because when this is achieved, it means a sprinter's shoulders and neck muscles are relaxed and not strained, making the strides more efficient. At first, few players got it right, but throughout all subsequent drills, Gareth Chilcott ran up and down purposely making a 'gurning' face which reduced spectators to fits of giggling.

In fact, Gareth seemed a bit at odds with many of the new drills. The polymeric exercise, whereby you had to bounce two-footed over three hurdles without pausing, proved especially difficult. Gareth would hit one of the three without fail and finally gave up, muttering that he didn't jump on people with two feet anyway so this wasn't much use to him.

When it came to weights, we were all embarrassed by the fact that Judy Oakes was far stronger than any of us. Although she had trained at this, even the big forwards were way down on her weights. When Mike Winch demonstrated the rapidity required for the explosive pushing of, say, shoulder presses, you could see some of the players' jaws drop. Of all the facets of training that were overlooked, systemised weight training was the one that never became standard. The major difference between today's professional players and us is the improvement in strength gained from such programmes. Though I tried to incorporate a proper training schedule with weights, there were just not enough hours in a day to travel, work, eat, do all the other team and individual practices and maintain a consistent weights programme.

These new methods saw a stark divide develop in the squad. Many of the older, established players were of the view that nobody could judge their rugby by looking at how many press-ups they did nor how quickly they could, or could not, run repeated 400-metre sprints. On the other side were some mostly younger internationals, and those on the fringes of the team. We believed in the new methods and saw that whilst they were not a precise guide to a player's ability, the fact that a player scored highly meant he had been working hard and was therefore likely to be in a better condition. Given the previous fitness standards had been so low, this could hardly be a regression.

From the outset, I went at it and determined to feign unconcern about who thought what. The truth was that on the drive back to Nottingham I would run over in my mind, again and again, every drill, every answer, every conversation, and berate myself for mistakes made, or things I thought I should have said, worrying about what impression I had left and if I had upset anyone. That I did this will surprise some, but this goes to prove that it is difficult to define a person's true nature without knowing them intimately. I so wanted to succeed that I could not bear the thought of failure, and even fleeting consideration that I might fall short was intolerable because it would prove the taunts made by my negative side were well founded.

Training camps abroad meant four days of drills and competitive team sessions. Some were held in England but two were in Portugal. They were held at different times of the year, but over the New Year became the fixed time for the four-day camps. Other athletes used the camps, like Steve Backley and Great Britain's field athletes and runners. They used to look askance at the way we trained. They went out before the sun got high, did a 50-minute warm-up, a 45-minute session, then retired to rest. They then came out in the early evening when it was cooler and repeated this. We went out at 10 a.m. and worked until 1 p.m. We went out again at 2 p.m. for another two hours when the heat was at its most intense, and in both sessions beat the shit out of each other.

Afterwards, in the evening, whilst the athletes sipped water quietly, we drank ten pints and played games in the bar. Steve Backley, being a good sport, asked to join in one of these games but chose the wrong one. There is no way to rationalise the punching game, as to any outsider it must seem insane. The participants form a circle and then punch the person to their right in the jaw; he then does the same, and so on. The game never gets to an end because although the initial blows are nothing more than taps, the temptation to increase the weight of the punch is too great. At some point a 'light-hearted' set-to occurs.

For reasons known only to him, Steve chose to stand between John Hall and Dean Richards; both are over six-feet-three and weighed seventeen stone plus. When Hall clipped him, he asked what he had to do now. As he turned to his right he was met by a snarling Richards, so he said he didn't want to pass on the punch, whereupon Hall clipped him again. Summoning up the courage to turn again towards Richards, he was confronted by the police constable, who had stretched himself to his full height and was now almost foaming at the mouth. We let him leave: it would have been cruel and unusual not to.

These fripperies gradually disappeared as it was eventually accepted that the new way was here to stay, and for good reason. We had a long way to go and we would find out through a number of hard lessons just how far. Nineteen eighty-seven found England at the start of a four-year evolution that would see them reach the World Cup final in 1991. You would not have put a lot of money on this back then because the squad was a mixture of the inexperienced and talented and the experienced and not so blessed. The approach to all elements of preparation was changing, as were the personnel.

As with my absence from the England v Wales Students game years earlier, timing played no less a part in my full international rugby career. The Five Nations of the 1987 season approached, with the final England trial taking place at Twickenham. Trial teams were selected with the notional Test team labelled the A team, whilst the possibles were the B team. Now discontinued, these trials rarely changed a selector's mind and often produced embarrassing defeats for the A team. Trial games demonstrated the importance to a player and a team of having the right psychological state before and during games. A player picked in the A team knew that, barring a disaster, he was going to be picked. Therefore, although he knew he could not simply go through the motions in the trial game, his choice between conservative and cavalier was always the former. The converse was true for his opposite number and if risky options did not come off, a B-team player had lost nothing. When they succeeded, confidence grew and so on.

In my final trial Graham Dawe, the Bath hooker and Cornish farmer, got the nod and played well enough to maintain his then top ranking. I was very upset. So upset in fact that I talked at length about the game to the coach Martin Green, highlighting things that proved that I, rather than Dawe, had played a better game. They did no such thing, though I believed so at the time. In any event, as with many selections, they preferred another player. And subjective as is selection, that was that.

In fact, that little soap-box barracking of Green did me no favours in his eyes. Through my Nottingham teammate, Gary Rees, I later heard that Green's response to my tirade was that he thought I was a smartarse. He was not the first or last to come to this conclusion.

The team chosen to face Ireland in the opening game included Graham Dawe and seven other Bath players. In the pack were Chilcott, Dawe, Redman, Robinson, Hall and Simpson; in the backs, Trick and Hill. This tactic by England to attempt to emulate the success of their foremost club has been tried a number of times by a number of countries – rarely with success. The Welsh team of 1990 was a further example, as they selected from the Neath team, which at that time was sweeping away all their Welsh club rivals.

The reason this rarely works is that players and units that appear all-conquering at club level benefit from the fact that their rivals usually have specific areas of weakness. Moreover, even if opponents have some better players, this advantage is overcome by the overall effect of a cohesive team. Against good international teams there are no weaknesses. There may be areas of lesser strength, but this is not the same. Further, provided there have been sufficiently consistent selection and preparation, individual players who might be outplayed by superior units in club games can become greater than the sum of their apparent parts.

The president of the RFU that year was John Burgess. A passionate, some said professional, Lancastrian, Burgess had proved successful with the North of England team, but actually had one of the worst coaching win:loss ratios of any England coach. His penchant for getting involved with the team was concurrently irritating and endearing, but never proved useful.

In one meeting at the Petersham Hotel, the team headquarters for a long time in the 1980s and '90s, we assembled to be addressed by Burgess. A bright and blunt man, Burgess had a reputation for speaking from the heart and becoming emotional during his addresses. As he began he pulled out what seemed like a huge wad of notes, which engendered an inward sinking feeling. 'Look, lads, I've just got a few things I'd like to say.' He held up his notes and then took hold of his half-rimmed reading glasses that were attached round his neck by a thin chain. As he swung them up to flick the stems either side of his head, one of the stems bent inwards and poked him in the eye.

'Oh, fucking hell.' Splutter splutter. Such was his reputation that nobody laughed, even though I could see a few faces quickly covered by hands. 'I'll start again.' Another swing, but this time the other stem bent and poked the other eye. This was too much. An expectant, nay nervous, audience burst into peals of laughter from which he couldn't recover and he had to abandon his declamation.

Nevertheless, Burgess was determined to show he was fully behind the team by visiting the dressing room in the hour before kickoff. He was not the first or the last to do this, but at least his visits produced merriment and not the resentment that later visits by committeemen provoked.

His special touch was a strong handshake and a good-luck kiss for each player. The latter continued until Mickey Skinner actively jumped the queue and grabbed him, shouting, 'Burge, come here,' and proceeded to stick his tongue down the startled old man's throat.

Before the Ireland game, Burgess again came into our changing room. As the weather was filthy, some of the players dipped their hands in powdered resin that was supposed to make their palms sticky and aid the catching of the ball. As Burgess got to our full-back, Marcus Rose, he did not see that Marcus had dipped his hands in the resin, and when they embraced and Burgess planted his obligatory kiss on the grinning player, Marcus patted him with both hands several times up and down his back. He left the dressing room with several massive palm prints of this resin all over the back of his very expensive beige cashmere coat. The atmosphere created by captain Richard Hill's exhortations disappeared amidst gales of laughter.

The game was a disaster, with England being bullied about the park and our backs unable to do the basics in the teeth of biting wind and rain. Though I did not say this at the time, Graham Dawe did as well as any hooker could have done with a slippery ball and destabilising gale at throw-in time. Nevertheless, it did not look like a good performance from him or the others. We lost.

The second game against France at home saw an escalation of Hill's cries for blood to be spilled. Just after the kickoff, Graham Dawe leapt up and rolled right over the top of the formed maul. He later smacked Pierre Berbizier off the ball; I couldn't see why he was marked down for this.

The next match, away to Wales, saw the infamous punch from Wade Dooley on Phil Davies; everybody ignored the fact that the brawl was started by Steve Sutton trying to hit one of the English second-rows. As the match involved several flare-ups, there was a clamour for disciplinary action. The RFU dropped Hill, Chilcott,

Dooley and Dawe for behaviour they deemed unacceptable and for bringing the game into disrepute.

I never agreed with Dawe being dropped on these grounds, though naturally I felt he had not been better than me anyway. Nevertheless, this stroke of fortune from his misfortune gave me my first cap in the final game against Scotland at Twickenham.

I remember the call from Mike Weston telling me I had been selected in place of Dawe. I was in the hovel that passed for my house, an old student place in Radford, Nottingham, where one of the few things that worked was the telephone. When I replaced the receiver, I jumped in the air and shouted, 'Yes, Yes, Yes!'

# 9

## The Start of Something Big

### Five Nations Championships 1987–9

The Six, or as it was in my playing days, Five Nations is a tournament that is often derided by the rugby cognoscenti in the southern hemisphere as being a very poor relation to their own Tri-Nations. They refer to the standard of rugby played and sometimes have a valid point. However, it is less valid when they go on to automatically link superior technical quality as being superior in terms of attractiveness and enjoyment. For such concepts involve not only the technical standard on the field of play, they involve all facets of a tournament.

The point about the Six Nations is not just the quality of rugby, which differs markedly from season to season; its 100-year history cannot be crudely dismissed by assessing it using one criterion only: who wins and when. For beyond statistics lie individual and collective memories for players and supporters alike that encompass so much more. Further, taking into account the political and geographical proximity of its combatants, many of the fixtures have symbolised, to differing degrees, contests that were about more than just sport. The ancient rivalry between England and France, the political enmity between Scotland and England, and

108

Beware of the Dog

the historic difficulties between the Irish and the Scottish all resonate quietly in the background of the annual matches between the countries.

On top of the above, the traditional trips made by thousands of fans to the capitals of their adversaries have become, for many, fixtures as immutable as the rugby around which they are based, and memories shared by these people form the basis of many a barroom anecdote. The extent of the enmity is perhaps overstated, but ask players and fans alike and they will attest to the fact that it is never far from the surface. Marketing men from the southern hemisphere would bleed to be able to implant a fraction of these extra features into their competition.

My introduction to the Five Nations came in an unlikely, unjustified, but very welcome manner and it was in the perfect setting: at home, against Scotland and one of my schoolboy heroes, Colin Deans, the Scottish hooker. At the time, I could not have chosen a better scenario. Furthermore, England's form had been poor up to that point, so any improvement would be seen favourably.

The week before my first cap dragged on, and I was desperate to get on the field, but a few days before the team met, I was out sprinting and something in my left foot appeared to crack. I hobbled about, not knowing the extent of any injury, and though it eased and did not feel like a break of any kind, I still could not walk without pain. I am glad I did not know how long this injury would dog me because, had I known, I would have been pessimistic about my chances of going through the constant pain for such an extended period of time.

When I got into camp, the physiotherapist, Kevin Murphy, tried ice and massage, but nothing seemed to make it recede. In the end I just gritted my teeth and bore the discomfort. Nothing was going to stop me from taking the field and gaining the thing that I had sought for so long. If anybody had looked closely at the figure that went across to speak to a group of well-wishers, they would have noticed a slight limp that, though I tried desperately hard to conceal it, indicated that I was having trouble with my left foot. The training sessions prior to the game were difficult, but by that time I was taking high doses of painkillers that helped mask the problem slightly; in any event nobody brought up the subject of my fitness.

My feelings and thoughts during the morning and leading up to my first cap were similar, in part only, to those experienced by others who have been in the same position. Pride, joy, fear and so on are all there, but what makes an account interesting are not these common emotions, but rather the specific personal ones. And those memories differ for each player.

I remember sitting in my room, which looked out over the Thames and from where the rooftops of the Twickenham stadium were just visible, and thinking of the thousands who, like me, had walked to the ground with anticipation framed by their own hopes for their team. Where were my mother and father right now? I knew they had got on the early-morning coach from Halifax to travel to the game, but had they got across London? Where would they be sitting? Then I began to think back to the times they had run me to school on Saturday mornings to meet the coach for away games. How much did I owe them for all the sacrifices they had made to raise me, take me in, love me? Who else did I know in the crowd but was not aware they were attending? How many people would watch me on TV that afternoon? What if we lost? If I played badly, let all these people down, could I bear the shame afterwards?

I then thought back to the Saturday afternoons when I and the rest of my school team watched the Five Nations games at school, having returned from a morning game. What had I thought of the players I had seen representing their country? There was an otherness about players who had reached the pinnacle of my sport. I certainly never had the remotest belief – though all schoolboys carry hope – that I would achieve anything remotely similar.

After the brief forwards meeting in the morning, the squad assembled as usual in the team room around midday. The theme tune to *Grandstand* blared out, the opening shot came from Twickenham, and shortly after I was mentioned as winning my first cap. It was when a picture of me came up on screen that I suddenly thought there may well be schoolboys looking at my picture in the same fashion as I had done many years earlier. It was at that point that the full magnitude of what was about to happen descended on me. I thought that in the days prior to this one I had become inured to the pressure that surrounds a first cap; I was wrong.

In the after-dinner speeches I now make, I sometimes try to encapsulate what it is like to win a first cap, and though it does not really get close to the same intensity, the best analogy I can come up with is this one: I ask people to take a second to think about what has been, up to that point, the hardest test of their life. It could be something academic, it could be a driving test or similar. I then ask them to add to this picture several other factors. Imagine that for the last ten years nearly every waking thought has been bent towards trying to get into a position to be allowed to take that test. A few days beforehand, somebody calls you and informs you that the following Saturday, you will now take the test; and between then and now, all manner of media call you and write about your likely performance during the test; some say you shouldn't be taking it because there are others better suited. On the morning of the test, you realise that not only will it be taken live, in front of your loved ones, but also in front of 60,000 others; when the TV rights are syndicated, maybe as many as twenty million people might watch you.

That is about as near as I can get an audience and the reader to understanding the pressure that at that point landed on my head. A better way to have to deal with these issues as a player is to come on as replacement because they are then all condensed into the brief time he has to remove his tracksuit and get on to the pitch.

Part of the reason for my previous nonchalance was that I had been in the squad for three games of that Championship. Surely I had a good idea of what it might be like actually to play? Not a bit of it; nowhere near.

An apposite parallel might be the different perceptions of a driver and a passenger. Even if the passenger is navigating, he is unlikely to remember the route as clearly as the one who steers, accelerates and brakes. Even if the passenger's recall of the route is similar, he cannot, by definition, have the same experience as the driver, for he has not had the responsibility for safely negotiating the car to its destination; he has viewed the journey as a bystander (or is it by-sitter?). Therefore, although this was not the first time I had travelled to Twickenham for an international, making the short journey over Richmond Bridge, the trip on 4 April 1987 was not like any before or since.

When I arrived at the ground, I went out on to the pitch. It was a grey but dry day, and I walked across to a group of Old Crossleyans who had come down to mark my first cap. I tried, as best as I could, not to limp as I walked, but was glad to get back into the changing rooms.

I have already remarked on the way in which each step up in level drew forth from me the expectation that this was the new height at which my shortcomings would be cruelly exposed. However, with my first cap, this was only partially true, and the lessening of that terror was welcome because I had enough to deal with without having to deal with irrational fear. No, this time I had the knowledge that Graham Dawe had survived at full international level, and I believed I was at least his equal; *ergo*, this was not a level that would leave me completely exposed, though it still had the potential to make me look foolish if I played at anything below my best.

For some things I have the retention skills of an amnesiac goldfish; for rugby, although it is not photographic, I have a memory able to recall whole swathes of games. I find it sad that many players can only say of their first cap that the day was a blur and that in concentrating so fully on what they had to do, they recollect little more than glimpses.

I can recall much of the game, and a few events stand out in particular. In an early scrum, facing the titanic Iain Milne and Colin Deans, I hooked the ball but it hit John Hall's knee at flanker and rebounded into their side of the scrum. 'You've got a lot to learn, laddie,' was the mild mock from Deans, to which I inwardly raged, 'We'll see about that, you Jock twat.' Not an entirely respectful thought about an idol. The game went well and England played with a fluidity that had not been apparent during the pitched battles that had previously made up our assault, both literal and figurative, on that year's Five Nations Championship.

About twenty minutes before the end of the game, we were well ahead, and barring something extraordinary, were going to record our first win in our Five Nations campaign that year. An injury had stopped play and the crowd in the old North Stand began singing 'Jerusalem'. The intimacy of the old stadium has been lost with the building of the super-stadium that now exists. People will find this difficult to believe, but when I threw the ball into the lineouts, I was no more than six or seven yards from the front row of the crowd. It was possible to hear individual comments very clearly when you were that near, and over the years I did hear a huge variety of comments; good and bad. I remember saying to myself that I must remember this moment because it might never come again. I listened; I absorbed the voices, and at that point I was satisfied that I was indeed an international rugby player.

The inaugural World Cup of 1987 took place in Australia in between my first cap and the start of the 1988 Five Nations Championship. I returned from that World Cup as the notional incumbent for the hooking berth, but my tenure was supported only by a handful of caps, few more than my rival, Graham Dawe. As such, it was akin to starting the battle for the number-two shirt afresh. Fortunately, the foot injury that I had developed shortly before my first Five Nations cap and that went on to plague me throughout the World Cup was to disappear swiftly and well before the start of the 1988 Five Nations campaign, thanks to some spectacularly successful orthopaedic help. This left the ground open for an even contest between Graham and me.

In addition to my miracle cure, my obsessive adherence to the newly introduced training methods and regime was beginning to pay dividends. During the next four seasons, I worked so hard that I became an athlete. OK, not a true one, but a rugby player's version none the less. I smile wryly to myself when I am now caricatured by some as a dinosaur, and my playing is dismissed as that of an old meat-head forward. Nobody embraced the new horizons more eagerly than I did, and my independently recorded sprint times show that, on occasion, I was quicker than several of the England backs over thirty and sixty metres.

If I am honest, it was almost down to the toss of a coin whether Dawe or I was chosen for the opening game of the 1988 season. But I got the nod and, save for a brief spell in 1990, I did not relinquish the shirt until I retired eight years later.

The 1988 Championship saw us steadily improve, but we opened with losses to France and Wales. The opening game in Paris was notable for the first cap of probably one of the most technically adept props ever to play for England – Jeff Probyn. In concert with Probyn's Wasps teammate, Paul Rendall, we took three strikes against the head by taking the French front row so low that their hooker, Daniel Dubroca, could not properly strike (the ball was put in straight in those days). Each triumph resulted in the obligatory exchange of punches as the scrums broke up, but as any old front-rower will tell you, the pain was as nothing to the inner satisfaction of those strikes.

We lost 9–10 and would have won, had we converted two glorious chances, and Les Cusworth, the fly half, showed a fraction of his ability in attack when it came to the more prosaic duties of defence. The winning penalty came from a dropped scrum that was sent turf-wards by Probyn after a bad hit. In a later and typically slanted report, John Reason wrote in the *Daily Telegraph* that the scrum had dropped because I was too small and not strong enough to scrummage at that level. This allegation came from an off-the-record conversation he had had with Probyn, who had to give some reason for the scrum's collapse, and chose to blame me. Jeff is like a brother to me: we bitch and moan at each other in private, but against outsiders we are solid. When I discovered that he had been behind the story, his betrayal sent me into a paroxysm of rage. Jeff offered no defence when I brought it up, saying, 'I had to tell him something – and remember, Brian, never shit on your mates; unless you really have to!'

It was in that game that I received six stitches, and the scar is still visible on the right side of my forehead. In a typically powerful surge on our put-in, the French drove and we got slightly twisted, and as they drove on, our second row collapsed underneath us and we were driven backwards. As all three of us fell on to our backs, I, as with all hookers, found myself in the uniquely uncomfortable position of having both arms pinned behind my props. As the French front row gleefully drove over the top of us, all I could do to avoid Dubroca's foot stamping on the middle of my face was to turn my head slightly so that he caught my forehead and not my nose.

In those days, the blood bin was not enforced and I got up from the scrum bleeding, but smiling, trying to hide the fact that he had indeed hurt me. I waited several minutes until the start of a lineout to seek treatment: it was psychologically important not to allow an opponent to know he had got one over you. I ran off the pitch to get stitched but knew the labyrinthine corridors of the Parc des Princes would take several minutes to negotiate so that I could get to the medical room. I therefore insisted, in language that made even me blanch, that I was stitched in the tunnel without anaesthetic. This sounds either psychotic or tremendously brave; the truth was that I was so angry and had so much adrenalin coursing through me that I would not have felt an attempted amputation. I returned determined to have my revenge, but though I sought a suitable moment for retribution, I did not find one. It was nevertheless noted for the future.

The Welsh beat us by scoring two tries at Twickenham, and we went to Murrayfield improved but bottom of the table. We had to get a win. This was achieved in a manner that was so boring it rightly prompted fury from the Scottish coach Derek Grant, who, when congratulated by Geoff Cooke on the game, simply snorted, 'What fucking game?' I couldn't disagree, but then what did he and everyone else expect? We had to get the win, at any cost, to preserve the improvements that had started to occur. Had we not bludgeoned the Scots, it is likely that the pressure for 'all change' would have been insurmountable. In any event, I wryly noted several years later that my 'Grant-like' reaction to similarly negative Scottish tactics in the 1995 Grand Slam decider was not also acknowledged as a fair point.

The final game saw us hammer Ireland at Twickenham, whence came the turgid anthem 'Swing Low, Sweet Chariot'. Chris Oti's hat-trick of tries in the second half saw the adoption of the song that would spawn a thousand headlines, form the basis of even more puns within lazy journalistic prose, and forever doom the England team to be celebrated by the singing of a negro spiritual that could not be further in its original meaning than that afforded it today. I hate that song: not for what it was; for what it has become. Still, it could be worse: it could be 'Flower of Scotland'.

Of the remaining seven Five Nations Championships I was to play in, we should have won six and grand-slammed in five, but such is the rivalry within these games that we inevitably made mistakes and did not achieve all that we ought. The 1989 Championship saw us fall short by drawing the opener against Scotland, and though we won the next two games, we lost 9–12 in Cardiff despite dominating the match for long periods.

The benefit of the passage of time leads me to conclude that for the England team in which I played over those years, there were a number of games that stand out as representative of the team, its players and the stage to which it had developed; further, that there are a few games to which can be traced longer-term effects on its style of play or the sort of players who, from a certain point onwards, were favoured.

To the winner is given the writing of history, and in rugby terms this means the southern hemisphere gets to do this. As it has taken all but one of the World Cups since 1987, it has been able to construct the world of rugby in images it desires and reshape rugby history to suit. If anybody had the time, the will, or the motive to study the styles of play of the teams from both hemispheres between 1985 and 1995 (and the advent of professionalism), they would, if fair-minded, be forced to disavow the now-common belief that northern hemisphere teams, especially England, were boring and forward-based, whilst their southern counterparts were all things beautiful and expansive. It simply is, and was, not true.

By way of one example only, I invite you to consider the 1988 match at Twickenham that marked Will Carling's first game as captain. We beat an Australian team containing the likes of Campese, Farr-Jones, Lynagh and Tom Lawton (all nineteen stone of him) 28–19 in a game that was as open and free-flowing as any that can be pulled from more recent archives. Played under laws whereby the team moving forward retained the put-in but was allowed to ruck properly, this game on its own gives the lie to the claim that England did not play expansive rugby, and that old laws were archaic to the point that they had to be changed in order to move forward into the new realms of professionalism. Those intent on retaining their carefully constructed façade of north-ern=bad, southern=good, like to avoid such games because they do not fit their argument, but this game remains a complete refutation of such claims.

We built on the style established in that game against Australia, and although our Five Nations results of 1989 were not what we had been hoping for, progress was definitely being made. No less an authority than Bill McLaren told me at the time that he was thrilled by the way England were playing. Then we ran into a seminal moment at Murrayfield in 1990 that was to change our outlook and approach for a good three seasons – if not longer.

# 10

## Rugby Goes Global

### The First Rugby World Cup, 1987

The RFU voted against the establishment of a World Cup. They said it would encourage professionalism; they were right.

Even so, at the time you would not have predicted this tournament in May 1987 would eventually become the third most watched global event behind the Olympics and the FIFA World Cup, certainly not if you were in Australia witnessing England's challenge for the William Webb Ellis Trophy.

England's preparation was poorly planned and mistakes from previous tours, especially the 1984 South Africa tour, were repeated. It may have been inevitable that these mistakes were made and that the RFU had to experience a tournament to understand what was required to compete in one; there is an element of truth in this, but there were still basic things that were done badly. The players still had memories of the jollies they had enjoyed in the very amateur days, and they did not realise that this tournament was to mark a watershed in the game. From that point on, teams and tours were to become progressively more professional; the latter were to be planned in detail and larking about was virtually to disappear.

The coach was Martin Green, an intense man who thought deeply about the game and about his contribution to the team; but though he tried, his natural reticence limited his effectiveness. One incident gives some insight into the way his persona came across to the players: after scraping himself quite badly on some coral whilst diving, he was fined in one of the players' courts for infecting the environment with the tropical disease 'Greenicus non Smilicus'.

I cringe now that I contributed to the levity that accompanied England's off-field approach. Though this did not reflect my approach to training and playing, it was symptomatic of a lingering ignorance of what was required to compete with the very best in the world.

Dean Richards and I disembarked at Sydney airport wearing Ronald Reagan and Mikhail Gorbachev masks. At least I got Deano to be Reagan. The fact is that we approached the competition as if it was a normal tour. England, at that time, were poor tourists anyway, but the dynamic of a tour is different from that of a World Cup.

What nobody knew as they watched Mr Gorbachev walk in a stilted fashion across the tarmac towards Immigration was that I was still carrying the chronic injury to my left foot that had developed just before my Five Nations debut earlier that season. Worse, it had swollen hugely on the long flight and was so painful it was all I could do not to be sick from the effort of making myself walk to passport control. As the injury to the top of my foot had not yet been diagnosed, I had no way of effectively treating it. I honestly did not know whether I was going to be fit for the first game, never mind the whole tournament. Throughout the tournament, in fact, I ended up taking painkillers to the highest dose I could every day until we were on the plane home, but I had no alternative.

I had only been capped once, in the final game of the Five Nations. Graham Dawe, the other hooker, whilst no incumbent, had three caps, and though he had been dropped (unfairly, but highly conveniently) for alleged indiscipline during the first three games of the home internationals, there was a general feeling that, as we were now far from home, we would effectively be back on par when it came to the Test hooking berth. Had I any doubts about the nature this rivalry would take, which I had not, there was no room for ambiguity when Dawe shook my hand and said, 'Let the battle commence.'

The first round came earlier than expected and in an unconventional manner. We found ourselves side by side in a gym, slowly doing laps to warm up. As everyone else eased out their air-weary legs, we registered the other's proximity. I jogged a bit faster; so did he. He accelerated slightly; so did I. I began striding; he responded. He started a near sprint; I matched him.

We were oblivious to the fact that all the other players had witnessed this insanity and had stopped to watch. By way of encouragement, they started to clap and cheer, which made us both break out into a full sprint. Round and round we went, stopped only by coach Martin Green's intervention to try and stop us wrecking ourselves before we even got on to a field. Had he not intervened, I believe neither of us would have stopped until physically exhausted, or the other had quit.

As this 'warm-up' ended, I went to see Kevin Murphy, England's long-serving physiotherapist and one of the kindest and most loyal men you will ever meet. I told him the full extent of the problem and confessed that I did not know if I could make the training session. We had worked together on this injury before the Calcutta Cup game that year, and he was surprised that it still remained, but then again as neither of us knew what it was, it was difficult to know what to do. He padded the arch of my foot, which eased the pain a little, just sufficiently for me to do the session through solidly gritted teeth.

Any pictures of me during the tournament that were taken whilst we relaxed will show that I always have socks and trainers on, even in stifling heat. This was to hide the mass of tape and padding that I had to wear to keep my foot in some sort of working order. I was not prevented from playing at full tilt, but dealing with the aftermath of the swelling and pain became a trial of increasing severity.

I tried my best to disguise my injury, but the management were not fooled. When they pulled me to one side, I had to admit that I had a problem, but assured them it was of recent origin and not something that would prevent me from being available for the first game against Australia. Their response took me aback, but in retrospect they were right to warn me that if I did not do a full training session the next day and at full pace, I would be on the first plane home. They were justifiably angry that they had brought a player who might not be fit enough to take part in the competition. They could fly out a replacement, but that would mean inconvenience that they should not have to face; it would also mean the player had insufficient time to learn calls, moves and so on before sitting on the bench.

The morning of the crucial session, Kevin again padded and strapped my foot and ankle tightly. I wanted him to give me a painkilling injection, but he rightly told me that if it required such extreme measures to manage the injury, there was no point because he would not treat any injury with daily injections. There was little point deferring the test of the foot: either the arch padding would keep it manageable or it would fail and I would seek a proper solution back in England. I was far from confident, and I sat alone in my room thinking my career was about to end.

By this time, the rest of the squad had heard about the ultimatum. I don't know how; I did not tell anybody and Kevin would never break patient confidentiality. However, it had spilled, and the black humour of the forwards manifested itself in Messrs Rendall and Dooley starting a chorus of 'Underneath the Arches'. My legendary sense of humour failed me, but I got through the session.

A combination of the increasingly effective anti-inflammatories and Kevin's *ad hoc* treatment of padding the arch of my foot got me through not just that session, but the rest of England's campaign. Had I gone home, who knows what? Dawe and I might have swapped places, with me having to watch him play out an extended career.

Kevin saved my rugby career, and something similar was to occur on two further occasions. On such fortune is based many a long-term international career. Luck or fate; it matters not, but I never stop feeling the debt I owe to the skill and kindness of my medical saviours.

The intensity of the subsequent World Cups dwarfed what passed for pressure during this competition. The media coverage in Australia was low-key at best, and though it may have been different in New Zealand (which was co-hosting the tournament), this made no difference to the teams playing their games across the Tasman Sea. Rugby union was, and still is, a minority sport in Australia and the coverage matched its status.

One of the most difficult aspects of touring, and one that has to be thought through and dealt with effectively, is the non-playing and training hours. It is, or was, accepted that on tour there would be 'downtime'; witnessed by the fact that there was an appointed social committee, a players' court and tour rules. To current professionals, much of this will exist only in stories from older former players, but they were very real. I know: I was the court prosecutor on most tours.

The absence of, or limited, travel in a World Cup makes it an unusual experience. On normal tours, you move after every Saturday and Wednesday game. There is a succession of packing and unpacking, coaches, airports and just hanging about; lots of hanging about. In a World Cup you are based in one place for the pool games, and move only in the knockout stages; even then you might possibly stay in the same place, or return to it at some point. After training and the obligatory meetings, whether needed or not, there are many periods that are not sufficiently long to allow you to do anything tangible, but quite long enough to make you thoroughly bored.

As a player, I learned that it took conscious effort to plan for these periods and I had to get into the frame of mind to deal with them without succumbing to the temptations available in that particular town or city. In Sydney in 1987, though England did attend to training and games with seriousness, the out-of-school hours showed that our minds were not focused. At the time, I would have rejected this criticism; and to be fair, it was only possible to see this when I had played in later World Cups, for which our preparation was far better.

There is little of note to say about our performances in the pool games. Wins against Japan and the USA were expected and achieved. We didn't excel, but we were not poor, and we remained confident that we could progress. The game that effectively decided which country topped the pool was the first one against the co-hosts, Australia. We only lost 6–19, in a game played at the remarkably unattractive stadium called the Concord Oval, but we were never close to winning. In fact, the single memorable fact from the game is a remark made by my then Nottingham teammate, flanker Gary Rees. It goes down as one of very few witty remarks that were actually said during an international game. Many are told on the dinner circuit, but most are urban myths.

David Campese, that well-balanced advocate of all things English, was awarded a try even though he did not ground the ball properly. Out of the corner of his mouth, Reesy muttered softly to the referee, 'You one-eyed wanker.' Not sure what he had heard, or more likely disbelieving what he had heard, the referee said, 'What did you say?' whereupon Reesy replied, 'Oh, deaf as well.'

Between the pool stage and the quarter-final, we went to the resort of Hamilton Island; we should not have done. After the distinctly downmarket hotel in Rushcutters Bay (which had been our Sydney base until then), Hamilton Island was a paradise. Every type of water activity was available, as was golf, and so on. The squad tried to do everything, and management did too little to stop us. Readers could say that we were responsible for our own preparation, and in part that would be right. However, in those amateur days, and with us not understanding the challenge properly, more should have been done to educate us as to what was required; and resorts like this should never have been on the itinerary. At that stage of a World Cup, it is right to have rest and recuperation, but a quiet slice of luxury, without multiple strenuous activities to divert attention and sap the energy, would have worked. This mistake is compounded by the fact that I was told the RFU specifically chose the retreat and inspected it. Nice job if you can get it.

Coming second in the group gave us a fixture in Brisbane against a Welsh team that had not looked particularly good in the pool games and that had had to travel from New Zealand for the quarter-final. Although we had also had to travel to Brisbane, we had a much shorter trip to make than the Welsh. We believed we would beat them if we played well; in fact we were quite confident. This belief turned towards expectation when we found out that their fantastic lineout jumper, Robert Norster, had a bad ankle injury. In fact, looking back, we were even a little cocky about our prospects once the Norster news was confirmed.

It did not matter what state Norster was in when he took the field: we were so poor that we didn't deserve to progress. That game was one of the worst in World Cup history, made difficult by a terrible pitch at Ballymore, the Brisbane ground. It descended into a slow-motion contest, in which neither team played well, but Wales scored tries and we managed one solitary penalty.

We had not approached the tournament properly and this defeat made it quite plain that we were behind most of the senior nations in the world. In retrospect, that loss and especially its manner were vital in hammering home to us just how much work had to be done.

The manner of our ejection did not just cause disappointment; it was deeper than that. I believe that that was the point at which any remnants of reluctance to embrace the recent training regime were removed from the senior players; that is when the recent caps became determined that their careers, even if brief, should not contain defeats like this. There was simply no point in devoting so much time and effort if this was what lay at the end.

The inaugural World Cup was won by New Zealand. I wonder what odds you would have got on a bet that, at the time of writing, they would still not have won another.

When I got back home from Australia, I was fortunate to be referred to Barry Francis, one of a handful of orthopaedic specialists practising in those days, and a man who knew his subject well. After my gait was assessed on a treadmill, he then examined my left foot and told me that the spring tendon that ran along the bottom of my foot was not reacting properly. It is one of the few tendons in the body that is meant to move, and mine was restricted so that it was pushing together two bones in the top of my foot; hence the pain and its refusal to respond to conventional treatment. By taking plaster casts of both feet and making adjustments to the moulds, he produced a template from which orthotic insoles were made by a factory in Scotland. Three days after wearing the insoles the pain disappeared. It was a magical resolution to a problem that at times had felt so bad I wondered if I would ever be able to play again.

I was now free to set about making the changes that I knew were necessary. Previously I had thought I trained diligently. I had, but this applied only to the times when I was doing the sessions. From now on, I had to alter the way I approached my leisure time as well. These were still amateur days and I still enjoyed big nights out after games, but midweek drinking gradually decreased; by the time my last World Cup came round eight years later, I hardly touched alcohol midweek, and for two periods, pre-Lions tour 1989 and pre-World Cup 1991, I did not drink at all for six months. It was time to move on and up.

# 11

## One of the Others

### The Lions Tour to Australia, 1989

If there had been an 'otherness' about the international players I had watched as a schoolboy, the British Lions were by some way again removed from reality. The words of rugby correspondents were all that was available to try to evoke the atmosphere of a Lions tour because so few games were captured on film. When I experienced my first tour, I realised what an impossible task this was without the benefit of moving images.

The first letter I had ever received from the Four Home Unions Committee, which ran the Lions, was when I was still at Nottingham University in 1984. It came as a complete shock and, looking back, it showed that they must have sent hundreds of provisional availability letters. When I opened the letter, I thought it was a prank by the bar boys, and so at first I treated it flippantly, until they all denied sending it.

By the summer of 1989, against all expectation, I was, at the age of twenty-seven, on the verge of being accorded the greatest accolade a player could get on this side of the world: a place on the British Lions tour of Australia.

Though I made it into most pundits' squads, nobody had me in their prospective Test team. Conventional wisdom, as wise as it conventionally is, was that to counter Australia's giant hooker, Tom Lawton (anything between eighteen and twenty-one stone, depending on which source you read), the Lions would pick Ireland's seventeen-stone Ulsterman, Steve Smith. It was like a mantra: Steve Smith for Lions hooker. It was all I heard, all I read about and all I thought about. As far as it went, the theory about why he should be picked was fine, yet it had two flaws: first, it was bollocks; secondly, I would have my say before any Test team was chosen.

As previously stated, I did not drink for the six months prior to the tour, and after an uncomfortable initial six weeks, it didn't bother me. It certainly made a difference to my fitness, and by the time the tour came along I was flying. It was one of only two periods in my life when I have been as fit as an athlete. It was a state similar to being on a caffeine-high all day. I looked forward to punishing interval-running up steep hills and shuttle-sprint sessions that left me curled up in the foetal position, gasping, but knowing the pain was worth enduring. When I went to bed, I was asleep within thirty seconds and when I awoke I was instantly alert, usually thinking about what training sessions I had to fit into my working day as a solicitor.

At first my friends at the rugby club and elsewhere thought the fitness kick was a three-week blast, and they often tried to persuade me to have a quick one. When they realised what I was doing and the fanaticism with which I approached it, they gave up. To some of them it must have seemed strange and sometimes rude. On one run along the Nottingham canal towpath, I ran past a popular cocktail bar, the Baltimore Diner, with which I had a more than passing acquaintance. On the return run, two of my friends had come out to stand on the path and have a chat; I ran past them, saying I couldn't stop, leaving them open-mouthed at the snub. Touchingly, they organised a Sunday afternoon bar extension in our local pub, the Sir John Borlase Warren in Nottingham (no all-day drinking back then), and a surprise party to celebrate my selection. I didn't drink; there were things to do.

The composition of that Lions squad was not particularly controversial. There was a slight Anglo-Scottish bias, but this reflected the form and experience of the players. The 1989 squad contained many players who had accumulated substantial numbers of caps and this experience was to be badly needed at crucial points during the tour.

There was extensive coverage of the compelling 2009 Test series between the British and Irish Lions and South Africa. The extent and depth of this coverage has given viewers far more insight into why the Lions are special. However, although the explanations given by former players and management go some way to identifying the uniqueness, it is impossible to describe properly what can be a sublime rugby experience for players and supporters alike. My own attempt will add to the available information, but it is offered with the following caveat: to really know, you have to have 'been there'.

There is no real parallel in British team sport to give a flavour of the Lions; the nearest parallel would be the old Home Championship games in football. Now discontinued, these games rarely touched technical heights, but they were eagerly awaited by players and fans. Imagine those countries putting aside their rivalry for one tour, every four years, whilst the players tried to forge a united front against, say, Brazil. Furthermore, could the supporters of each country bond in a common cause? In rugby terms, that is what the Lions try to do on each tour.

It will be claimed by some that the example given is not credible because football is a more passionate game, and to expect people with such levels of fervour to combine is not feasible. Nonsense. That rugby fans have crap chants does not make them lesser supporters; the level of a person's patriotism or passion is not measured by how loudly they shout or sing; nor by the frequency with which they curse; nor by whether they are prepared to assault opposing fans. That rugby fans do not do these things does not make them less proud; it means they are civilised. Any player who has faced the Haka can tell you about intensity; rugby has it in abundance.

Lions teams today find the assimilation of players easier because many play in the same clubs or against each other in various competitions. Until 1995, when the game went professional, it might be the case that some players only faced each other during Five Nations games or the odd traditional fixture. In 1989, therefore, there was a level of suspicion and caution when we met to attend to the administrative formalities, get our kit and take the fitness tests required before anyone was allowed on the plane.

Gollum's ranting tried to remind me that I should not be there; I would fail; who did I think I was? What also scared me was that I had tried as hard as I could to prepare for this tour. I was fitter than at any time in my career before or since. If I could not succeed having given my all, there was nothing more I could do. This had occupied my thoughts on the journey to the hotel, getting stronger the nearer I got; by the time I was in the changing rooms before the Tests, it was almost overwhelming. I managed to get a moment of clarity and told myself that few players got this opportunity and that, having done so much work, was I really going to back away, leaving myself with years of regret?

I ran on to one of the pitches and found that Finlay Calder, John Jeffrey and Derek White were the only players changed. As I arrived, there was a cursory exchange of greetings and they suggested a game of touch rugby. What? Two-a-side touch rugby? I thought they were joking. I learned from that point onwards: Finlay didn't joke about such things. So we played a ludicrous game for a few minutes during which I felt the single-minded way the Scots treated even warm-ups.

When we were all assembled, I went and stood next to Stevie Smith. He was far bigger than me, but I had planned this moment for a long time. I wanted to make my case, and in the sprints and shuttle runs, I made sure I finished first in the group. When it came to the recently introduced 'beep test', I looked across at some of the players and could see looks of resigned dread.

It is a simple test: you run from one line to another twenty metres away. Touching and turning on that line has to coincide with an electronic beep. After a certain number of beeps/turns, the machine announces that you have reached level one and the beeps get slightly faster until the next level is reached, and so on. You then have to carry on running and turning until you collapse with exhaustion. Simple. In fact, it is a torturous test, not least because it is boring. There is nothing to distract you from the pain you know is coming and which can only increase. Being in the right frame of mind can add one, possibly two, levels to your score. There is a point at which you feel you cannot run any more, but the reality is that your body will allow you to continue for another couple of minutes – if, and only if, you have the requisite determination. The first time I did the test, I dropped out at the first point. When I became more familiar with what the test required, I learned to push through that false nadir. When the groups' results were collated, I had recorded the highest score of any forward.

After training, I stayed out and did extra. This bemused some and drew calls of 'creep' and 'arse-licker' from the policemen in our ranks. But as we left the field, Finlay approached me and said how impressed he was with my fitness and attitude; one of the big three of captain, coach and manager had taken note.

Recent coverage of Lions tours has featured the ploys used to engender team spirit. I do not remember anything similar on my tours or on those before 1989. Though I had wholeheartedly embraced the physiological side of preparation, the psychological one was different. I did not think it spurious, rather I believe that sports psychology has good practitioners but also some charlatans. Any voiceover with an American accent instantly makes me deeply sceptical, if not outright cynical.

Others had the same instincts. One year the RFU handed out a set of cassette tapes on which were recorded a number of visualisation exercises. Quite against copyright, the RFU appeared to have bought one set, then made multiple copies. We were told to study them but I did not get further than the first exercise. A soporific American voice encouraged me to stand six inches from a wall, shut my eyes and then imagine myself first falling towards the wall and then away from it. I started sniggering, and though I did try, I couldn't listen to any more of the tape without seeing one of a host of those hilarious infomercials that offer the universe for $29.99. The following weekend I gave Dean Richards a lift to London and I asked him about his reaction to the exercises. His reply still amuses me: 'I don't know. I taped Elton John over mine.'

The only bonding events I recall were old-fashioned drinks at the bar. I decided to come off the wagon; for the greater good, of course. Unfortunately, after six months without practice, I could hold only a disgracefully small amount before gibbering. As I had done all the work that would have any lasting effects on my fitness on tour, I need not have worried about falling off the wagon. In any event, the training sessions throughout the tour were hugely competitive and the infrequent binge sessions had no serious effect on my, or any of the other players', fitness.

I can vividly remember receiving my Lions blazer with its beautiful braid Lions crest. Mine didn't fit. One of the seemingly ineluctable laws of touring back then was that none of the formalwear ever fitted properly. I do not know how a succession of clothing sponsors managed to achieve this feat, but it became a standing joke. The arms of my blazer were more suited to those of an orangutan. Other players' trousers either came halfway up shins or fell well over the bottom of their feet. In addition to clothing, we were each given two pairs of Church's brogues. We were happy with this as they are high-quality footwear, but they posed one problem: the soles were so shiny that they proved lethal on any wooden floor, and from the fitting room, loud thuds were heard as several players ended up flat on their backs.

The differences between the countries' styles of play quickly became apparent on the training field. The Scottish traditionally played a rucking game. England was a more effective mauling team. After several discussions – arguments actually – the coach, Ian McGeechan, had the final say; rucking it was. The reason I and my fellow England forwards made this an issue was that we had played against Australia in 1987 and 1988. Scotland had toured New Zealand in those years, and we were convinced their rucking game would not be effective. We were right. A few games into the tour it became obvious that the Australians were adept at countering this style of play, and we adapted our game to include driving mauls. This comforted the English, especially Dean Richards, who later refined the art and turned it into a religion at Welford Road.

The tour was managed by Clive Rowlands from Wales. I knew of Clive's reputation, but also remembered the offhand remark he made following a Welsh loss to one Home Union country, after which he was asked, 'Where do Wales go from here?' He replied, 'Oh well, I suppose we will just have to go back to beating England every year.' As soon as I got to know him, it was obvious that his talkative, excitable manner sometimes got the better of him, but he was a master at dealing with difficult situations and protected us when the inevitable accusations came from the Australian press over all manner of things.

There is no man alive who knows more about the Lions than Ian McGeechan; as player, selector and coach he has been involved in tremendous highs and lows over the years. On the '89 tour he was the coach and it was the first time I had come into contact with the quietly spoken Scot, known by all as 'Geech'. When we chatted, I was impressed by the depth of his preparation for the tour. He was meticulous in his analysis and forthright when he communicated.

An example of his thoroughness was shown when he told us that he had asked one of his rugby contacts in Australia to watch the Wallabies' matches for the year preceding our arrival. I do not know how his contact found out, but Geech told us that the Aussies had a move from the scrum that they called 'Queensland'. It had worked so well in opposed practice sessions that they shelved it, intending to use it in the Lions series. When we heard this called in the first Test, we stopped the move before it went over the gain line.

Although I was unhappy about Geech's decision to play a ruck-ing game, one of his most impressive traits was his willingness to accept his mistakes and make appropriate changes. Geech had the humility and nous to know he was not always right. When it started to become apparent that the rucking policy was not work-ing, he quickly accepted the alternative of driving mauls, which the Australians found more difficult to counter and which attracted more of their forwards, giving extra space for our backs.

Clive and Geech both have sides to their character not often seen publicly: a streak of ruthlessness and an intense loyalty that meant they understood that at times it was necessary to fight fire with flame. When the Aussie press started to portray our forwards as violent thugs, the management supported us fully. As England players we had been used to craven apologists as spokesmen, but it was the manner in which they mounted our defence as much as the fact of it that impressed me. Where they could, they dismissed the accusations out of hand. When there was some culpability, they insisted the behaviour of the opposition was also scrutinised.

Roger Uttley was the assistant and forwards coach and he had a difficult tour because of the antipathy of the Scottish forwards. It was clear that they did not rate his style and they took little trou-ble to hide this fact. I felt sorry for Roger as the tour progressed, because the players gradually took over the sessions, giving the impression he was doing less and less. I thought Roger had limi-tations as a coach but he had the sense to leave well alone when it became clear we were capable of sorting out our own affairs. I was appalled by the purposeful slight towards Roger at the end of the tour when he was given a clearly inferior gift to those presented to other management figures for their efforts on tour.

An unconvincing win in Perth started the tour. I had not appre-ciated the geographical isolation of Perth from the other major Australian cities nor the resentment felt by the Western Australians at the fact that they produce 70 per cent of the country's wealth and yet are largely ignored. The wealth of Perth's élite is amply demonstrated by the magnificent Royal Perth Yacht Club at

Fremantle. We were invited for an afternoon's gentle racing on board a number of their members' yachts, and had a fantastic time. Bob Norster, the Welsh lock, does not have the photograph he wanted of the occasion because he unwisely gave his camera to an ageing member and asked him to take a snap of our crew. As the man struggled with the complexity of the very expensive camera, it slipped from his hands and slid slowly towards the edge of the harbour. The reaction on our faces went into slow motion as we viewed the man's desperate crawl to intercept the treasure. Just as the poor man reached out for the camera, it dropped over the edge and into the water. I didn't know whether Bob was about to explode or cry. He should have joined the rest of us: by then, tears were rolling down our cheeks.

Before we left, Finlay thanked our hosts for their generosity and a tremendous afternoon's entertainment, made special by the effort that had obviously gone into planning the event. Demonstrating the life of the über-wealthy, a voice from one of the members near the bar said, 'That's all right, mate, we do this every Wednesday anyway.'

The game was not notable, but the difference of approach towards immediate pre-match preparation stood out as we changed for the game. The England dressing room had, over the last couple of years, gradually become less animated and quieter as we developed a settled team. Mike Teague and I were therefore taken aback as we watched the Scottish players bouncing off the walls, screaming, 'Come on! Get into it!' Gavin and Scott Hastings were smashing into each other like Rock and Gravel, the Slagg Brothers, who drive the Boulder-mobile in *Wacky Races*. We had to go and change in an adjacent room.

We flew to the east coast, where the tour proper would begin. Wins against minor provincial teams built a momentum that made us confident of our chances against the major provincial teams and in the looming Test series. One of the arts of Lions management is to engender competition for Test places by picking players in different combinations so that they do not get the comfort of knowing they are first choice. This has to be balanced against the need to play the likely Test XV *en bloc*, to give as much time as possible for the players and units to familiarise themselves.

From reasonably early on in the tour, the Saturday team became reasonably familiar. Against all expectation, including my own at times, I won the hooking berth in the Saturday team. I did not go beyond having a perfunctory relationship with Smith until the end of the tour and he was a fine man, but I had not the character to be able to separate personal interaction from the sporting battle. Players like Jason Leonard did not mind amiability with their opponents and familiarity did not diminish his efforts when they met on the pitch. I could not do this. It is a sad fact that I only got to know and enjoy the company of several players after I retired.

Our first real challenge came against Queensland at Ballymore, in Brisbane. Whatever is claimed to the contrary by the Australians, the incident that provoked our admittedly physical approach to games thereafter was the trampling of Mike Hall, the Welsh centre. Lying nowhere near the ball on the ground, Hall was danced on by the Queensland pack. It was precisely the type of play about which the Australians were to complain hypocritically many times, in increasingly strident and hysterical tones, right to the end of the tour. Am I inventing this whingeing? Not according to the confession of the then Australian assistant coach Bob Templeton, who told me during his coaching stint with Harlequins a few years later that he had been against the policy of public pressure, as he felt it looked weak. He was right.

As Hall received treatment, Finlay gathered the forwards and made it plain that we would accept no more of that treatment of any of our players. Though the Queensland team had been perfectly prepared to condone their own rough play, during and after the game they whinged about us matching like for like. Even a casual study of the game demonstrates that it was the Hall incident that marked the beginning of our refusal to be put upon. This led to several brawls during the game and a series of incidents involving the Queensland hooker, Mark McBain. Under severe pressure in a retreating scrum, McBain hooked his ball and then collapsed the scrum to prevent us driving them back any further. Not only is collapsing scrums illegal, it was particularly dangerous for our front row, moving forward at speed. If our second row had not stopped pushing when we collapsed, there would have been a danger of our necks being forcibly pushed into our chests and hyper-extended.

I quickly realised this was a purposeful act and, when the referee refused to act, despite my informing him reasonably clearly, I took Bob Norster aside and told him that if this happened again he was to kick McBain. It did, so he did. At one point McBain's head was festooned with cuts, of which much was made post-match. When he complained, I told him that it was simple: if he stopped collapsing, we would stop kicking him. He didn't, so we didn't. I was, and am, unapologetic about instructing Norster to react in that way. Scrummaging is a difficult and dangerous pastime without deliberate and repeated collapsing, done merely to prevent embarrassment. To anybody who finds my attitude unacceptable: sorry, I do not think I should repeatedly risk serious injury and not take preventative measures, particularly when officials refuse to resolve the issue. You can say that I should not have taken the law into my own hands. You can say that *ad infinitum*. It was my neck, not yours.

The following day, it started. An orchestrated press campaign, highlighting only incidents showing us as aggressors, peppered the sporting pages without a scintilla of objectivity. Personal slurs were also made against Dean Richards and Wade Dooley, making mention of their private jobs as policemen. One hack described our pack as 'Atavistic Apostles of Anarchy'. I remember thinking that, whilst this was brilliant alliteration, it was of little use if the reader was Gareth Chilcott.

Curiously, the press seemed not to notice the punches, stamping and illegalities of our opponents. I do not seek to refute or even deny our culpability, but at least I am honest in admitting it existed. I thought at first that the complaints would wane, but I was wrong. As they became ever more extreme, I and the rest of the team knew we had the Australians rattled. Alan Jones, the former Wallaby coach, later wrote that he thought the strategy of complaint was a deliberate attempt to deny the fact that the Lions pack was well organised and superior.

The last major hurdle before the Test series began was the game against New South Wales. Everyone in the Lions squad paid particular attention to the starting XV for this game. In all but name, it would be the Test team the following Saturday. My form had been good and I believed I would be given my chance to win a Lions Test jersey. After I was named in the team for the NSW game, I turned my attention to the player I would face, and the fact that he was young and inexperienced further raised my expectation of dominating the scrums and being able to get around the field as I had been doing in previous games. The rookie's name was Phil Kearns and he turned out not to be the patsy I had expected: in fact he was big, solid, and although he posed me no problems, neither could I impose myself on him.

The game did not have the physical malevolence of the Queensland game but we were stretched to the final whistle, winning by two points. This meant we went into the first Test undefeated and looking forward to a hard Test series.

Our confidence was shattered at the Sydney Football Stadium as we were given a hiding by Australia. We did not manage to compete effectively in any phase of the game, and in the lineouts in particular their tall locks, Campbell and Cutler, dominated possession. The scrums were even, but the only time the game was evenly balanced was at the kickoff.

If anybody wants to study the effective use of ball and decision-making, they should watch the performances of Nick Farr-Jones and Michael Lynagh, the Aussie scrum half and fly half respectively, for that eighty minutes. No one has ever played a perfect game, but they made so few errors that realistically it was pretty close to ideal. Farr-Jones's distribution was swift, he knew when to take on the back row and especially when not to throw out rubbish. Lynagh released his outside backs in space, but it was his kicking out of hand that stays with me. Time and again I got up from scrums or rucks to see the ball rifling past me, bouncing a foot inside the touchline, leaving us to trudge sixty metres back. We were pinned in our own territory for so long that scores were inevitable and we were trounced 30–12.

It is not difficult to imagine the mood afterwards. It was not just the margin but the manner of defeat which went so deep. We had failed to test them in any aspect of the game. So comprehensive was the loss that it was difficult to see how we could work towards squaring the series. For a few hours after the game, the atmosphere was not just low. I and most of the team that had taken the field were stunned.

At the post-match meeting, Finlay was typically candid when he simply said, 'Make no mistake about it, there will be changes.' These words were delivered in a voice that immediately reminded me of John Laurie playing Private Frazer in *Dad's Army*. Normally I have difficulty repressing an irreverent tendency to giggle when I find levity during solemnity; this time I was too down even to smile.

The Aussie press reports were gleeful: it was good for the game that the bully boys had been sent packing. I think that this, as much as anything, snapped us out of self-pity. To any scribe who penned such words, I give thanks. Had the reporting not been purposely vindictive they would have written about magnificent performances by the Aussies and we would have had little or no praise. The fact that they chose to be spiteful made us angry, and that, coupled with a second Test that might see us lose the series, was enough for us to anchor our preparations for this most crucial of matches.

Bob Norster was one of the best lineout technicians to have played the game. At six-feet-five, he was not especially tall for an international second-row, nor was he well built. It was his timing, nous and refusal to be intimidated that set him apart from most of his contemporaries. He managed the no mean feat of dominating Wade Dooley on more than one occasion. So the fact that he was replaced by Dooley for the second Test shocked some players and many who watched from afar. As the Norst (as he was affectionately called by the Welsh players) was something of a father figure to the Welsh contingent, there was a lot of bad feeling amongst the Welsh players over this decision.

The truth was more prosaic: Steve Cutler, his Wallaby counterpart, was simply too tall for Norster to get near him when the throw was on target. It was felt that Dooley's more direct approach might unsettle Cutler, who was an athlete, not a wrestler. I did rediscover my ability to giggle inappropriately, along with Mike Teague, who also suffers from this affliction, when Wade was given a pep-talk by Roger Uttley on the morning of the second Test. Roger addressed Wade thus: 'You are replacing one of the best second-rows in the world; a man who has everything; good hands, athletic, superb. And you're in, because you're big.' Now, if that doesn't make you want to go out and bite the heads off chickens, I don't know what will.

There were other important changes and some of the longer-term antipathy between the English and the Scots may stem from the fact that two further Celts were replaced by two Sassenachs: the first, Mike Teague, had recovered from earlier knocks and took the blindside from Derek White, which was hard on Derek as he had been played out of position in the Test, but Mike's selection turned out to be most significant; the second change was the inclusion of Rob Andrew. Rob had not been in the squad at the outset, but he replaced Irishman Paul Deans when the latter was injured. His late call-up was greeted with no enthusiasm, and a few of the Scots openly rubbished the decision. What happened when Rob played in his first game on tour midweek surprised even the England players. His first of a number of clean breaks was electric and he played seemingly without restriction. His replacement of Craig Chalmers was deserved and it increased the England contingent in the starting XV to eight.

As we could not specify any areas of particular Australian weakness, it was difficult to know how we should move forward. In the end Finlay simply said that we had not become a poor team overnight. Moreover, we felt that the right team, bar one or two, had taken the field and would surely not play that badly twice in a row. In addition, we knew that Australia was unlikely to play any better and that Farr-Jones and Lynagh would struggle to repeat the near-perfect games they had played. That was it – not much to work from.

A midweek win against ACT in Canberra, during which an early deficit was turned around into a handsome win, meant that, instead of going into the second Test cowed and bloodied, we went into that game intent on bloodying the noses of what was becoming a triumphalist Australian press.

The Brisbane Test has been named the Battle of Ballymore (on account of the ground at which it was played), but in truth it was never that bad. From this game came the reputation of that Lions team as a bunch of thugs, with little or no brains or ability. In fact, whilst we did beat the shit out of them, there was only one general free-for-all. There was no gouging, phantom punching from behind, spear-tackling and the like. What we did do was hit every breakdown with ferocity and we rucked any Aussie player near the ball out of the way and with venom. Had we been wearing All Black jerseys, nobody would have made a comment about the ferocity of the footwork, although to be absolutely candid, I don't include in this assertion the kick from Dai Young to the head of Steve Cutler. Whilst it did not connect with any force and caused no damage, I cannot defend it, and Tom Lawton in particular took exception to it, wading in with fists swinging.

The other incident that was the focus of media attention after the game was a brawl that was started by two of the least likely culprits. One scrum half standing on another's foot is not usually the signal for World War III, but Farr-Jones reacted angrily to Robert Jones doing this as he tried to feed the ball into the Aussie scrum. His two-handed shove was met with a token left hook from the diminutive Welshman, and then it started. One Aussie journalist accused Finlay Calder of deliberately holding down the French referee so that he could not whistle and intervene. Yes, that is how preternaturally biased they were. A free-for-all began between the packs that, when quelled, saw us well ahead on points. It was termed one of the most illegal acts perpetrated on Australian soil, but bearing in mind that police constables Dooley and Richards, police inspector Ackford and solicitor Moore were involved, I hardly think that 'illegal' is the right epithet.

The game was otherwise fiercely contested and our forwards dominated, with Mike Teague rampaging over would-be tacklers in the first of two performances that would see him deservedly awarded the Man of the Series accolade. Nevertheless, if there is a hallmark of Australian teams it is their refusal to quit; you hardly ever see an Australian team thrashed. In a game that swung towards either team for periods, the precociously talented Jerry Guscott gathered his own grubber kick, scoring under the Aussie posts to seal a famous 19–12 victory.

It was a remarkable performance given the severity of our loss in the first Test. But the Aussie press, intent on denying us any credit, launched into us with allegations that at times bordered on the hysterical. Again and again, unwisely, Aussie players came out and stated their disgust at our physical approach. They could not point to a litany of serious foul play, as per the previously listed acts, for there were none. They had been physically beaten and could not stand it without whingeing. It is ironic that the Aussies are so fond of the accusation 'whingeing Pom', when they are by some way the greatest exponents of this art. Comment in defeat is not automatically whingeing; there are times when it is right to make play of something serious and unacceptable. In that game there was one free-for-all, in which players stood face to face and traded blows; nothing underhand, nothing done on the sly. The fact is, they lost 'the biff', as they call it, and did not like it.

Tom Lawton was quoted in the press as saying that if this was the way rugby was played by the Lions, he wanted no part of it.

Later that day, we happened to be watching a tape of the most recent Bledisloe Cup between Australia and New Zealand. To wry amusement we watched the same Tom Lawton tread right on the head of the Kiwi hooker, Sean Fitzpatrick. Having replayed the incident a few times we took the tape to the management and asked for it to be released to the press at the next meeting. They did not want to do this, and at the time of the decision I was angry, as I felt that this sort of incontrovertible evidence of hypocrisy should have been used. I now think I was wrong. That we took whatever abuse they threw and met it with indifference, provoked yet more lurid headlines. The more extreme things got, the greater became our belief that we had seriously destabilised them.

Not surprisingly, the atmosphere in our camp was transformed, but it was also restrained because we knew the job was not finished. Again, the reliable Aussie press highlighted nothing positive. They ignored the hugely powerful runs of Teague, the brave defence of David Sole, and the skilful audacity of the young Guscott, preferring instead to invent conspiracies such as our plan to take out the referee in the last Test. In retrospect it is all highly amusing; at the time it served merely to stiffen our resolve.

Before a game, it was rare for my body to feel absolutely right. There was always something that felt tight, some worry. In the hour before the deciding third Test at the Sydney Football Stadium, I changed early and tried to get into my routine of pre-match exercises. In those days, the team did not warm-up collectively on the pitch before the game, and it was very much an individual's choice as to what he did to prepare. After five minutes of stretching in various contorted positions, I stopped. I was ready. With this unusual physical feeling came a similarly atypical certainty that we would win this series. Had I known the minute margin that would separate the teams at the final whistle and the enormous effort that I and the team would have to give, that conviction would have been lessened; but I did not know, and the fact is that I never thought we would not win.

The commitment of both sides was raised from the levels of the second Test, and up front the battle was much more even. We made liberal use of Rob Jones's ability to pinpoint high box kicks to their wingers, David Campese and Ian Williams, both of whom had shown their dislike of this tactic in the second Test.

The winning try was a classic for only one reason: it came from a horrendous blunder by Campese. For many years, he has been the critic of all things English, but although he was one of the greatest wingers ever to play the game, most people enjoy a bit of *schadenfreude*. Trying to summon a spark of genius within his own in-goal area, Campese flung out a misdirected pass meant for his fullback Greg Martin. When it went to ground, Ieuan Evans gleefully fell on the ball to score, following this act with a few words of comfort for the distraught Campese. I can still remember the commentary of that most supportive of Aussie commentators, Chris Handy: 'You don't do that in your own in-goal area. You don't pull on the green and gold jersey to play that sort of Mickey Mouse rugby.' It couldn't have happened to a nicer bloke.

Although we resisted waves of thrilling counter-attacks from Australia, they eventually forced a scrum only five yards from our line in the dying minutes of the game. Michael Lynagh lined up for an attempt at what was a reasonably easy drop goal. As the score was 19–18 to the Lions, it would have won the game. The following will have been forgotten by nearly everyone who watched that game, but not by those in the depths of the front row, where these things matter, and such events become as priceless as victory itself. We had no problems with the Aussie scrum in any of the Tests, despite conventional wisdom that a giant hooker meant inevitable superiority. This scrum demonstrated that this theory was/is complete rubbish. Taking the scrum lower to the ground than Lawton wanted, we managed to make him struggle to hook back the ball cleanly. With a slight shove, and keeping the front row low, we took the ball against the head and the danger was cleared. I remember thinking as we controlled the ball and it was kicked to touch that this was personal vindication for the slight regard I had been given before the tour.

The end-of-series dinner was not an occasion of sobriety and restraint. To their credit, the Aussie players gritted their teeth and mixed, but unusually it had been made a mixed dinner with partners attending. None of the Lions had their partners at the dinner, and when the drink flowed, our behaviour caused a few raised eyebrows. I only remember part of what was a spectacularly vulgar and immature celebration on my part.

My old Nottingham teammate, Steve Holdstock, was at the time playing in Sydney for Manly, and he and some Australian friends and partners sat on a nearby table. Towards the end of the dinner, I went over to chat to Steve, and one of his Aussie friends asked me to have a drink with him. I grabbed a bottle of red wine and said, 'Right, I'll have this one,' and handing him a similar bottle said, 'You have that one.' His wife looked daggers at me and told me not to even think of it. He was about to defer to his better half when I challenged him wittily by saying, 'Come on, you soft Aussie bastard, drink it.' We started together but when he had consumed about two thirds of his bottle he collapsed and I tried to drag him back up whilst being berated by his wife. Failing to get him off the floor I finished my bottle and his, and the rest of the evening I do not remember, though it had not finished; not by a long chalk.

I cannot recall any of the following but I must have staggered from the hotel and wandered the streets of King's Cross for some time, gradually wending my way along the road that led to Manly. The following account comes from two British journalists who were covering the tour. As they sat in the back of their taxi on their way over the Sydney Harbour Bridge, they saw what they thought was a vaguely familiar figure running towards them, in the fast lane, and against oncoming traffic, doing airplane impressions like those done by many a five-year-old at weddings. As they drew almost level with the idiot, they recognised me, stopped their cab and dragged me into it and to safety.

This was the Lions series victory for which I had worked so hard and for so long. We remain the only Lions team ever to lose the first Test match and go on to win a series. The trip was special for many reasons, on and off the field. We played as friends and comrades; played with a free rein and in an unapologetic physical manner. The Australians like to deride our achievement, and in the litany of alleged violence they neglect to mention two things: we did not start the rough stuff, we finished it. Further, bar the Dai Young incident, any remaining confrontation was face to face, giving them the opportunity to give as good as they got. As I think back, I realise I missed the opportunity to savour the sweetest of triumphs with a leisurely evening in a fantastic city, and I can only come up with one phrase: what a half-wit.

# 12

## 1990 and All That

The Five Nations of 1990 has to be seen in the context of the British Lions tour that had taken place the previous summer. The respect gained and given during the efforts of the winning series against Australia had several effects. Players and men who had harboured deep suspicions, me being one of the most sceptical, had been forced to acknowledge that former rivals were not only good players but, as men, were worthy of respect. It did not matter that personal dislike remained. John Jeffrey and I are unlikely ever to exchange Christmas cards, but I cannot, with any candidness, deny his commitment and loyalty to the cause, nor overlook the way he bore the disappointment of seeing Mike Teague take his Test place and become Man of the Series. In the end, I would have fought toe to toe with him because he would have done no less for me. Personal lessons like these do no man any harm.

However, with the bonds that had been forged came an intimate knowledge of players' strengths and weaknesses. In addition it created, if anything, a heightened rivalry, because nobody wanted to be found lacking in the game immediately after they had bared their soul. Added to the usual type of rivalry between opposing teams, was one that resembled the rivalry between siblings. It was not abstract this time; it was deeply personal.

The England team was given a lift both in the form of the returning Lions players and by the fact that we now knew we could compete with any team anywhere in the world. Success could not be guaranteed, but we had closed the gap that existed between the two hemispheres. We had made up the bulk of the winning Lions Test XV and we knew that *en masse* we were the best team in the northern hemisphere. This will lead some readers to conclude that this was evidence of the arrogance that they say led to England's downfall against Scotland in the Grand Slam decider. Confidence in a sportsman is essential, and often those with the most confidence hit the highest notes. Invariably this is mistaken for arrogance, yet I do not think this was the case. Even looking back, I still do not think it was so.

The 1990 Championship opened with us beating the Irish 23–0 at Twickenham. It was an incomplete performance, but to prevent a team from scoring is rare, and it showed the measure of our dominance, though the points did not come as freely as we wanted. This was followed by England's first win in Paris for many years when we beat the French soundly, 26–7.

Playing at home is always an advantage, but given the weight of other external factors, such as historic rivalry and so on, this is exacerbated when it comes to this particular championship. The number of away wins recorded over the years is ample proof of the difficulty of winning on the road. For England, Paris had become a graveyard of results: team after team, some containing very good players, had not only failed to win but even to play well. It was second only to Cardiff in terms of nightmare venues for an England player.

Approaching a game against France required a special mindset if you were a forward, particularly a front-row forward. All of theirs were immensely strong and took pride in scrummaging to the maximum on every ball. It was usually the case that an opposition hooker would try to strike on my ball or a wheel was attempted. The eight-man shove was used regularly, but selectively, usually according to the position of the scrum on the field. Against France, the weight came at you every time.

We called the effort involved 'kitchen sink' scrummaging: that is, you threw everything at it. This did not mean driving, as packs are illegally allowed to do today; it meant absorbing the huge pressure and keeping as stable as possible from start to finish; very, very tiring. Fortunately, the introduction of Jeff Probyn into the front row helped enormously because he was able to take and scrum so low and to hold it there so that more of the pressure went up over his shoulder. Probyn's contribution to England was always underrated, especially by the captain, Will Carling, and the coach, Geoff Cooke, both backs, who had no idea what he actually did and how much effort he saved the rest of the pack. They assumed that the sulking and general unhappiness that came from us when Probyn was dropped was simply due to the old guard sticking together. It was not; it was because we all knew the importance of his contribution to our and the team's success.

When I saw Probyn's head appear to my right and almost near my right boot, I knew all was well. It did not matter if his opponent was a power-lifter or five stone heavier; the anatomical difficulty in trying to get underneath a low object makes it near to impossible. Probyn destroyed front rows, and for this reason he was singled out for treatment. There are different kinds of courage. One definition of it is someone who refuses to be intimidated and who, in the face of punishment, continues doing that thing that attracts the punishment, taking it no matter what is dealt out; thus it was with Probyn.

The weather in Paris on the day of the match was filthy. There was no sign of springtime and a gale blew and swirled around from all directions on the field. As if this were not sufficiently difficult, sheets of rain sporadically added to the challenge. This game demonstrated fully the difference made when a team has a kicker who converts early and difficult penalties. Simon Hodgkinson's penalties, in the most difficult of kicking conditions, gave us the foundation from which to gradually pull away from France. Importantly these successes had two contrasting psychological effects.

For the England pack, they were rewards for discipline: taking some French hits, refusing to retaliate and taking the resulting points. To the French, each kick increased the frustration of the team and, even more importantly, of the crowd. In the ten times I played against the French, when they played with confidence and had the support of the crowd, they seemed to be irresistible. The other side of this beatific adoration was the unsympathetic disappointment expressed volubly by the crowd when things did not go according to plan. We would try to achieve, first, a quietening of the Paris crowd and then, if all went well, the sweet sound of discordant booing and whistling; over many games, it was a sound I was to hear again and again. This hostility only served to increase the French team's frustration and opened them up to yet more disciplined provocation from us. Our approach was: never hit back and certainly not in the open; if you did hit, do it first and take whatever comes back without complaint. Cynical – yes; effective – yes; painful – indubitably, *oui*.

Compared to the days of English diffidence or infrequent promise, our performance this time was one of near-total concentration in which the French side was dismantled, and we scored three tries, two of which were belters. The comprehensive nature of this win led not to self-congratulation but to demands that we do what too few England teams had managed previously: maintain that level of performance and concentration in successive matches.

As it happened, we did what was demanded and more. Although I do not remember much about our win against Wales at Twickenham in the next fixture, it is probably one of the three games with which I am genuinely content. This will sound absurd to most, but Gollum has managed to taint so many performances by amplifying my mistakes that, when I recall the games, my performance feels it has no merit. Of all the many scars inflicted by this little monster, the pleasure lost by the warping of what should be good memories is perhaps that for which I bear him most hate.

Up to that point of the 1990 season, the Welsh club game was about Neath. A strong-running and abrasive pack, quick ball and effective finishing had seen Neath hammer all their rivals to the rhythmically guttural chant of 'Neath, Neath, Neath'. It was great to watch and involved great skill, but it wasn't real. By this, I mean that it was impossible to play that way at international level, unless teams were horribly mismatched. Nevertheless, Ron Waldron, the then Wales manager, fell into the same trap as had the English selectors a few years earlier by picking a club team, augmented by a few players from other clubs. Wales became Neath – or was it the reverse? – expecting to play the same way and with similar results.

I watched the available footage of Neath very carefully and it was obvious to me that the principal reason they had been so dominant at club level was that they were fitter, stronger and more abrasive than their opponents. When opposing teams had a few players who could match these qualities, they only had sufficient numbers to delay the inevitable. Player for player, the advantages enjoyed by the Neath players did not exist at international level. Further, the continual pick and drives initiated by the Neath forwards almost invariably gained ground at club level. The better, bigger defences in the Five Nations easily absorbed such thrusts, and often the attempts served only to slow down good ball and frequently to lose it.

Welsh rugby was actually slipping into depths not previously experienced, but I do not believe that a Welsh side had previously been beaten and battered in the way that the Wales XV was that day. Almost everything we tried worked. It is not fair to suggest Wales did not give it their all; they were overwhelmed and we played very well. Time and again we got quick ball and put together sweeping moves – another style of play that does not exist if you are one of those who maintains that that England team played only ten-, nine- or, sometimes, eight-man rugby.

Early in the match, I was at the bottom of a ruck when my head carelessly came into contact with the boot of my former Lions front-row teammate, Mike Griffiths, the Welsh prop. The dull thud signalled a blow that did not knock me out, but did make me 'heady'. My shirt showed the blood that came out of a cut to my head that later required stitching. I cannot say to what extent that blow contributed to the way I played thereafter. What I can say is that I wish I had been stamped on more often if that was what it did for me.

Fear of inadequacy makes me react sharply against much of the criticism concerning what I was or did as a player. Much of the time I should be better able to ride negative opinions, but what did and does really anger me are assertions that are demonstrably refutable by simply viewing the available evidence. Of the sort that I was: too small to scrummage effectively, too slow and clumsy, and an adherent of grinding rugby. All of this is countered by watching those eighty minutes. It is a valid point of view to claim I showed too little of the above skills and played negatively too often; but it is then a question of degree. I am well aware of my failings and inadequacies as an England player; indeed, the fact that I have chosen to defend myself is a sign of insecurity. But when it comes down to it, I know that I tried as hard as I could, gave what I could, and nobody was prouder of the shirt than I was.

My favourite memory of the game, of the few available, was my sixty-yard touchline run from a pass at the front of a two-man lineout from Wade Dooley. When I was out of favour some years later, trying unsuccessfully to resurrect my international career, Tom McNab kindly wrote to me, enclosing a picture of the run which shows me with a 'jelly jaw'. I cry more freely than most men and do not apologise for this, but that small, thoughtful act reduced me to private tears during what was a dark time. To that Scot, I give many thanks.

The press and public reaction to the win was unqualified praise, and it was as a result of this that talk of a Grand Slam being inevitable emerged. I did not utter anything similar, and, as far as

I was aware, neither did anybody connected with the England team. As a team, we purposely stressed the need to continue in a professional manner and that we had no right to assume an entitlement to success.

It had been ten years since England's last Grand Slam. I remember watching Bill Beaumont being chaired off at Twickenham amidst a surging crowd; nobody thought it would take more than a decade for the feat to be repeated. Not only had England fans had to get used to losing, they had always been subject to taunts that their team had little flair. Like it or not, the rugby we played in the first three games of the 1990 Championship was exciting and showed what we could do and the direction we might have taken had that season gone to plan.

We stayed in the Peebles Hydro Hotel, near Edinburgh, from the Wednesday night before the Scotland game. It was a cosy and quiet hotel without any of the excitement and angst that was building up in Edinburgh; it was thought that detachment was the correct way to minimise the pressure that would increase steadily until it reached its climax on match day.

Training was good and Will Carling and I had a number of conversations about overconfidence; it was an issue that we were acutely aware of, and had there been recognisable signs of this, it would have been addressed. The discussions about the game were candid, and the Friday morning run-out before the press was as good as it gets. When I started playing rugby, I had read about All Black sessions during which no ball was dropped; that session was the same. As I jogged off the pitch, I recognised the brogue of the wonderful Bill McLaren, who had a quick word to wish me all the best, and he added that he did not recall a Home Unions country's training session of that pace and quality. Yes, we were confident: when a man of McLaren's stature and integrity makes those sorts of remarks, you can be nothing other. It is a cheap jibe to say that we were haughty. Much of the English media hype around us may have bordered on this, but the team itself was not arrogant.

This will be disputed by some Scots, but these are the people who cannot say the word English without attaching the word arrogant. I remember a perfect example of this bigoted attitude coming from a Scottish caller to a radio phone-in programme: he gloated over the England football team's exit from the 2002 World Cup in Japan. 'The trouble with yous, is that yer all sooo arrogant; before the Cup started yer manager said yous thought yous could win it.' I remember clearly what Eriksson had said: he thought that England had the ability to win the Cup; not that England would do this. If he had not said this, he would have been criticised for not expressing confidence in his team.

Now that I have had time to go through all the events surrounding the Scotland match – and, believe me, I have gone through them hundreds of times – I realise there were small points that were not noticed, things that were not right. They are obvious now, but I have asked myself so many times whether I or anyone else should have recognised the subtle way we lost focus before the game. I have concluded that we probably could have done little about it because it was not until the searing lesson of defeat had been applied and after the passage of time that these things have been recognised. It is difficult to explain how faint the loss of focus was, but that is all it takes on such occasions. That is one of the enduring attractions of sport.

I have had the benefit of talking about the match at length with one of my two Scottish friends, Finlay Calder, the 1989 British Lions captain. Having been given authoritative material about Scotland's preparation from a man who is incapable of saying anything other than how it is, I think I can now give as full an account as any about how things turned out. It is as disinterested as I can make it and it is not until this point, nearly twenty years later, that I can wade through my natural but unjustified bitterness and attempt to be objective.

Though this game has come to represent the triumph of the little nation against the over-mighty neighbour, the truth is that it was never as one-sided as portrayed; but there were a number of reasons why we were the favourites. If both teams played to their full potential, we were a more talented team than Scotland. The Lions selections and performances just before the Five Nations were reliable evidence of this. What was not given sufficient import was the fact that in many of the Lions Test positions filled by English players, their immediate rival was a Scot. We were better, but not hugely so, and the Scottish Lions had shown ability and character in winning all the pre-Test games. What this meant was that Scotland needed no miracle to beat us; all they required was that we did not play as well as we could and that they played somewhere near their best. It does not matter whether we lost because we failed to do so or because of Scottish pressure. Nor am I claiming that we lost the game, rather the opposite: they won it.

In addition, the manner of our wins up until then contrasted with those of Scotland. Their previous games had been scrappy, and not many tries were scored; the fact that the Scots had managed to fashion wins in each game was partially obscured, in comparison with the way we had thrashed the same teams. The fact was that suffocating defence and the converting of limited opportunities were the hallmarks of that Scottish team. It played to its strengths – and that description is realistic, not derogatory. Furthermore, the Scots, rightly, had no truck with criticism that suggested they were dour: who cares, as long as you win?

From the Scottish point of view, the psychological preparation was straightforward. It was 'backs to the wall'; 'nobody rates us'; 'that fucking arrogant little numpty Moore', and so on. There was so little genuine expectation of Scotland winning that there was little pressure on the Scottish team. Anything they could achieve would be more than most people thought they would. Today, no Scot will admit to pessimism before the game, but I have taken the trouble to dig out as many papers and as much footage of the coverage of the last few days before the clash, and hardly any Scottish writers, pundits or fans expressed any confidence, and some even predicted an easy England victory.

The freedom given by being able to go out and fight without fear of blame is huge. More importantly, it allows the specifics of the task in hand to be addressed without distraction. The more distant I become from the match, the greater is the significance of these respective Scottish and English mindsets and of how they affected each team.

Scotland's tactics were simple. They would use their home crowd to pressure us throughout the game. They would move our larger pack about the field, and at all costs try to prevent it being a set-piece game. They would use quick tapped penalties and free kicks, short or quick lineouts; anything unexpected that would stop us settling into a pattern of play. If sufficient disruption was caused, they would seek to turn mistakes into scores.

Allied to these tactics, the easily generated anti-English fervour was reinforced by the genuine political antipathy felt by the country towards the English Thatcher government, particularly as it had been trialling its new system of local rates, known as the poll tax, north of the border.

Carrying the moniker of 'favourites' is something that not many teams or individuals can bear; even fewer absorb it with ease. We were the first England team for many years to be so heavily favoured and to even the most jaundiced eye we had been playing with freedom and were beginning to fulfil the promise shown when we had beaten Australia two years earlier at Twickenham.

The promise of England's first Grand Slam for ten years saw the fevered activity of the media increase to a pitch I had not experienced up to that point. Will Carling and the management were quick to remind us of the fact that nothing tangible had been won, and I think the players understood this. The difficulty with facts, opinions, and indeed any piece of knowledge, wanted or unwanted, is that once absorbed it cannot be completely erased. By way of an example, one of the papers posed the question 'Is this the best England team ever?' Although I put the paper down and told myself not to entertain the question, at times my thoughts lingered over the matter, and though swiftly dismissed, the fact is that this question had intruded and would not have done so had I not happened upon it in the first place.

I also think that we did not give enough thought to how Scotland would approach the game. We did concentrate on our game and some people say that it is legitimate to 'let them worry about you'. We did discuss the way we thought Scotland would approach the game and we were correct, but only in generalised terms. We knew they would want a broken game in which our forwards were moved about, and they would want to prevent us from developing any pattern. We knew that the Scots had used the high kick to the fullback and wingers in every game of the Championship. They had an effective chasing game and this, aided by the baying of their home crowd, would undoubtedly be tried many times during the match.

However, we did not go beyond this and did not consider exactly what moves or ploys might be used to put this strategy into effect. An example that actually comes from the game was the use of trick lineouts. Twice, Scotland used players who normally would not be receivers, and with one throw to Finlay Calder at the front of a lineout, they made thirty yards. Telling each other to be alert is not the same as looking for specific plays that might be attempted.

The other vital issue we did not sufficiently stress was our discipline. We specified that we must not give kickable penalties away and were confident that we were a disciplined side. In previous games, especially against the French, we had withstood all manner of provocation, and the number of penalties conceded had been low. Knowing that Scotland needed to unsettle us, we should have predicted the small niggling things that happened in the game. Let me make it plain: I do not decry Scotland for one moment for using such tactics. Had we been properly focused, they would not have worked and they did not involve foul play. When describing the game later, I will highlight two such incidents that in the end would mean the difference between winning and losing.

As we arrived at Murrayfield, I could tell the atmosphere was going to be different and it was not going to be pleasant. There were more supporters at the ground than was usual so far in advance of kickoff, and although the 'welcome' we traditionally received was not warm, the comments made were laced with invective and had a genuinely hostile edge, as opposed to usual sporting banter. This didn't bother me – in fact I liked any sort of reaction. Far better that than ineffectual comments.

Stories of legend are now told by many Scotsmen who claimed to have been present. If they are all telling the truth, there must have been a crowd of 200,000. The famous Scottish walk on to the pitch is celebrated as an act of Wallace-like defiance and some Scottish players have embellished the story to claim that fear could be seen in our eyes as they marched forth. Bollocks. The truth is that we were at one end of the field when they came on to it. I did not even realise they had walked on to the turf at first. Their gesture may have drawn from their crowd the hoped-for rallying call, but I do not think it affected anyone in our team.

Those who were present will know that a gale was blowing straight down the field, and I am not exaggerating when I use that term. It was actually difficult to throw the ball to the tail of the lineout without it being pulled off-line by the wind. Winning the toss, we decided to play into the wind; the thought being that, in international games, the first twenty minutes are often frenetic, with neither side able to establish much cohesion. Often, by the time the side that has the advantage of the wind gets into their stride, they have little more than about fifteen of the forty minutes in that half in which to use the advantage properly. This choice was not controversial and was adopted by most teams because most times it turned out to be right.

Hindsight is the most marvellous of tools, but I now think it was the wrong decision; though I did not think so at the time. In games of this significance, away from home, the first thing needed is to quieten the home crowd. This means not attempting moves that are complex and that might end up with the opposition turning over the ball. It means making back-row players, who are intent on getting amidst your backs and causing mayhem, tackle repeatedly so that they cannot disrupt you. Control is what is sought. It is far easier to do this with a gale at your back, when any reasonable kick will keep the opponents pinned in their own twenty-two. With this advantage, you can do what they want to do to you – hit high kicks and bury the catcher. No crowd roars in anticipation of their fullback being hammered, even if he catches the ball.

In addition, the fact that Scotland went into half-time with a lead gave them the belief that victory was not only possible, but only forty minutes away. It meant the crowd screamed their approval for any act that proved positive for Scotland. They roared approval for lineout catches, tackles, anything, for the whole of the second half. The lead also sustained the Scottish forwards in the last quarter of the game, when they threatened to tire. Having made so many tackles, the Scots were naturally beginning to feel the effects, but the fact that they were in front, allied to the fantastic support given by their crowd, provided sufficient succour in their time of need.

Had they been behind, although they would still have had the support, they would have had to create rather than destroy, and tiredness makes the former more difficult – as we found out time and time again when we launched attack after attack, only for them to break down at the last.

The anticipated aerial bombardment did come but did not produce much for Scotland. So difficult was the wind that even kickers of the quality of Craig Chalmers found it difficult to put kicks into positions where an England catcher received man and ball. Often his kicks were short or rolled over our dead-ball line. However, though these kicks did not catch us out, the fact that they rolled dead kept us in our half of the field and more importantly in range of their kickers, should we concede penalties; which is exactly what we did.

I previously mentioned discipline. We were not a team that gave away unnecessary penalties as a rule, as our record up to that point proved. Yet in the first half, we gave away two needless penalties, reacting precisely the way Scotland had planned. The first came when the Scotland front jumper in the lineout, my Nottingham colleague and friend (and dentist) Chris Gray, shoved Paul Ackford off the mark where the lineout was to be set. It was niggling, not threatening, but Ackford responded with a punch, got caught and they kicked the penalty. The second came when David Sole, their loose-head prop, wrestled with Jeff Probyn who took the opportunity to stand on him, got caught and they kicked the penalty. In a game that was always going to be close, not least because of the weather, we gave Scotland six points without them having to create anything. Against such a strong wind, we had few chances to replicate the expansive rugby we wanted to play, but we scored from a scintillating break from Jerry Guscott who hit the line at pace and put Rory Underwood over the line.

The only other time we got near the Scotland line was for a series of five-yard scrums that were to become the subject of much debate and misinformation. The decisions made have been wrongly singled out as the cause of England's loss, so here is the accurate version of what happened.

During the only other period spent in the Scotland twenty-two in the teeth of the gale, we were awarded a penalty five yards from their line when they killed the ball at a ruck. I wrongly asked the referee for another scrum. Although I was pack leader and notionally vice-captain, I should not have made the call as it was the prerogative of Will Carling, the captain. I spoke without considering whether our fullback Simon Hodgkinson might kick the penalty.

The scrum re-set, I hooked the ball and we went for the drive again, and again it was collapsed by Burnell, who ended up lying across the tunnel, parallel with his own goal line. When the referee asked what we wanted to do, Carling, who had made sure he arrived promptly, asked me what I thought and I said we should have another scrum. In saying this, I took account of the fact that if we scored a try in this fashion it would be a body blow for their forwards. Moreover, I had this time considered the strength of the wind and, even though the kick was one normally considered routine for a kicker of Hodgkinson's ability, there was no certainty that he would be successful. Indeed, Simon later said that he thought his chances would have been no better than even. I also knew that if the referee made Scotland scrummage without collapse, we would push them over the line; and alternatively that he would award a penalty try if they did collapse.

Carling thought about it, agreed and asked the referee for another scrum. Legend has it that I overruled Carling (who had wanted a penalty kick) and that is wrong. Whilst I effectively did this by asking for the first scrum, that decision was of no consequence because we were to get two further penalties, and thus no different circumstance resulted as a consequence of my impetuosity.

We set for the put-in, I hooked the ball and, as we drove forward, Burnell again dropped the scrum and we were awarded another penalty. The same discussion between me and Carling took place, and he nominated another scrum.

Today, any referee would have been marching between the posts to award a penalty try for repeated infringement, but referee David Bishop would not take this step, even though he obviously thought Scotland was responsible for the repeated collapses. At this, the third five-yard scrum, I hooked the ball but it bobbled about in the second row and shot out of the side of the scrum behind the feet of flanker Peter Winterbottom. It was hacked downfield and the opportunity was lost. Even had the penalty been successfully kicked, the decisions to take a scrum rather than kick at goal made a difference of only three points. Compared to the six points given away through thoughtless indiscipline, it was of less import. Furthermore, a tactical decision we made in the second half was to prove the final error and led to Scotland being awarded a try against the wind.

When asked today whether he made the correct decision, Carling says that he asked the wrong person. Who else should he have spoken to? Moreover, with the second and third penalties, he had the option of accepting or rejecting my advice. Just because he accepted what I recommended does not make the decision anybody's but his.

We went in at half-time with the score standing at 9–8 to Scotland. We were calm, as the lead was not insurmountable. We agreed that we needed to make full use of the wind and reminded ourselves that having this advantage would not in itself bring us victory.

The second half was a whirlwind of flying blue and white shirts as both sides piled into the rucks, and although we made use of the wind, we still tried to play expansive rugby at times and in conditions that were not suitable. One such misguided attempt was to seal our fate. For God knows what reason, when we had a scrum with our put-in centrefield on the halfway line, we decided to do a back-row move. From that position the ball should have been drilled deep into the Scotland twenty-two for them to have to work their way up the field against a wind that was, if anything, getting stronger. From the base of the scrum, Mike Teague knocked the ball on. From the resultant put-in, Scotland ran down our blindside, chipped ahead and their winger Tony Stanger dived for the ball and was awarded a try. You may note I do not state that he touched the ball down, because he did not. It wasn't a try, as admitted later. Even so, neither I nor anyone else in our team questioned the try, as it appeared he had done things correctly, and without the aid of TV replays, David Bishop was right to award it at the time. Could you make a case out that Stanger should have done the right thing and admitted he did not score? Are you kidding? He would have been lynched.

Scotland defended desperately for the last fifteen minutes but we found we could not make the final pass count. It is no good now pointing out that they killed the ball repeatedly. We would have done the same; and they got away with it. The truth is that we had not maintained our discipline and did not establish control. They had executed their limited game plan properly and with no little character. They did not 'want it' more then we did; they played their game better than we played ours. I have no issue with their win.

When the final whistle blew, I was enveloped by hordes of

delirious spectators swarming on to the pitch. A few commiserated with me with sympathetic lines but I was beyond hearing. I cannot describe what I really felt at that moment of loss. I was desolate and numb. Up to that point, all had been going perfectly and the perfect ending had been wrenched away. One of sport's cruellest or finest aspects, depending on which side you are on, is the fact that its gladiators win or lose in public, in the full glare of the media and of the millions watching at home or in bars. The knowledge of such an audience heightens, exponentially, any emotion accompanying the moment when victory or defeat is apparent. If this chapter had a small video clip of my face at that moment, there would be no more need for words.

The dressing room was silent for a long time after the final whistle. As I emerged to board the bus back to the hotel, the press surrounded me and I could only comment tersely; I was too close to tears to do anything else. As if trying to erase another painful memory, similar to ones from a distant past, my memory does not record much of that evening's dinner. I was still stunned. The following day, I wrestled with a decision I had not expected to have to make: the previous week I had accepted an invitation from Chris Gray to attend a Sunday luncheon function at the Myreside clubhouse in Edinburgh. Could I now face the reception I would undoubtedly receive?

I had to brave it. It would have been cowardly not to have done so. I went and took all that came my way and congratulated Scotland on their Grand Slam. An achievement I firmly believed should have been mine, ours, as the better team. I endured the torment, which to be fair was eased by a number of Scots who were decent about the way we had played the season and who gloated as little as they could allow. However, for every second of the experience, and I exaggerate not, at the back of my mind was repeated the phrase, 'I would rather die than allow the Scottish to do this to me again.'

# 13

## Harlequin FC

Harlequin Football Club is the correct name for the rugby club everybody knows as Quins. They play in the following colours: chocolate, French grey, magenta and light-blue quarters. On the wall of the old Committee bar, they used to have an old photograph of the five former Quins who were internationals and Members of Parliament.

Harlequins is a rugby club unlike any other. The foppish image of talented dilettantes was to a certain extent justified, but a few years before I joined in 1990, they had started to assemble a useful team under coach Richard Best.

I had considered leaving Nottingham when I left university: the place where you go to university is never quite the same when all your friends leave. However, Nottingham was a great place and the rugby club was making big strides, so I had decided to stay, and under the tutelage of Alan Davies I gained my first England cap and toured with the British Lions. I finally decided to leave after nine years because I wanted another challenge and because, even though it was a city, Nottingham was sufficiently small for people to know all about your movements.

The decision was made after someone asked me about the blonde with whom I had been to the Theatre Royal the previous Wednesday. When I asked where they had been sitting, they replied that they had not been there, but a friend of a friend had brought this up at a dinner party. Even though there was nothing untoward, I didn't like it.

Having made the decision, I thought about where and what I might do – always making the decision dependent on there being a senior club within travelling distance. At first, I thought about returning to Yorkshire. On my visits home, I saw the place differently from when I was being brought up there. It is a fantastic area and Leeds, the largest city, had begun to develop rapidly. Many of the best law firms outside London were based there and I went for an interview with Hammond Suddards.

I was interviewed, rather flatteringly, by the head of the firm and six of his fellow partners. I liked the firm. I liked the people and had another meeting at the firm's flat on Sloane Street. The only thing was that the nearest senior club was Orrell, across the Pennines, just outside Wigan.

I didn't have any problem with joining them but when I looked at the practicalities of training and playing, I knew it would be difficult. It wasn't the mileage, but the fact that it would mean travelling on the M62 three times a week at rush hour. Sometimes stationary, other times slow, and for a few days each year closed, the M62 is a nightmare bettered only by the M25. I just didn't want to do it.

I considered moving to Bristol and would have had Bristol, Gloucester and Bath within easy distance. At the time, Bath was the premier club in England and, though it would have meant a war with their hooker Graham Dawe, I made enquiries with Jack Rowell, their coach. However, I understand that when he put the possibility to the senior players, there was a very stark divide in opinion. Some were very keen, others resolutely against. It appears that I wasn't the sort of person that would fit in at Bath.

Though I would normally bristle at the suggestion that I was not suitable for any club in the country, in retrospect it was probably right that my joining would not have worked out. Each club has its own culture and Bath was a very local club. Though the players went at each other unmercifully, to the outside world they presented a united front and were very loyal – very like Leicester. Graham Dawe was a favourite at Bath for his honesty and fearless play, and had I managed to overcome this challenge, there would have been friends of his who would not have forgiven me. I admire that sort of loyalty.

For a long time, I resisted a move to London because, wrongly, I did not consider it a place where I wanted to live. This was not based on any facts and therefore was even more inexplicable. I chatted to people from Quins and Wasps. Both were good clubs and both were willing to help find me a decent job. However, in terms of ambience, they were very different. Temperamentally I should have joined Wasps: a more earthy club, where I could also have joined Paul Rendall and Jeff Probyn, my England props.

The honest reason for my deciding to join Quins was because of a landscape. Though this sounds like a quote that should feature in Pseuds Corner of *Private Eye*, I had fallen in love with the view from the top of Richmond Hill. England stayed at the Petersham Hotel, halfway down the hill, so when I wanted a quiet moment of fresh air I often walked along the top of the hill. The view is the best of any in London. The sweep of the Thames as it bends towards Teddington is flanked by fields, and in the foreground there is a working farm where cows roamed in summer. Near by is the magnificent Richmond Park with its deer and fabulous walks. In contrast, Wasps was then situated in Sudbury, where admittedly you could get a very decent curry, but I doubt anybody has ever made a landscape portrait of any part of the borough.

As I continued to ponder the move, it was announced that the then Quins hooker, Jon Olver, was leaving to join Northampton, having accepted a teaching post near by. This was the final factor, Quins it was.

I discussed things with Colin Herridge, an RFU

With Thelma, my foster mother:
at least I was cute for a few months

**Executive**

REV. JOHN W. WATERHOUSE
O.B.E., M.A., B.D., *Principal*

MR. T. OWEN BUCK, B.COM.
*General Secretary*

MR. ALAN A. JACKA, M.A.

MISS MARY P. ASHBEE

REV. GORDON E. BARRITT, M.A.

## NATIONAL CHILDREN'S HOME
AND ORPHANAGE

*Founded by Dr. Stephenson, 1869*

**HIGHBURY PARK, LONDON, N.5**

**General Treasurer**
SIR HAROLD BELLMAN
D.L., J.P., LL.D.

Remittances payable to the
National Children's Home
and Orphanage

**40 BRANCHES**

Telegrams
Childsaver London N.5

Telephone
CANonbury 2033 (5 lines)

CIH/CW.

14th August, 1962.

Mr. and Mrs. R. Moore,
13 Pharoah Lane,
Illingworth,
Halifax, Yorkshire.

Dear Mr. and Mrs. Moore,

        Further to my letter of May 9th, in which I said we
had no news of a little Chinese boy, I now write to tell you
of a baby who is half Malayan and half English. His name is
Brian Kirk, and he is 7 months old. Date of birth 11.1.62.
Miss Blount, of International Social Service, asked me to make
some enquiries about this baby, who is in a temporary foster
home in Birmingham, and who is available for adoption.

        One of our Child Care Officers in the Birmingham area
has seen Brian, and describes him as follows:-

"Brian is a beautiful, bouncing, bonny boy of just seven months.
He eats and sleeps well, and seems very happy in his foster home,
where he has been for 4 months, and the family are all very
attached to him, and he has been no trouble at all and they
consider him very intelligent. He already says "Daddy", and he
gets around on the floor, and is trying to pull himself up on the
chair also. He does not look very oriental and is not very dark
skinned. His mother is a ▮▮▮▮▮▮▮▮ of 23, and comes from
Yorkshire, the exact town is not known, but is almost certainly
not Halifax. Mrs. Bush, Moral Welfare Worker, is checking on
this.

The earliest description of me in one of many letters concerning my adoption;
it just shows how wrong you can be

The rainbow family: from back left to right – Mother, Gwen, Father – middle left to right – Elizabeth, Ai-Lien, Catherine – front left to right – Paul and me

Dorothy and Ralph, my extraordinary parents

Me as the predatory striker for the Halifax Under 11 football team; shame about the haircu

Colin who? On my way to winning the *Victor Ludorum* at school

It was sometimes like street fighting: the Old Crossleyans first XV squad that won the *Yorkshire Post* merit table in 1979/80

I will not yield: curry-eating competition with Dylan Davies,
the Loughborough prop, 1983

Turning to my parents in the stand after a first-cap victory against Scotland
at Twickenham, 4 April 1987

My farewell presentation after my last game for Nottingham; I could barely speak in trying to hold back the emotion

M'Lud, I give you a sanctimonious prat

Is it a bird? Is it a plane? No, it's superdwarf; me in the process of charging down an Australian kick in the Second Test against the Lions 1989

*Rugby World* Player of the Year 1991

On a 60-yard dash against Wales in the 1990 5 Nations. One of the few games with which I was genuinely content

My constructive advice to Wales' Andy Allen in the same game is given short shrift

Joy after Carling scores the winning try against the French
in the 1991 Rugby World Cup quarter-final in Paris;
we thought it was coming our way

Despair – we lost; what else is there to say? World Cup final, Twickenham,
2 November 1991

My first wife, Penny

'Let's be 'aving you': PCs Bayfield and Dooley about to effect an arrest on Jean-François Tordo of France in the infamous 1992 game in Paris where two of his colleagues got their marching orders

Have you heard the one about . . . an unusual moment of levity for me; the All Black pack didn't get the joke

They call this 'doing your nut' in New Zealand; an impromptu haka of victory against the All Blacks in 1993 at Twickenham

I was actually singing the national anthem

It's only a scratch; I've had worse – in need of running repairs after foolishly headbutting Sean Fitzpatrick's elbow in the Third Test against New Zealand in 1993

All in a day's work: the Springbok forwards leave their calling card on my
back during the Second Test at Cape Town, 1994

Fifty caps up. Running out to face France in the 5 Nations
at Twickenham, 4 February 1995

Altered body mass probably led me to my fifth drug test in a row in the 1995 Rugby World Cup – it is actually the pads that make me look bulked

I went seventeen years with punches, knees and kicks but broke my nose only once when it came into contact with George Gregan's head v Australia, quarter-final Rugby World Cup, 1995

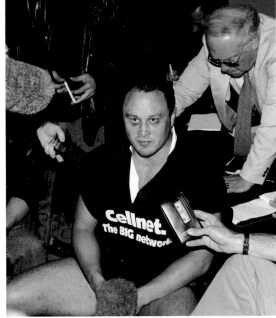

My second wife Lucy, mother of our daughter Imogen May

**DO YOU HAVE THE BALLS TO JOIN IN?**

ON JUNE 9 GET YOUR KIT ON AND HELP US RAISE MONEY TO FIGHT MALE CANCER.

To pledge money or for more information call 0906 3022 502

I think I got the plum position. Campaigning with fellow sportspeople against male cancer

Everybody wrongly assumes it's a life of luxury being a commentator – Eddie Butler and I perched on top of the Shed at Gloucester

Like other things, skiing became a serious business – too much bottom edge on this turn

Move over Valentino, there's a new kid in town; coming out of Clark Curve at Brands Hatch with the California Superbike School

My third wife Belinda, mother of our daughter Larissa Holly

My daughters, Imogen (left) and Larissa: being with them is the closest I get to being complete

Committeeman and a man well liked and respected within the England squad for his work as press liaison officer. Colin was always a players' man and although he looked more an archetypal Alikadoo than most, in reality he was pragmatic and moreover a thoroughly decent and honest man.

There were rumours about my move similar to those of many players who joined Quins: that I was being paid, if not openly, certainly indirectly. I do not know about anyone else, but between me, God and the Inland Revenue, I can honestly state that the only thing that Quins did for me was pay the first month's rent on my flat that had to be paid in advance. As the Quins treasurer will confirm, I never made an expenses claim in all the time I played at the club.

I took up a post in the corporate-finance department of Rea Brothers, though moved back to law whilst still at Quins. There was a view, mistaken, that these jobs were sinecures. In fact, nearly all the careers that were aided by the Quins business mafia were ones in which, once the opportunity was given, it was up to the individual. The times of spare capacity went in the late 1970s, and you have to remember that the other people fighting for those careers were determined to succeed as well.

People often joked about Peter Winterbottom's transformation from farmer to Eurobond dealer. Yes, Quins did open the door for him, but thereafter he proved himself and was accepted. Those who made this joke do not understand the nature of the City, especially the trading business. They seem to think that London is a place where people get fabulous salaries for doing very little. When a team of traders is put together, it cannot afford to carry anybody. When trades happen in hundreds of thousands of pounds, mistakes lose money and lose it big time; those responsible are out of the door, no matter how iconic they may be in the rugby world.

The season I arrived, Quins had recruited a group of players who belied their dandy-boy image, and an eclectic bunch they were. Though Jason Leonard's school may have been specifically approved by Her Majesty, I doubt you could call it a privilege. Add Yorkshireman Peter Winterbottom, Geordie Mickey Skinner and the like, and you see that the makings of a good team were there. We had a talented squad and would win the Pilkington Cup and reach the final twice more. On the right day, we were more than a match for any team. However, for reasons I can only partially define, we never came to dominate English club rugby as perhaps we might have and as Bath had done.

As expected, Quins was very different from Nottingham. Although the players got on well and we did mix with some of the supporters, there was never the unity that exists in many regional clubs. There were relatively new supporters and others who had been members for many years. These groups had totally different attitudes to the game and to the club. At Quins, there were a few players and many fans who had been public-school-educated. Many were from very wealthy families. They had different values and perspectives on life and rugby.

My first game for Quins took place at Twickenham. Quins had the agreement of the RFU to play fixtures there, I think, in return for letting the RFU use the club grounds on international days. It turned out to be the last time the club chose to use the RFU HQ and the reason was obvious as I ran on to the pitch for a game against Llanelli. Two thousand people in a 50,000-seater stadium produced an eerie effect. Having played there when it was full, it was disorientating to see almost all the seats empty. What noise there was echoed mildly and then was lost.

During the game we had a problem with the Llanelli front row, as they continually collapsed the scrum to avoid being shoved backwards. Their tight-head was Lawrence Delaney, who had played for Wales, but in that game was terribly unfit. After yet another collapse, I warned him politely to desist from this dangerous practice. The next scrum went down and I leathered him. He didn't complain; he knew he was in the wrong.

We won the game comfortably, but in the bar back at the Stoop I was standing having a beer and overheard the conversation of two elderly gentlemen. Unaware that they were within earshot, one asked the other, 'What do you think of this Moore chappie? He's a bit of a rough type, isn't he?' The reply was equally unfavourable. 'Yes. I'm not at all sure we want that at the club.' Unusually, I decided to let it go, as I didn't actually believe their description was either unfair or unflattering.

Training was never dull at Quins, thanks to the quality of the players and the idiosyncrasies of Dick Best. We had an irregular relationship during my time at the Stoop and my final year was one of armed standoff. However, as a sessions man there were few better, even if some of the things he introduced I am convinced were to see whether we really would do something so crazy.

I did train very hard and almost all the time took training seriously. One of the very few times I broke this rule was after a lunchtime meeting in the City got out of hand. After several bottles of distinctly reasonable red wine, I realised that it was almost time to leave for training. I grabbed my kit and turned up on time, but reeking of alcohol. As soon as Peter Winterbottom rumbled this, I knew I was in trouble. Sure enough we went into one of the many grid sessions at which Best majored. This meant four players, each standing on one corner of a large square, holding tackle shields and numbered one to four. Two men in the middle worked together, one feeding the other with the ball and the receiver driving into the corner man whose number had been called out by Best. He then drove him back a few yards and went to ground, laying the ball for the supporting man. The receiving player carried on until the whistle blew. It was hard work.

When it got to my turn, Best just happened to be watching our group. When he saw it was my turn to receive, he called endless diagonal runs, as they were the longest and the usual minute went into two and then three. 'I'll teach you to turn up pissed,' he roared. 'Was it a good year? We'll probably see it in a minute.' I slogged on, trying desperately not to vomit and avoided doing so only by a few seconds when he finally blew the whistle. I didn't do it again.

There are many theories about the inability of our team to maintain a consistent challenge for league honours, particularly given the amount of talent that was at our disposal. We should have been able to challenge Bath and Leicester in the league, but we did not manage to do so, though we had the odd win against the two teams that regularly swept all before them.

Quins never emulated the fraternity of a provincial rugby club. Wasps and Saracens managed this by manufacturing a grudge against 'fashionable' Quins, the lah-di-dahs. The geographical spread from whence came the Quins players meant that few socialised with each other away from the club.

When it came to the public support for the club, this too was difficult; in contrast with Bath, for example. There, in sporting terms, the club is the centre of the town. Everybody knows the players. Some live next door, all are recognised and, if successful, lauded. It is not difficult to establish an identity and a sense of purpose when this geographical proximity exists. No sport dominates London. It doesn't even manage to do this in a single borough like Twickenham, where many inhabitants have no interest in rugby and simply live there because it is a nice area. An evening out in Bath means going to bars in which the players are well known. This enhances the sense of community and belonging felt by players and public alike. In London, this only happens in Richmond, and even then, in not more than a handful of places.

Also, as many of the Quins players had jobs in the City or in the professions, they had social circles away from the club. When I was at Nottingham, most of the players lived within half an hour of each other and socialised together away from the club. The simple practicalities of living in London made the establishing and maintaining of a tight-knit group far harder and, with alternative lives available, players came together mainly to play and train and went out together only after games. As many of the players had high-pressure careers, it was not possible for them to saunter through the day with their mind wandering to rugby.

Then there was the international dimension. Most of the players in the first-team squad were either internationals, or were on the fringes of the full or second England XV. A few were internationals with other countries. At one point, Quins fielded a team containing fourteen international players, the non-capped player being the much-missed number eight, Richard Langhorn. I believe they still hold the record for the most club players to play in a World Cup final – eight: Halliday, Carling, Leonard, Moore, Ackford, Skinner, Winterbottom and Coker, the last one being the only winner, the bastard.

The removal of over half the squad for international training and games did not help either the social or playing cohesion. From one week to the next, the players focused on entirely different goals, used different moves, with different calls and faced different physical and emotional challenges. Add to this the end-of-season tours and it is evident that international players' fitness requirements alone differed markedly from that of club players.

I do not believe that I ever consciously gave less than my all for Quins, but there is no doubt that in some games I did not play as well as I and those watching expected. In retrospect, I am not sure what I could have done to rectify this, because it was not deliberate. I never felt it was less important to play well for Quins, but practical matters like the attritional nature of Test matches meant that my body had only just recovered by the Thursday before the next game and inevitably that took its toll.

When Will Carling told me that, if he could, he would prefer to just play for England, I dismissed this as what I thought was the typical selfishness of the man. I realise now that I misjudged the comment. There is no doubt that it would have been preferable to be able to focus on one objective for a sustained period. The present system, whereby the Six Nations period stands alone with the players playing only internationally, means it is easier to compartmentalise club and country.

Some clubs that also had large international contingents managed to meld their players with better effect, but when the dissimilarities I set out above compounded the dislocating effects of club v. country, Quins could not do so. However, over a short series of games, or in any singular game, Quins were capable of beating any side. It is for this reason that, as a cup side, Quins were rather more successful, reaching the final of the Pilkington Cup three years in succession between 1991 and 1993, winning one and losing two. Two of those Cup games stand out for me.

The 1992 final when we lost to Bath must be one of the greatest of all finals. In a pulsating game, Quins had Bath on the back foot for most of the match. In particular, we dominated up front, and in the lineout shut them out almost completely. However, in their redoubtable way, Bath kept in touch; not for nothing did they have an unbeaten record in finals.

The scores level at full time led to extra time that was as combative and absorbing as the first eighty minutes. With the very last play of the game, Bath managed to win a lineout and from forty yards Stuart Barnes dropped a goal to win them the game. Gutted? Yes and no. I have never been one for lauding magnificent losses, but there is a difference between losing a game in which you played well and gave your all, and losing one in which you made tactical blunders or did not perform. I wasn't happy, but I had to bow to the resolution shown by Bath and the coolness of the final kick.

The following year's Cup campaign was eventful, if ultimately unsuccessful, as we lost to Leicester in the final, which I missed because of injury. The quarter-final at Blundellsands, the home of Waterloo, brought back memories for me and not good ones. When I played at Roundhay and later Nottingham, Waterloo was on the fixture list and nobody liked playing them. This was not because they were especially good, but because they were a cynical and dirty side. Their pack had a number of players who were not talented, but were intent on punching, kicking and gouging whenever they got the chance.

By the time Quins travelled to play them, their bullying players had largely retired, but the unpleasantness lingered with me and I made no differentiation between the past and the present. Though we won comfortably in the end, there were furious disputes and allegations after the game.

The Waterloo fullback had to go to hospital and I was accused of punching him. The truth is that I was probably responsible for the contact that did the damage, but it was due to my hitting a maul hard and the swing of my forearm as it went to bind. It wasn't deliberate. In addition, during the game there was a complaint from one of the Waterloo forwards that some of us were wearing illegal studs. Three of our pack were made to change boots before we were allowed to carry on.

After the game, one of their backs, a certain Austin Healey, walked into the press conference backwards with his shirt raised to show the rake marks all over his torso. Had I known then what I know now about Austin, I would have made certain there were an infinitely greater number. They whinged and whined about all aspects of the game, but majored on the studs, which they called rugby-league studs.

A few days later, it was announced that there was to be an enquiry by the Middlesex Committee, the relevant county body. Leonard, Snow and Moore were summoned to answer the charge of wearing illegal studs and more importantly of changing boots after the inspection of the referee before the game. Although it wasn't a full RFU enquiry, the Middlesex hearing had to be taken seriously as they had the power of suspension and, for Jason and me, the fact that we were established internationals would attract publicity and condemnation. We were role models, weren't we?

We went for the highest free legal representation. This just happened to be Edwin Glasgow QC, one of the top advocates at the bar and a Quins luminary. We met at Edwin's small mansion in Thames Ditton on the Sunday morning a week after returning from Waterloo. Jason and I arrived early, Snowy was late. We decided to start anyhow and I gave a true account as far as matters related to me.

I explained that we had arrived at Waterloo, and despite there being several large changing rooms available, we found them all to be locked. We were then herded into a very small room that had no roof and was adjacent to the public toilets, meaning not only was it ridiculously cramped, but anything that was said could be overheard. This was a deliberate act by the home club. It was unacceptable and it generated a mood of spite that carried on to the pitch and was visited on their players.

As usual, the referee came in to check studs, but at the time I was in the toilets and he did not notice my absence and did not inspect my boots. I was wearing not the rugby-league studs alleged, which were longer and sharper than those allowed in Union, but normal studs with washers. This had the effect of making the stud longer, though not sharper, and gave extra purchase. I had got the ruse from the French, who not only played with washers but also League studs; I had played against France only the previous week and used the same configuration, which was passed by the international referee. This time, I was technically illegal, but as I had not been the subject of examination by the referee, I could not have deceived him.

Jason just lied and denied changing his boots. He did this with an uncomfortably innocent face.

As we were finishing our accounts, Snowy walked in and Edwin told him that we had given him our stories about the affair and would he mind giving his story. I couldn't believe it when a slightly shocked Snowy said, 'What, the real one?'

At this point, the legal nous of Glasgow QC leapt forth and he leaned to me and said, 'Mr Moore, would you like a moment with your client?' I would, and Jason and I took Snowy into the next room until he recovered from his temporary bout of amnesia.

We went before the Committee with no chance of being found guilty. During the week, Martin Hobley, a Quins prop and captain of Middlesex, sent a letter stating that he and all the Middlesex forwards had used similar studs to those worn by the three of us and this had been with the knowledge of the Middlesex management. Faced with a problematic case, confronted by a leading QC, and with the prospect of looking like hypocrites, they went through the motions and we went free.

We faced our local rivals Wasps in the semi-final. Any loss to Wasps was accompanied by chants from the Wasps dressing room of 'One team in London' or 'If you want to go to heaven when you die'. Quins didn't go in for such vulgar gloating; better to act as if our wins were merely the natural order of things and thus not notable.

The semi-final was held at Sudbury and we won 14–13 in a brutal and sometimes spiteful game in which both sets of forwards cheap-shotted the other wherever possible and anyone on the wrong side of a ruck got it. The Wasps flanker Buster White to this day insists on showing me the scars that I gave him at one ruck. Well, he shouldn't have been there.

There were many characters at Quins and it would take several chapters to log the incidents I remember from even a few of them, but I think some are worth sharing.

Alex Snow was a baby-faced second-row educated at Harrow. His family were titled and he had the regulation accent. He was, however, a good second-row, dextrous and unafraid to get stuck in. He is now the CEO of one of the country's leading mid-cap finance houses and by all accounts a bit of a hatchet man in business. Snowy was a perfect example of someone whose persona and mannerisms, whose views of the world, were moulded by his upbringing. When we first met, it would have been easy to characterise him as a typically arrogant snob, but when I got to know him I realised that he was as much a product of his upbringing as was I. His real world was simply different from mine.

I didn't realise until I played for Quins that they were hated, sometimes playfully, sometimes not, by all the senior clubs. In particular, Quins had always had a hard time when they played Orrell. This stemmed from when Quins lost to them in the Cup and it got into the paper that one of the Quins members had said, 'My God, we've been beaten by a layby off the M6.' That type of dismissal is not forgotten in Wigan.

Orrell away was not a glamorous fixture, and we went by train on the Friday night before one game. As we alighted at Wigan station, Snowy raised himself to his full height and said, 'Do you know, it actually smells of shit.'

His grandmother, Lady Snow, uttered another immortal gem when she was confronted by the commissionaire at the door of the Committee Lounge. When asked for her ticket, she dismissed the doorman with a wave of her hand and added, 'Get out of my way, you silly little man. I had an affair with Wavell Wakefield.'

The 1994/5 season, when I captained Quins, was a disaster. We only escaped relegation by winning our last game away at Gloucester, and the whole season was a trial. I found that the style of play I wanted to play, ball in hand but with some structure, was openly criticised by some players, Will Carling in particular. As things got worse, I became more intense; and as often happens, the harder I tried, the worse it got. In addition, I had to focus on the forthcoming 1995 World Cup in South Africa and deal with the emotional and practical difficulties surrounding the break-up of my first marriage. I had met my wife, Penny, the year after I left university. At the time, she was still a medical student and we were together for over ten years, marrying in 1992. I was twenty-four when we began our relationship and she lived through all the years I played rugby, bar the last. All this meant that, during the season, my head was never in the right place for long enough. Of the many things I got wrong in rugby, this was one of the most painful.

It seemed to me that, as the end of the World Cup would see my retirement from international rugby, it would be as well to cut myself off from the game altogether. I had played senior rugby for seventeen years and, at the age of thirty-three, was reaching the age around which most players considered giving up the game. In addition, most of those years had been at the highest levels of rugby and the dedication required to play at that level had grown each year. Although I had not suffered any severe injuries, the physical side of the game had also intensified and would, if anything, do so further. Though this conclusion came after months of prevarication, once it was made, I wanted the end to come quickly.

Quins' final game had to be won for the club to avoid relegation. We had to go to Gloucester, never an easy place to play, and this time their crowd had the delicious prospect of sending down a bunch of London dandies. I had made my decision to retire from club rugby at the beginning of that week but I knew that, as soon as it was announced, I would have all sorts of requests for interviews, and that was something I just could not face. I was so emotional but was not able to identify the reasons for this properly. Being in that state, and feeling as if I would either explode or dissolve into wretched tears (not least because of the rage I felt inside me at being unable to understand and control what was going on in my head), I was afraid that my answers might be even more obtuse than usual.

I sent a very short paragraph to the Press Association the day before the game. In it, I detailed that I was to retire from club rugby after the weekend's game, and from all rugby after the World Cup. I made sure it went out sufficiently late that it could not be covered the following morning. In retrospect, I was wrong to deal with it that way as I now have few articles to mark my years in the club game. The reports of the game included partial résumés of my career but were not what they would have been had I given the authors enough time to do their job properly.

I shall never forget the generosity of the Kingsholm faithful. Gloucester were in no mood to do us any favours and playing that day at hooker for the Cherry and Whites was an emerging player called Phil Greening, who ran and handled like a back and impressed me from the start. We won the game, to the disappointment of our many nationwide fans. I remember saying that I had seen the future of England hooking and it was called Phil Greening. He went on to represent England, though not for the extended run I foresaw, as he seemed to lose focus at times. Nevertheless, he was a very good player.

As usual, throughout the match I received the usual vernacular welcome from the Gloucester fans whenever I came within earshot and when the final whistle blew, I found myself in front of the infamous Shed. I turned round to see who had shouted, 'Oi, Moore' and, as I did so, the man who had shouted for my attention started clapping me. He was joined by those around him and I walked the whole length of the pitch and received a very moving ovation from fans who were loyal Gloucester supporters but who had the generosity to mark the passing of my career, one in which I think they recognised I had given everything I could for the national cause. It was a very special moment, produced by a special set of fans.

When I came off the pitch, I was met by Penny, my wife, who unbeknown to me had driven from London to see the game. She had done so despite the fact that we were in the throes of breaking up, and on top of the huge surge of emotion produced by the Shed's parting actions, this was more than I could bear, and I found that I was unable to speak for several minutes. I found the final press conference an ordeal that I could only deal with by being uncharacteristically flippant.

It was not to be my last game, although I thought so at the time. My years at Quins had been much like my life in general: gloriously flawed, with moments of triumph, yet marked with disappointment at missed opportunities and mistakes made.

The circumstances surrounding my eventual departure from the Harlequins were undignified and should have been avoided. The acutely distressing circumstances of divorce and all the attendant emotion, added to the terror I felt about retirement, made me want to cling on to the one thing that I had found to be a constant up to that point in my life: rugby. It was a mistake, though, made for reasons I thought sound at the time.

Before the start of the 1995/6 season I called Jack Rowell, the England coach, to discuss the reversal of my announced retirement. I thought at the time that, if there was a chance that I could retain my England place, it would be sufficient reason to carry on and deal with the tremendous commitment this entailed. Rowell assured me that I would be viewed no differently from previously, and if my form warranted it, there would be no problem retaining my place.

I told Harlequins about my change of heart, and the reaction of Dick Best was so less than wholehearted that I should have anticipated problems. Simon Mitchell, the former West Hartlepool hooker, had joined the club pre-season, being lined up with another north-east player, Mick Watson. Naturally, I would have to fight with the replacement who had been sought, but I felt more than capable of doing this.

Though I was picked for the first few games, at the crucial pre-Christmas period, when the players' form would be assessed for England's Five Nations challenge, I was selected one week in two, and then one week in three. This effectively ended my chances of retaining my position with England, though I did not receive a cogent explanation for the selection decisions. A standoff ensued in which Best and I both refused to make the phone call to clear the air. Both of us probably had a case as to why the other should make the call, but neither of us took this step and in the end I simply faded out of the set-up. It was a poor way to finish my time at the club. I felt, and still feel, I was not allowed to go out with dignity.

During the 1996 Five Nations, I did some media work, but watched no other rugby. Of the rest of that season, I honestly cannot recall what I did, other than party very hard. It remains a blur of late nights, although I now accept what I denied at the time: that I was close to being out of control. What arrested the slide towards an embarrassing fall from grace was the fact that I had unresolved issues with rugby and the terms on which I had left. My subsequent season at Richmond RFC proved to be my lifeline.

# 14

## Failures No Longer

### The 1991 Grand Slam

Having lost to Scotland in the memorable 1990 Grand Slam decider at Murrayfield, England toured Argentina in July and August of that year. Although we were told that players who had toured with the Lions in 1989 need not tour, I took the view that if I did not go and my then rival Jon Olver played well, there would be a temptation for the selectors to retain a winning team; and then, despite what might have been said, I would find myself out of the team. I should not have gone: after almost two years of continuous rugby, my body was shattered and needed rest.

In rugby terms, the tour did little for English rugby, other than to confirm which young players definitely were not capable of playing internationally. There were some points to note. The series was drawn 1–1 and Jason Leonard won the first of 114 caps in the first Test. I remember packing down with Jason for a session of scrummaging against a standard Rhino machine. As soon as he took his bind, I thought, 'Christ, this lad's strong.' Nobody could predict he would go on to win a record number of caps and be regarded as one of the best props in the world but, for an eighteen-year-old, his power was extraordinary. The fact that in both Tests he coped with Roberto Grau, a renowned scrummager, gave a hint of what he might achieve.

The other significant fact was that the tour saw the start of a decline in my relationship with Will Carling, which was always uneasy, and hence a parallel decline in my influence within the team. The catalyst for the deterioration was the fact that they selected only one specialist tight-head for the tour. This was not an oversight, rather it was a deliberate decision born out of a complete lack of understanding about how scrums work and the roles of both props therein. To outsiders, binding on the left or right of a hooker is akin to playing on the left or right wing; but the parallel is wide of the mark. The job of the loose- and tight-head differs significantly: it means using a completely different set of muscles and levers, and the body positions are very different. Although from the outside they do not appear to be dissimilar, that is not the case and few players have been truly competent in both roles.

What this selection meant was that in opposed scrummaging practices, the pack that contained the out-of-position prop got mullered. After one such disturbing training session I raised this with Carling and voiced my complaint, explaining the problem fully. I was basically told to get on with it and that it was not his problem. This worsened the mutual suspicion between us. He thought I was undermining him and was envious of his captaincy. I thought he felt insecure and threatened. He was correct that I was envious of his captain's role, but he was wrong about me undermining his authority. If anything I quelled some mutinous elements. I made points such as the one above because I knew what I was talking about and it needed to be made by somebody. Our relationship never really recovered from that moment. In retrospect, there was fault on both sides and we failed either to recognise or to accept that we were both flawed characters, with those flaws concurrently driving and limiting our achievements in most areas of life.

Enough introspection. It was the Argentina tour that spawned a legion of stories that were nothing to do with rugby and that are recounted fondly and at length whenever players from that tour meet.

We were the first team from any sport to tour Argentina since the Falklands War eight years earlier. As such, we expected a degree of hostility and did encounter this in Tucumán, a provincial industrial town. However, we began the tour in Buenos Aires, a beautiful city, and home in my opinion to the most beautiful women in the world. During an evening out in the first week, I got talking to some English-speaking residents. When the subject of the Malvinas came up, they maintained Argentina's claim to sovereignty but said that they had never wanted to go to war to back that claim. They explained that the repressive regime they had been living under at the time meant that nobody was able to protest openly about the decision of General Galtieri to invade the islands. No criticism was made to us of the British defence of the Falkland Islanders, and as a result we were not received badly on the tour; on the contrary, the local people were keen to talk and drink. We did plenty of the latter – all in the name of diplomacy.

Outside the games, the social side of the tour was a huge success, which probably accounts for some of the lack of success on the field. On the third morning of the tour, the two dudes-about-town Victor Ubogu and Chris Oti excitedly informed us that they had discovered a brilliant place full of gorgeous friendly women. That night, we trotted along to the Cutty Sark bar and entered a room that had a small bar in one corner, very much like one of those home bars constructed by an enthusiastic but talentless DIY fanatic. There were a number of evenly spaced tables with two chairs and at each table sat a stunning girl with a single drink in front of her. I turned to Victor and said, 'You idiot, this is a brothel!' I had read about such places and how they might look. Victor denied this and insisted the girls were really friendly, which was hardly surprising given their profession. My claim was quickly confirmed by Victor's short conversation with two of the girls, who offered something called the 'bang bang special'.

An important matter required attention before we could plan for the tour's first court session: we needed a new judge. Paul Rendall had always filled this role, hence his nickname of 'Judge'. In his place we appointed the West Midlands policeman and Moseley prop, Mark Linnet.

It was traditional at the end of a tour for there to be a players' revolutionary court. This turned the tables on the court officials who had handed out punishments during the previous sittings. Linnet's punishment was that he had to wear, beneath his formal dress of tour blazer, tie and trousers, a lurid bikini that was several sizes too small for his ample figure. On a limited number of occasions, whenever a certain word was shouted out, he had to perform a striptease wherever he was at the time. The first call came in an airport concourse, but after the second, which came just after the security scanners, it was decided that it should be withdrawn on the grounds that he was enjoying it too much.

In a normal tour court, a number of officials were required. I was chief prosecutor, assorted second-row players were made court enforcers, and the court sneak, Mr X, went to the eminently qualified Jon Olver, known to all as Vermin. Mr X's role was to agitate for information on which we could base a variety of charges. He was frequently called upon to give evidence, but due to the clandestine nature of his activities, he did this disguised in a hat and dark glasses. As a court official, his testimony was irrefutable and he sent many players to their doom.

Mickey Skinner provided two of the tour's best stories. Having been late for training again, he and three other players were made to run back to the hotel after training, about four miles. Roger Uttley, the coach who imposed this penalty, sportingly did the run with them, but as Roger was super-fit this gesture did not impress the miscreants, especially as we encouraged them warmly whilst getting on the coach. Roger set off bounding down the street, followed less swiftly by three of the players with Skinner bringing up the rear. When he considered the other runners were out of sight,

Skinner stopped and got in a taxi. We saw this from the bus and tried to alert Roger to it but failed because of the traffic noise.

For the rest of the journey, Skinner waved from the cab, which followed our coach as we crawled through traffic. As we neared the hotel we saw Roger standing atop the entrance to the hotel, which resembled the police patrol positions on the side of motorways. The taxi overtook us and we stopped in waiting traffic. As we watched, the taxi, now seemingly unoccupied, edged slowly up the ramp towards Roger, stopping a couple of times. It reached the apex and then did the same on its way down the other side and then drove off round the corner of the hotel and out of sight. During this journey, Skinner had lain on the floor in the back of the taxi repeatedly asking if a tall man who looked like Mr Potato Head was still standing there. When he received the answer 'yes', he had told the cabbie to drive a bit further. As we got off the bus, we saw Skinner walk back round the corner and approach Roger and say, 'Rog, have you got any money for the cab?'

Skinner's lack of punctuality eventually got him a warning that serious measures would meet any further lateness. We all gleefully registered his absence at the start of one morning meeting a few days later. He did not appear and we left for training without him, each of us making suggestions as to what punishment would be given. Half an hour into training, Skinner appeared, accompanied by our diminutive liaison officer, whose first name was 'Fafa'. In broken English, Fafa proceeded to tell us about Skinner apprehending a would-be burglar caught in our team room. I had my doubts as soon as Fafa started to describe how Skinner had wrestled the man to the floor and heroically summoned the hotel security staff. However, the story was accepted by the management and players, and training resumed. It was not until we were on the plane home that Skinner confirmed what I had suspected, that this was a lie concocted to avoid the serious trouble he knew he was in when he overslept because of a heavy night.

I could fill many more pages with similar stories, but the above show that today's players will never have that kind of tour. But then they are paid well for their efforts and unfortunately they can't have it both ways.

Argentina flew to London a few months later to play a reciprocal Test match. For the first and only time during my international career, I was dropped. I was naturally very unhappy about this, and at the time there were serious political rows with the RFU over the amendments made to the laws concerning amateurism. Suffice to say that I was at the heart of the arguments with the RFU and in particular with the then secretary Dudley Wood. At the time, I strongly suspected the decision was political and that I was being singled out as a troublemaker. This feeling was heightened by the fact that the first words Will Carling said to me after the news broke were 'It's not political'. Given that I had not alleged this, it seemed too coincidental. In retrospect, I was wrong to think this. I had been playing almost continuously for two years and should not have toured Argentina because I was shattered. The truth was that, at the time, Jon Olver was in better form and deserved his cap.

The game was an easy win for England, but the game is memorable for one incident. The eighteen-year-old, nineteen-stone prop, Federico Méndez, gained his first of many caps for the Pumas and was also sent off. His haymaker that decked Paul Ackford was worthy of Mike Tyson. As Ackford staggered from the field, supported by the medical team, he did a convincing impression of Bambi on ice. At the after-match dinner, people kept walking past his table, throwing their napkins on the floor and shouting, 'Bring him out! Bring him out! My boy's had enough!'

During the next few months, I was able to recover my form and regained my place for the 1991 Five Nations Championship. The atmosphere in the team was markedly different from that of the previous season. The searing experience of Murrayfield the previous year had had a profound effect on the psyche of the team. We were again favourites to win the tournament and the team was highly experienced. The strong feeling was that if we did not achieve a Grand Slam this year, then we would have failed. Moreover, given the fact that the second Rugby World Cup was to be played in England later that year, with France sharing a few venues, if we had any pretensions to being world champions we had to have the psychological boost of going into the competition as *de facto* northern-hemisphere champions.

The above description is a summary of the mood within the team, but the practical effect of that mood and the desperation to win a Grand Slam was that we abandoned our development of an expansive style of play. Winning that prize rendered all else secondary and, given that our pack was one of the best in the world at that point, it was to this strength that we turned.

Our opening game was in Cardiff, where England had not tasted victory for over twenty years. Good and bad England sides had lost at the Arms Park, and playing there had become a thing of dread.

Many elements of our preparation were changed and some proved to be inspired alterations. It was alleged that the unique atmosphere of the Arms Park, the singing, the fervour, had intimidated previous England sides. I cannot say whether this was so, but I loved the confrontational ambience and the fact that the crowd not only sang in tune, but also in harmony. It did send a shiver down my spine but that *frisson* was not one of fear, it was of relish for the battle to come.

Nevertheless, to address any lingering neuroses, Geoff Cooke had recordings of the Welsh national anthem blaring out over the public-address system at Kingsholm, the Gloucester ground, during our training session on the Wednesday night before the game. In addition, the policy of stopping just short of the border until the morning of the game was abandoned. The luxury of the St Pierre Golf & Country Club, Chepstow, England, was eschewed in favour of the more prosaic charms of the Crest Hotel, Cardiff, Wales – two stars at best.

There were a number of reasons for the change in accommodation. As the Crest actually backed on to Cardiff Rugby Club, it was little more than a 150-yard walk to the National Stadium. The coach trip from Chepstow to Cardiff, on the morning of the match, took about an hour and, although for club games players travelled further, nobody wanted to be on a coach a minute longer than necessary. Furthermore, although this could be the product of a warped mind, it always seemed to be the case that we set off in sunshine and as we crossed the Severn Bridge it darkened and began to rain. On top of this, the cosy atmosphere of a country-club hotel contrasted starkly with the hostile reception we received once in Cardiff.

By staying in the heart of Cardiff for the two days preceding the game, we were immersed in the antagonistic tone that accompanied any visit by England. When Saturday arrived, we had had our fill of comments such as 'Don't know why you're bothering', 'Bad luck on Saturday' and banter from people I suspect had Tourette's Syndrome. When I watched the film of our walk to the dressing rooms a couple of hours before kickoff, I was struck by the expressions of anger on many faces. By the time the whistle blew to start the match, the desensitisation process was complete.

We beat Wales comfortably, but the fact that we scored one try, a forward drive finished by Mike Teague, and kicked seven penalties, drew unfavourable comment. We did not care. England's first victory in decades was also relegated to the inside back pages because of our refusal to talk to the media after the game. The background to this was linked to the growing antagonism between the RFU and the players regarding the former's determination to keep the English game amateur. Things had got so bad that we had decided to take what was an unprecedented stance, and an already upset RFU Committee were apoplectic and threatened to sack Geoff Cooke because, although he had no part in the decision, he would not condemn our action nor drop any of the ringleaders, of which I was one. I never established any sort of rapport with Cooke; I often thought he had an active dislike of me, but I admired his refusal to be cowed by a bullying bunch of Colonel Blimps. It took great courage.

Although we tried not to let it do so, there is no doubt that the antagonism affected the team. Whilst it promoted unity in adversity, it was fatiguing to have the threat of deselection hanging in the air; to feel there was a section of our own governing body that was not acting in our best interest. As I sat in on a number of meetings about amateurism, I suspected that there was politicking behind my back and that some on the governing body did not want me there at all. Consequently, I had difficulty in sticking to the subject in hand when what I really wanted to do was leap across the table and throttle the bastards. Against this background came our next game – the Calcutta Cup. No fixture could have added more pressure; this time it was personal. Our failure the previous season had given my Gollum an invaluable weapon to use in moments of doubt, of which there had been many since that day. For months after that loss, there were nights when I was unable to sleep, haunted by my failure, remembering the taunts and the criticism that ensued.

Before the game, Paul Ackford neatly encapsulated our position as a team when he said, 'If we don't win, we've got nowhere else to go. It will be the end. The team will have failed twice and we cannot allow that to happen.'

There was no more to be said; the details had been covered midweek. On the morning of the game, all the faces in the team meeting were stern and remained so throughout the journey to Twickenham and into the dressing room. Our backs usually tried to maintain a relatively light-hearted approach before the game, but they mirrored the forwards in their determination to gain revenge, at least in part, for the agony of the previous season.

As we stood for the anthems, the Scottish players were smiling and pointing. We just glared. The moments before the kickoff saw the extraordinary sight of Rob Andrew and Craig Chalmers, both fly halfs, exchanging insults.

My approach to that game was utterly cynical, shaped, in part, by some of the stories related by Scottish players that we had turned up the previous season in an arrogant mood; that we had cowered as they made their walk on to the pitch, and similar nonsense. I always tried to play with aggression, even overtly so, but I was not a cynical player. However, I was so desperate not to lose again to Scotland that I was guilty of tap-tackling John Jeffrey without the ball, obstructing runners – anything to gain an advantage. I did not enjoy this approach but for that eighty minutes I did not care. We won 21–12 and reasonably comfortably. That part of the job was now behind us.

Although our next win, away to Ireland, was scrappy, we were just happy to negotiate a typical challenge from the Irish forwards and a typically filthy Dublin day. We had won the Triple Crown but by that time this meant nothing to us. We needed the Grand Slam.

Had we described the perfect scenario in which finally to achieve our goal, we would have asked for the fixture which was scheduled to be our final game: France at Twickenham. That game was hyped like few have been before or since. All the old clichés – Agincourt, Waterloo and Trafalgar – were included in ever more sensational headlines. It was one of the last internationals to be played before the wonderful old wooden stands made way for impressive, but impersonal, modern concrete replacements. Few will now recall the wonderfully warm atmosphere generated by the old stadium. In terms of facilities and capacity it had to be altered, but the ambience of the new stadium makes it feel as anonymous as any modern venue.

Throughout all the time that I played for England, France had very talented players, but our game plan against them never changed: stop their runners on the gain line, and do not kick stray ball with which they could launch counter-attacks from anywhere on the pitch. Well, so much for the theory.

In the early stages of the game, we lined up across the field to chase a penalty kick. When it missed, the forwards ran to get into position to receive the resultant twenty-two drop-out. Undetected, the French scrum half, Pierre Berbizier, feigned to touch the ball down and instead launched a counter-attack from five yards behind his own line. His pass to Serge Blanco initiated probably the best try ever seen at Twickenham. A sweeping counter-attack, involving Sella and Camberabero, saw the latter chip ahead, gather his kick and put in a superb cross-field kick which was gathered by Philippe Saint-André, who scored under our posts.

We showed character to recover from that hammer blow, and eventually our pack took control of the game. With a series of punishing drives, we marched the French back down the field, and from one sustained assault on their line, we saw Andy Robinson dive over for the winning score. We also held our nerve near the end of the game and repelled repeated attacks from the French backs.

When the final whistle blew, a wave of pent-up emotion was released and several players jumped for joy; others sighed with relief. As the crowd surged on to the pitch they hoisted Will Carling aloft and carried him to the tunnel. I made my way into the dressing room and gave an emotional interview to Nigel Starmer-Smith of the BBC. I was then told that the rest of the players were going back outside to ascend the balcony used for presentations and accept the applause of a joyous crowd. As I went to join them, I was suddenly confronted by Gollum and felt I did not deserve to be part of this triumph. Why are you going out there? You know you were lucky even to get into the team – do you deserve to be seen with the greats of the game? Though I tried to shake off what I knew were illogical and frankly insane thoughts, I could not do so and did not join them. That is the reason I do not appear on the photographs of a celebrating England team that appeared on most of the front pages of the following day.

By the time the players returned, I had come round sufficiently to join in the spraying of champagne and the general celebrations. The RFU's first reaction to all this, obviously in the name of the anti-commercialism that they had loudly espoused in our discussion about amateurism, was to flash the message on the stadium's giant screens, 'Get your England Grand Slam merchandise'. It was later changed to 'Congratulations, England!' What hypocrites.

The end of the regular season did see another event that was both humbling and extremely satisfying: I was voted the 1991 *Rugby World* Player of the Year – so fuck you, Gollum.

# 15

## 'We Lost.' What Else Is There to Say?

### Rugby World Cup 1991

After finally gaining the elusive Grand Slam, England looked forward to the second World Cup. Though many from the southern hemisphere will not like or accept it, the fact is that the catalyst that transformed the Rugby World Cup as a tournament from incidental to indispensable was that it was held in England and that the home team reached the final.

Our preparation for the tournament was immeasurably better than in 1987. In part, the success of the British Lions in Australia in 1989 had given all the home countries a significant fillip, both in raising the standard of their preparation, but also more importantly in demonstrating to them that they could compete and beat the Antipodeans. (South Africa was still kicking its heels awaiting political change and readmission to official rugby.) We also had the satisfaction of going into the tournament as northern-hemisphere champions. We had a pack that was the equal, if not the better, of any team in the world. It had been together for three seasons and had provided five of the Lions Test pack that had battered the Australians and that was at the top of its game.

Our squad for the competition was not difficult to predict and did not cause any controversy. I was in form after recovering from the staleness caused by several years of continuous rugby and an Argentinean tour that was incredible fun, but on which I should never have gone. I was focused for the challenge ahead. My fitness scores were good and I wanted to face the rest of the world with a team that had a chance of winning. On the Australian tours with England of 1987, '88 and '90, we were never really near matching the Australians. It would be good to face them now on equal terms and at home.

The group stages put New Zealand in our group, together with Italy and the USA. Due to an odd pattern of tours, England had not faced the Kiwis since 1983. We had toured Australia four times and also played Tests against them at Twickenham. Conversely, the Scots had exclusively toured New Zealand. Such an imbalance would not be tolerated today, and the lack of first-hand knowledge would prove significant.

As hosts, we played the opening game at Twickenham against the All Blacks. The media interest was far higher than that of 1987, not just because of England's greater population, but because of the Grand Slam games of both 1990 and 1991, which had galvanised support for rugby in the faithful and attracted the temporary attention of fans of other sports.

The legend that is the All Blacks was still bolstered by the British press and thus lived on in the minds of players who had not yet faced a Kiwi team. No Kiwi players played in Europe and, though no player about to face them would admit this, their hard uncompromising teams were still regarded with awe.

We lost the opening game and this had two benefits. Firstly, although New Zealand deservedly won, I and the rest of the players realised when we analysed the game that we had made many errors as a result of rushing and forcing passes and plays. We had assumed that because this was the All Blacks, we would have less time, less space and would be under greater pressure than in any previous game; but though it was a good Kiwi team, it was not super-human. Secondly, the loser of that game was put into the easier side of the draw, with potentially a route to the final that involved games against France and Scotland.

We won the remaining group games and improved. As we did so, the press interest heightened, as it did for the Scots, Irish and Welsh. Rugby was a main topic in the sports pages, something that had never happened before.

As stated previously, a World Cup brings difficult periods of downtime that have to be usefully filled. The various distractions in 1991 were taken up with alacrity and sometimes provided unintended merriment. On an afternoon's shooting in Hampshire, for example, Jon Olver accidentally discharged the contents of his shotgun through the toe of Mike Teague's right boot. Hopping around instinctively in shock and not yet realising he had had an amazing escape, Teague was none too pleased by the sympathetic enquiry as to his health from Dean Richards that involved him asking Olver, 'Did you get the bastard?'

Unfortunately, for two players, Dewi Morris and David Pears, every other player played in at least one game. For various reasons, none of which stand up to much scrutiny now, Richard Hill and Rob Andrew were kept together for every game. The inactivity of Morris and Pears became embarrassing for the squad and I didn't know what to say to either player, knowing how cruelly they felt their isolation. That both players took their part in anything that was asked of them and publicly never voiced their disappointment and anger is a huge compliment to their character. In their position, I doubt I could have reacted in the same way.

I am often asked to name my favourite international game and this is difficult because the best bear a relation to their context, the opposition and so on. However, one game stands out, and of any game in which I played, this is the one most indelibly etched on my mind: the France v. England game at the Parc des Princes. This quarter-final of the 1991 World Cup was a game unlike any I experienced before or since, either as a player, spectator or commentator. Indeed, it is so indelibly etched in my memory that it evokes not just visual images, but also sounds, smells and touch.

It turned out to be probably the most brutal game of my career. The reasons for this were many; some were obvious, but others are not widely known. Of the latter, a number involved incidents that happened only once and could not have been predicted. Each one was seemingly trivial, but when added together they heightened what was already a fraught atmosphere to a point where trouble became inevitable.

Games that take place in the knockout stages of a tournament necessarily produce more pre-match tension than those in the group stages. Knowing that there are no second chances puts players on edge, and this game was no different. To this encounter was added the historical background of centuries of conflict between England and France that included one war lasting over 100 years. This may sound fanciful, and indeed this issue was never raised in team meetings, but within the innumerable articles written before the game there were so many allusions to this rivalry, not least through the language chosen to describe the encounter, that I am certain this made some contribution to what occurred later.

The week before the game, there was a war of words to which I contributed as fully as I could. For the French, their captain Serge Blanco came out with comments that were not well received, such as his guarantee to the French people that in his last season of international rugby he would bring them the Rugby World Cup and dispatch us along the way. He criticised our playing style, and his tone was then adopted by the French press.

As a result of the strains generated by the above factors, we arrived in Paris in an already fractious mood. The build-up was good and we were confident, but there was a seriousness about the French that was not normal and that served only to intensify the tension. During the Five Nations, we had beaten France three times in a row, the last win clinching the Grand Slam the previous spring. However, we also realised that the French were capable of shredding any defence in the world if they were allowed. We knew how difficult it could be to play in Paris, and the physical challenge posed by the French forwards meant it was going to be rough, whatever the final outcome.

As with previous visits, we stayed at the luxurious Trianon Palace Hotel in Versailles, which used to be the servants' quarters of the centre of the Ancien Régime. The morning of the game, I went down to breakfast. As usual, most of the team were there. What was not usual was the silence as the players ate, each caught up in his own private reverie. I recall thinking that this was a sign that things were either very right or very wrong and that I could not tell which it was.

Sporadically, someone would break the quiet, but any exchange was brief before silence was again restored. I do not know why, but I suddenly got up and went outside. I walked up to where the gates and railings still stand in front of the magnificent creation that is the Palace of Versailles. A splendidly decorated place, its zenith was during the reign of the Sun King, Louis XIV. Unwisely, he was the monarch who famously declared, 'L'État, c'est moi' (I am the State). Within eighty years of his death, the French aristocracy was wiped out and *La République* was born. I knew there was some reason to like the French.

I tried to imagine the thoughts and feelings of the peasants who had stood in the same place hundreds of years before. Excluded and angry, they had assembled as a mob and I tried to picture them storming the gates. This dip into history reminded me that when we played the French we would be part of sporting history. Within a sporting context, our clash was an extension of ancient enmity. To be chosen by England to do battle on its behalf was a great honour. I returned to the hotel aware of the responsibility we bore: we must not lose.

I packed and went down to the team room for the final gathering. A few players were already there but again nobody spoke. The meeting was short because nothing much needed to be said. When a squad has been together for weeks, either on tour or in a tournament, it is a question of highlighting challenges posed specifically by the next opponent; issues concerning our own performance, calls, moves and so on had already been taken care of on the training field. Above all, the need for discipline was stressed several times. We knew what had to be done to beat a talented French side on their own soil; it was straightforward, but by no means easy. In fact, it turned out that the game was to demand of every England player his utmost commitment, self-control and bravery.

The silence continued as we boarded the coach for the fifteen-kilometre trip to the Parc des Princes, situated in the western suburbs of Paris. Such journeys are meant to be quiet, contemplative times when players sit with their own thoughts, listen to music, read or chat quietly. I was no different and would use the journey times to clear my head and to try and focus on my individual contribution.

The first example of the atypical incidents referred to above came when, for this occasion only, the coach was escorted on its journey not by the Gendarmerie, as normal, but by a detachment of CRS riot-police outriders. We set off on what would usually be a nightmarishly slow journey through the outskirts of Paris, but when we went through the first tunnel, which we rather surprisingly shot through, someone, I cannot remember who, came running from the front of the bus and told us that we had to come up front and look at something, though he did not say what. I and most of the other players then watched through the windows at the front of the coach as the CRS effected a rather idiosyncratic traffic-management policy: put simply, if a car did not move out of the way when requested to do so by a CRS policeman, he drew his baton and smacked the side of the offending car. In other instances, if the car did not move as quickly as required, the policeman kicked the front doors to make the driver move. Naturally, the forwards thought this was marvellous. What should have been a forty-minute period of calm reflection turned into a 100kmph white-knuckle ride, with players offering enthusiastic support, especially the policemen on our team, who were probably wishing they had similar largesse when on duty.

When we arrived at the ground, the atmosphere on the coach was buzzing, not sober as it should have been. The coach drove to the underground car park, and from that point on, we did not see daylight again until we ran on to the field just before kickoff. This unnatural setting was a portent of the gladiatorial contest to come, as we could hear the crowd and knew we were to perform for them shortly.

As we approached the door of the customary away-team dressing room, we were guided to another room, which was about one third of its size. When we were told the other room was not available, the pressure gauge went up a few more degrees.

Ten minutes before kickoff in a game of that importance, there is no point in saying anything complicated: details are either in or out of a player's head. A captain has to try and manage the mood, dampening or stoking it where necessary. Will Carling stressed discipline, tackling, and retaining possession, and he was right.

It took more than a few seconds to negotiate the labyrinth towards the tunnel, but as we walked closer to the sunlight, the crowd noise began to grow and with it the adrenalin that was by now coursing inside me. We had made a policy of sending our forwards out behind the captain when we faced France, as they themselves liked to send a message by showing their strength in this way. As we neared the right turn that would send us on to the turf, a small man wearing a World Cup blazer stepped in front of us and said that we could not go on to the pitch. He had no way of knowing that his intervention was placing another log, this time a large one, on a bonfire. He was asked why we could not run on, and he told us that we had to wait for the French. We told him in rather prosaic terms that we didn't want to wait for the French.

At that moment, a door opened from the corridor down which was the French changing room. A surprised French team filed into the communal area just beyond the view of the crowd; they thought that we had already gone on to the field. Nowadays it is not uncommon for teams to run out together, but I never played in a game where this was done and this was not the case in 1991.

Thus, you had two packs of forwards who disliked each other anyway; they had been subject to mounting pressure all week, and in our case had experienced a number of unique happenings that had further raised the pressure. For what seemed like five minutes, but in reality was only about forty seconds, both sets of forwards glared at each other, and when we locked eyes we did not look away, for fear of losing face. Then the muttering started: words under the breath such as 'I'll wipe that fucking smile off your face, you French twat', 'Remember these [six stitches]? I do', and so it went on. We got the order to go, and ran out; they stayed and ran out later, making the whole confrontation absolutely pointless from any perspective.

I tried earlier in this book to describe what it feels like to run on to a field to represent your country. The thrill astonished me every time I did so and never lessened in intensity; it is an experience that is irreplaceable. However, running on to the pitch at the Parc des Princes was different again and unlike any other entrance anywhere in the world. Not only were there the normal human voices roaring approval or opprobrium; not only did hands clap loudly; at the Parc you got bells, whistles, firecrackers, flares, live cockerels and the Dax band. As I ran into this cacophony, all those things hit me like a tidal wave and I, like all the other players, was lifted somewhere into the clouds. As if all this were not enough, we then had the national anthems. If you watch the line-ups during the anthems, you will see that several of the French forwards are shaking and in tears. That is how tightly coiled they were. At this juncture, the minds of both packs were somewhere in the stratosphere.

I have spoken to hundreds of fans, French and English, who were in the stadium for that game, and to a person they all agree with me that there was a strange malevolence in the air. Had that been a game of football, I have absolutely no doubt there would have been crowd trouble. The unusual nature of the crowd led John Taylor, the ITV commentator, to use the cliché that 'You could cut the atmosphere with a knife'. In fairness to Taylor, he was absolutely right to use that description, as the feeling was tangible.

Never before or since have I played in or watched a game that had anything remotely approaching that tone.

Given all the normal and abnormal pressures that had accumulated, plus our human frailties, I now believe it would have been impossible for that game to go in any other way than it did. The players might have been able to control the emotions generated by any one of the many incidents that occurred before the game; cumulatively I think these incidents made what subsequently happened inevitable.

In the middle of this maelstrom was the New Zealand referee David Bishop. Had he known about all the things that had occurred, he might not have come out of his dressing room. As it was, he was in charge of two teams intent on, well, let's just say, making their point. There is little a referee can do to defuse such tensions; it is a matter of managing the battles when they occur. I think Bishop did as good a job that day as could any referee in the world, having found themselves in that atmosphere.

A few minutes into the game, we won a lineout just inside the French half, and Rob Andrew hoisted a huge kick which was caught by the chasing Jerry Guscott, who was immediately tackled to the ground by Serge Blanco. The French captain later claimed our move had been a deliberate plan to injure him. That he received the temporary injury of stud marks all over his torso was not deliberate; it was, however, of considerable incidental benefit that our forwards found him lying on the wrong side of the ball. He was rucked out of the way viciously but legally, and given that the incident happened right in front of Bishop, who did not give a penalty, there is no substance to Blanco's claims.

Blanco's reaction was the worst possible: he complained and lost his temper. He was joined by Éric Champ, their unpredictable flanker, who stood nose to nose and lips to lips with Mickey Skinner. When Skinner refused to retreat, Champ shoved him away heavily with both hands.

Shortly thereafter, our winger Nigel Heslop hoisted a kick, and when Blanco caught the ball, hearing no whistle to acknowledge that Blanco had been awarded a 'mark' and was therefore not to be tackled, Heslop did what any winger should do and hit him with a tackle. This incensed an already angry Blanco, who rained punches down on Heslop and was assisted by Champ. As a result, Heslop was actually knocked unconscious and there was a five-minute delay whilst he was treated.

The game went on and so did the violence. I had my eyes gouged in the next scrum but, aware that Bishop was already under incredible strain, I tempered my complaint by saying to him that I knew he couldn't see everything but could he watch for any repeat of this serious offence. During play, we scored a lovely try when Jerry Guscott hit the line and drew Blanco to put Rory Underwood over in the corner. The booing and whistling that greeted our try was deafening and a sure sign that things were going well. At times, the French threatened to cut loose, and we had to defend desperately.

Had I not been one of those facing French players running at pace, from depth and with superb angles of support, I would have shared in the joy of watching them in full flow. That day, however, amidst these typical flashes of brilliance were interludes of kicking, charging, rucking and so on. I must make it plain that we were not in any way blameless in all this, but we managed not to commit such acts in front of the referee.

At one point, the enmity between the packs drew a comment from TV commentator David Kirk, the former All Black captain who had lifted the first World Cup. Usually erudite, Kirk, who had seen a few things in his playing career, simply commented, 'Jeez, these guys hate each other.' Coming from a Kiwi captain, this was saying something.

I can recall almost every play of the match in my head and there are many memorable moments and a few that were seminal. After our good start, the French slowly began to get on top, and towards the final twenty minutes of the match, the French forced a series of five-yard scrums on our line and they were within a penalty goal of drawing level.

I do not know how this has ever been measured, but I was told by someone that when international front rows hit together in a scrum, seven tons of pressure is exerted each way into that scrum. The front row itself absorbs the majority of this and it is very attritional. When a scrum collapses it means nothing to most observers, other than a delay, whilst it is being re-set. For the front rows it means taking another huge hit. In Paris that day, after three scrums in succession collapsed, something happened to me that, for some time afterwards, I hesitated to believe had occurred. Some readers will know that in moments of crisis it is possible for the brain to have scores of clear but disparate thoughts, and for this to happen in a fraction of a second.

If you study the video of that series of scrums, you will get no hint of what went through my head because it happened in a trice. I was on the verge of panic, because I was so shattered I did not know if I could stand up for the next scrum. At that point, something occurred, or rather it felt as if something spoke to me and asked, 'How many people would like to be where you are now?' and 'What will you do if you do not face this test? Where will you go?' Again, in a split second I felt a surge of energy, and with it came the conviction that from that point on until the end of the game I did not care if I got hurt or if I hurt anybody: I would do anything I could to win for England.

I take no pleasure in describing the events of the final twenty minutes. It was a war in which both packs levelled anything above grass height. What was captured on camera was probably a quarter of what went on, as players tore into each other legally and often illegally. Peter Winterbottom was caught on camera as he kicked the head of a French forward. Winterbottom was not a dirty player, and a cheap shot like that was totally out of character. However, what the cameras did not register was the act that drew his violent response: he had seen the French player stamp straight on my face at the beginning of the ruck. One act does not, in terms of jurisprudence, excuse the other, but niceties such as these were not really the order of that day.

The most visible act of defiance from England came when Mickey Skinner tackled the French number eight, Marc Cécillon, when he tried to drive over our line off the back of another five-yard scrum. Not only did Skinner stop him; he picked him up and ran him five yards backwards, whereupon the rest of us gleefully ran over the top of the likeable but unfortunate Frenchman.

Our 19–10 win was sealed when Carling jumped for a high ball and he and Blanco landed with their arms around the ball. As our pack drove the maul over the line, Carling ripped the ball from Blanco and the weight of the maul that collapsed over the French line helped him ground the ball. Jason Leonard scandalously and repeatedly defames me in his after-dinner speeches by claiming that after this score, and in the face of an apoplectic crowd, I ran down the touchline sticking two fingers up to them. That is a downright lie; I merely waved in the manner of a royal – which was infinitely worse.

Just before the final whistle, I had another surreal experience. I was running across the field, my head still cloudy after another blow from the Basque strongman, the fearsome Pascal Ondarts, when everything seemed to go into slow motion for a few strides. For some reason, I noted that the sun was shining but then thought, 'We are going to win.' This is what it is all about; all the hours of unseen slogging on cold January and February nights. This is the essence of sport: the best feeling in the world, to be on foreign soil, in your country's jersey and to win. It does not get better than this.

After the game, there was a special atmosphere in the dressing room. It wasn't triumphal because we knew what lay ahead, but there was deep satisfaction at having beaten a good French team on their own patch. In sporting terms, it had been a war and we had stood together. Experiences like this forge bonds that do not need the reinforcement of visits, calls or letters, and with the passage of time, I now appreciate that these bonds are rare and to be treasured.

The semi-final took place at Murrayfield, where we faced

virtually the same Scottish team that had taken the field against us for the clashes in the two previous Five Nations tournaments. If anything, the relationship between the countries, unions and players had deteriorated. The usual anti-English campaign, alleging arrogance (surprise, surprise) took place in the week leading up to the game, but with it came a variation, the significance of which did not dawn on me at the time. It was at this point, when we looked likely to reach the final, that Australian accusations began concerning our style of rugby. We had continued to use the power of our forward pack and had not returned to an expansive game. The statements were crude generalisations, and a proper examination of our games proves this. However, the accusations were widely reported and were picked up by the Scottish press. Previously nobody had raised the issue, and in any event I saw no reason why there was a duty by just one country, England, to play in a certain manner for the alleged benefit of the game. The rest of the squad had the same view; nevertheless the seed of doubt was sown.

The game was unremarkable, and although we only won 9–6, I never felt we were in serious danger of losing. Much has been made of the penalty that Gavin Hastings missed in front of our posts when the score was 6–6, but even had that gone over, I felt we had the capacity to win. The game was no repeat of the 1990 Grand Slam decider and we were in control for most of the eighty minutes.

After the victory there was remarkably little celebration. We knew our opponents in the final would be Australia, who were a very good team, with few, if any weaknesses. We had watched them dispatch New Zealand in their semi-final with something approaching ease and noted the fact that their tries came from their dangerous backs. I knew that we would have to play to our limits to win but I knew that our forwards had the edge over the Australian pack. And if our forwards controlled matters, as they had done up to that point, there was little the Australian backs would be able to do about it.

The difference between the extent of the media coverage the following week and that given to the corresponding week four years earlier was so marked that it took me by surprise. I had not taken into account the fact that, since 1966, no England team from one of the established sports had reached a world cup final. The coverage, in all forms of media, was saturating. I could not pick up a newspaper without some obscure fact being revealed about one of our players. Enmity within the media industry is well known but I was still staggered by the inventive ways each outlet sought to present a different slant on what was essentially the same story. Had someone proposed the notion that many years later I would be doing the same thing, I would have thought them mad. One of the papers, for example, had spoken to every player's former PE teacher. Fortunately mine, Peter Holden, could not have been nicer; I must have done something right in all the years I mithered him.

Amidst the deluge of predictions and analysis came an increasing stream of comments from the Australians in similar vein to those we had had before our semi-final with Scotland. Having raised the point, the British media naturally began to pick up on it, not necessarily because they agreed with it, but merely in order to debate it. The question of whether we were a boring team was put widely to various 'experts' as well as to a number of former and current players and coaches. Opinion varied, as it always will do, on an impossibly subjective matter, and even though my attitude was 'Fuck them', the real point was that Australia had successfully turned it into an issue.

I remember clearly the meeting that took place to define our tactical approach to the game. Geoff Cooke, Roger Uttley and Will Carling drew up a plan based on the premiss that we would not dominate the Australian forwards to anything like the degree we had done our opponents on the way to the final. Therefore, given this, we should plan to play a wider game on the assumption that we might even be shaded for possession. I have thought many times about my role in what transpired, and I think I have to shoulder some of the blame for the fact that, when this assumption was made, I did not challenge it with sufficient rigour. I did not agree with their assessment of the packs. Moreover, I had been on the Lions tour in 1989 when Campese, though a brilliant attacking force, had demonstrated his dislike of fielding high kicks; particularly the possibility of also being caught by a pack of forwards only too happy to be given a chance to answer his fulsome criticism of them in their own way.

I did voice my objection, but it was dealt with in the same way that other objections were dispatched, by a nod and then move on. I also made the point that we had not practised an expansive game and that I felt this discussion had been skewed by the Australian accusations. I should have stood and fought for my points until the meeting came to a standstill and there had been an exhaustive debate on the matter. As it was, I still left the room with the impression that we would look to play a slightly expanded version of our recent style of play. It was certainly not my or any of the other forwards' impression that we would play the way we did.

Strangely, I cannot recall much of the morning of the final, though I do remember sitting and thinking, once again, about all the people who were important to me, those who had helped me on the way to this point; and I also had to deal with an unusually severe attack of self-doubt raised by Gollum.

There was a fantastic atmosphere in the Twickenham crowd, but curiously, when I look back I don't think it was anywhere near the intensity of the crowd at the Parc des Princes two weeks previously. For me, this is sufficient proof of how much the historical background influences every game played between teams from the Five, now Six, Nations. The crowd was dominated by England supporters, but Australia had more fans than might have been expected. I doubt that anybody had been able to get a drink in Earls Court that afternoon. However, although there was healthy rivalry between the opposing fans, it did not have the edge that exists between, say, those from England and Scotland, or Ireland and Scotland.

The anthems came and went and I remember noting, as 'Advance, Australia Fair', the Aussie anthem, was sung, that only four years before I had seen PR people at Ballymore in Queensland handing out sheets with the words to that anthem, because many of the Australians were not familiar with them. How times had changed.

Expecting us to play with a slightly more expansive approach, I was bewildered by what happened during the next eighty minutes. Any semblance of a controlled game wherein we could pressure the Australian wingers and fullback with difficult kicks went out of the window and was replaced by a series of off-the-cuff dashes from one side of the field to the other. We only put up one ball on their fullback, Marty Roebuck, and it didn't appear to register with the decision-makers in the backs that he dropped it and that from the spilled ball had come a great chance to score. To this day I have no idea why this happened and nobody has explained it satisfactorily.

As I thought, our pack did dominate the Australians for large parts of the game; a fact acknowledged after the game by Nick Farr-Jones, their captain. In any event, anybody who asserts otherwise has to explain how it was possible for us to run so much ball if our forwards were not decisively on top. I still maintain that, had we played to our strengths, we would have maximised our chance of winning the game. I cannot be categorical, but what is more certain is that playing in a haphazard, unplanned and unfamiliar way, we lessened the one opportunity all of us, save Jason Leonard, had to be world champions.

Those who defend the approach taken that day have claimed that, had the forwards not been happy with decisions being made, they could have changed things. This is disingenuous because, as any forward will tell you, it is the job of the pack to produce ball and support runners and occasionally to drive ball at the opposition. Certainly, when your scrum half calls for the ball to be produced, you do not debate whether he is right to so demand. You just give it to him, and trust that he has made the right decision. Forwards engaged in the dirty business of mauling and rucking are not in a position to decide what is done with each piece of possession.

It may have looked as though we created many chances to score but we did not. Apart from the Roebuck dropped catch, the only two other genuine chances failed because of John Eales's tackle on Rob Andrew and David Campese's deliberate knock-on. I have no issue with what Campese did; I would have done the same, and he got away with it. The point I make about what he did is that, as he has been shown to be as cynical as the rest of us, I don't now want to hear lectures from him about the spirit of the game.

When the final whistle blew, the scoreboard registered our loss as 6–12. I was obviously very upset about losing but my feelings were tinged with anger because of the way we had played. I sat in the dressing room and could not speak for a good twenty minutes. I looked around at the forwards and they reflected emotions similar to mine: we had thrown away our chance.

I did not want to go to collect my medal. I felt that I, we, had let everyone down. It was of no consolation that the crowd gave us a warm reception. At the time, I was thinking, 'This is why England does not win; happy to cheer the gallant loser.' When various reporters asked me about the game, I simply replied, 'We lost.' When they did not receive my typically garrulous analysis of everything, they asked me, did I not think we had played the more attractive rugby? Was this not some form of moral victory? I rounded on them, perhaps unfairly, and in short told them I didn't give a toss about irrelevant points like that. We lost, what else was there to say?

The evening celebratory dinner at the Royal Lancaster Hotel near Marble Arch was something I could not face, and although I showed my face at the beginning, I slipped away quietly to a nearby pub with a few other players and chatted about the game and our disappointments.

In life, you get very few chances – possibly only one – to be the best in the world. When that chance is given, you have to do everything you can to win. If you deliver everything and still lose, then I think you should not be reproached. We did not do everything we could, because we could have played in a different way, a way that would have had more chance of succeeding. I reproach myself and have done so ever since with the ever-present aid of my *alter ego*. The team and I let ourselves and the country down and there is no easy way to seek absolution. I just have to live with it and try and gain sufficient acceptance and perspective so that it does not cloud the great times I had whilst playing.

I took home my loser's medal and put it in the loft. But even after two years, during which I had not looked at it again, its presence still haunted me and I threw it in the Thames. When asked about this on a TV show years later, I was so embarrassed at the foolishness of the act that I denied it. I had done the same to the trophy that I received when my school lost in the final of the Calderdale twenty-overs competition. All the intervening years had not taught me how to get a more realistic perspective on losing.

As if to deliver a further lesson in why the English don't win much, we were jointly given the BBC Team of the Year award in the end-of-year *Sports Personality of the Year* programme. The Great Britain 4x400m men's relay team had won gold at that year's world championships and should have won the award outright. I was mortified at having to be on the same platform as them and I could not look them in the eye. To compound this asinine decision, and with stunning insensitivity, somebody at the BBC decided it would be a great idea for our award to be presented by David Campese. I did not agree with the award or the presenter. Before the show, someone from the BBC came over and asked if I would mind being interviewed. I told him that I would be interviewed, but I would say exactly what I thought. When asked what that was, I told him that I did not agree with the award, as it reinforced the notion that losing should be celebrated. Further, that I could not believe the stupidity of inviting Campese to present the award. 'Don't you realise,' I continued, 'he will go home, laughing all the way and then tell Australia that we are such a pathetic country that our Team of the Year was the one they had beaten?' They interviewed Mickey Skinner instead.

# 16

## More of the Same, Please

### Grand Slam 1992, Five Nations 1993, Lions 1993

Records show that Grand Slams are not easily won; any side that claims one deserves recognition. Back-to-back Grand Slams are rare: only five times has a country managed this feat. Our 1992 Five Nations tournament could have gone badly but we were determined to add our names to this illustrious list, something that England had not accomplished for seventy years – and in so doing we would also find succour for our World Cup failure. The battles of 1991 had improved the team to the extent that lifting a successive Grand Slam proved to be relatively easy. In no game were we in serious danger of losing, and though we still had to fight for our wins, by then we were a side that could dispatch teams when we played well.

The coaching staff changed with Dick Best replacing Roger Uttley. Though I have had my differences with Best, he brought a fresh approach to training and was never less than entertaining. Our style of play became more ambitious because we slayed the spectre of Grand Slam failure and the 1992 season is the one to which I point when critics trot out their lazy and ill-informed claim that we were a dull, forward-orientated side. Over the four games, we scored fifteen tries, which exceeded the average by a large margin. Moreover, the majority were scored by the backs.

It was a relief not to have to deal with Scotland's irritating (in the right way) flankers Finlay Calder and John Jeffrey in our opening game at Murrayfield. Their absence highlighted the value to Scotland of their brave and often unrecognised work about the field, especially at the breakdowns. As we did not have to deal with one or other of them slowing down our ball, we were able to create momentum in our attacks and develop our range of attacking options.

In our next game, at Twickenham, Ireland felt the full force of the above options, as our backs ran in six tries in a 38–9 win. Jerry Guscott was sublime, and even I got involved with a touchline support run that sent Dewi Morris over in the corner.

The third game, at the Parc des Princes, presented France with an opportunity to gain revenge for being ejected by us from the World Cup. Prior to the game, there were the usual exchanges in the press, but no hint of the extraordinary events to come. I think that the hostility between the sides reached its zenith in this match. By that point, we had beaten France on four successive occasions. Naturally they were displeased by this but they were equally, if not more, affronted by the manner in which they had lost the games.

Traditionally, France picked rough forwards who compensated for any technical shortcomings by being able to batter opponents into submission. Yet in those four previous games, our pack had decisively won each encounter. To some extent, the French were the authors of their own misfortune because they continually picked one second-row who could not jump and they regularly made players play out of position. Their forward problems were exacerbated by their policy of playing non-specialist hookers, usually props, which meant their lineout suffered because these players could not throw in properly. Moreover, the expected advantage in the scrums did not materialise when they played against front rows that were technically sound. We never had any problems, provided we concentrated and regularly took two or three strikes against the head; each of which was followed by an obligatory punch-up. In my ten Tests against France, I played against eight hookers: Daniel Dubroca, Philippe Dintrans, Louis Armary, Philippe Morrocco, Vincent Moscato, Jeff Tordo, Jean-Michel Gonzales and Marc de Rougemont. Of these, only Dintrans, Moscato and Gonzales were proper hookers; all the others were non-specialist players. But all eight shared the common characteristics of being traditional French front-row forwards: strong, ugly and hard as nails.

The first scrum of the game set the tone. As the pressure increased, both front rows were forced up, and the French tight-head, Philippe Gimbert, gouged my eyes. Although this is one of the most cynical and dirty examples of foul play, one that could potentially blind a player, I kept my temper and did not react by swinging a punch; I merely removed his hand with mine. The referee, a schoolmaster from Belfast, Steven Hilditch, did not see what had happened, but he knew from my shouts and the pushing and shoving that something had occurred. Knowing he was under pressure, I said, 'I know you can't see everything, but can you not do something about this?'

Influencing referees is an art and each player has his own style. Sean Fitzpatrick and George Gregan, from the All Blacks and the Wallabies respectively, were never short of helpful observations. Martin Johnson was the English equivalent, and I tried my best, sometimes successfully. As with many allegations about me, the claim that I constantly spoke to referees is not true. It may have seemed like that, but I was well aware that no referee would tolerate constant talking; and more importantly, it would not have worked because a referee would eventually have become impervious to anything I said, whether or not it had merit.

I used to pose questions such as 'How did their flanker get in that position?' The posing of the question forced the referee to consider the point, and he would look out for it thereafter. Most referees did not mind a comment that was made in a light-hearted manner. In one game, the referee called me to one side and told me to stop trying to referee the game. He did not take offence when I replied that one of us had to do this, and as he hadn't seemed that interested . . .

We were in control of the game during the first sixty minutes, and began to play with freedom. Entering the final quarter of the match, we had scored four tries and the home crowd had gone beyond their usual whistling and booing: they were almost silent. As they quietened, the English supporters got louder, and when they began to rub it in, the French crowd was not pleased and began to hound their team.

It might have been this pressure; it might have been a case of 'Sod it, if we're not going to win, I'm going to take one of them with me'; it might even have been an innate tendency towards violence – whatever the explanation, something prompted the French prop Grégoire Lascubé to ruck Martin Bayfield's head whilst Bayfield lay prone and a ruck drove over him. This did not bother us, he was a policeman after all, but the touch judge intervened and Lascubé was sent off. I was taken aback because I did not see the offence and up to that point there had been little trouble and certainly nothing approaching that of previous games. As Lascubé walked slowly to the tunnel, I could feel the temperature of the crowd rise several degrees: it changed from passive dislike to overt hostility.

Lascubé's exit introduced ingredients that were guaranteed to aggravate the worsening situation. Moscato, who had been playing hooker and was doing well, was switched to prop to replace Lascubé. This brought into the front row a player who later captained France, Jeff Tordo. Although Tordo forged a reputation as a disciplinarian, this did not extend to his own play.

We lined up for the hit, but as we engaged with their front row, Tordo and Moscato butted Probyn and me. The scrum broke up with a flurry of punches and both front rows were hauled back by their second rows. My trumpeted restraint and policy of not retaliating in front of an official was temporarily suspended in the interests of self-preservation. The French were so enraged at what they perceived to be an anti-French conspiracy that they were no longer bothered about the result of the game: they would try to put someone off the field. When my safety was involved, I did not feel bound to follow team orders, and in any event, by this time, I was a fraction away from completely losing control. As a last attempt to avoid becoming involved in a brawl that would result in all the participants being dismissed, I turned to Messrs Dooley and Bayfield in our second row and told them that if, as I suspected, it was going to kick off again they should grab me and throw me out of the way.

When the packs were reset, Steve Hilditch warned Moscato, saying, 'Monsieur, la tête, non!' I looked across at Moscato, who either did not hear the referee or did not care about the warning given. He was crying tears of rage and Probyn, seeing this, thought it would be a wheeze to smile and pull a face at him. The front rows went down and Moscato butted Probyn. The scrum broke up once again, with players diving into a mêlée, some to prevent trouble, others to throw punches. I was dragged away by Bayfield, who grabbed me round the neck. The moment was captured by a photographer and it is a brilliant picture, apart from the fact that Bayfield's unnatural height, and my lack of it, makes me look like a dwarf.

Moscato seemed genuinely surprised and aggrieved to be sent off, and as he left the field I looked across at the French forwards. I cannot speak French with any fluency, but that was not necessary; all I needed to see was the look on the faces of the remaining six French forwards to know that for the rest of the game rugby would be incidental. The remaining fifteen minutes were the only time in an international game when my main concern was to ensure that I did not get myself into a position where I was defenceless. One or two of my fellow pack members did get into such situations and were lucky that the knee-drops visited on them did not cause serious injury. Again, I cannot claim that we were innocent of foul play, but the things we did were nowhere near as serious or as frequent as those of our opponents.

At the traditional post-match formal dinner, we were usually placed on tables that had players and Committeemen from both countries. On this occasion, the French sat on one side of the room, with us on the other. None of the players sought to alter the demarcation line, and even players from opposing teams who were friends thought it best to avoid fraternising for fear of provoking further incidents.

After the extraordinary affairs of Paris, even the Grand Slam game against Wales felt like an anticlimax. We won comfortably, with the only significant statistic being Wales's failure to score as we ran in three tries and scored twenty-four points. We tried to cut loose, but were insufficiently exact to finish many of the chances created. The atmosphere was flat, and although there was an attempt to celebrate as we had done the season before, it was half-hearted and soon subsided.

The 1993 Five Nations did not go well. It was by far the worst Championship with which I was involved during my England career. As that was the year of the British Lions tour to New Zealand, our poor play affected both England's standing within European rugby and the forthcoming summer tour.

I cannot account for the poor form of the rest of the England team, but I know why matters combined to dull my form, even when I continued to train assiduously. The litigation exercise I described in an earlier chapter became so important for my firm and for me that I could not refuse to devote the necessary time to run the cases. Furthermore, I wanted to do the work. It was challenging, but more than that I realised it would involve hearings before the highest courts in the land. Many good lawyers never get near the House of Lords, and if I am honest, such work was the perfect way to answer the whisperings of Gollum and of some members of the public that I was not a proper lawyer, that I was only employed because of my prowess on the rugby field, or finally, that I wasn't any good. However, the travelling, the long conferences and the concentration required resulted in the edge being taken off my game, and for the first time, rugby had to take a subsidiary role. As the House of Lords did not hand down judgement until the middle of 1993, my entire contribution during the Five Nations was compromised.

An injury at the start of the season saw Jon Olver gain another cap against Canada, and the team that had been settled for a long time, certainly compared to previous England teams, began to be broken up. The most significant change for me was the replacement of Jeff Probyn with Victor Ubogu. I did and do like Victor, but even he would have to admit that at international level he was nowhere near the equal of Probyn in the scrums. His selection was part of a wider initiative by the technical advisers to the RFU to move England's game forward – whatever that meant. The northern hemisphere has periods when it looks at the rugby played by its southern counterparts and concludes that anything they practise must necessarily be adopted. Around this time there was a fad for props who were mobile and for whom the graft in the scrum was a necessary evil. Australia was the strongest advocate of this policy and the most vocal in proclaiming that the scrum was only a means of restarting the game. I knew this was bollocks, and said so at the time. A decade later, I had to smile when the consequences of Australia's approach saw them destroyed in the scrum by all and sundry and losing games as a result.

England also started a misguided and ultimately futile quest to find bigger hookers. The logic, they explained, was that, as the southern hemisphere had big hookers, we had to match them. Being a small hooker, I naturally railed at this, but only partially out of self-interest. What the brains trust had failed to recognise was that the players to whom they referred, Phil Kearns and Sean Fitzpatrick, were hookers first and foremost, and just happened to be bigger than average; they were not selected for their size but for their ability. Moreover, James Dalton of South Africa was even smaller than me.

I remember posters appearing in changing rooms all over England. They were advertising for props, flankers, and even larger backs to attend sessions where any who showed potential would be put on a fast-track programme to master the art of hooking. My initial ire was quickly transformed to amusement as I watched a succession of wannabees struggle with the skills then required. I told everyone who cared to listen – actually it was anyone who could not escape – that there were two problems with this initiative. Firstly, most people had no idea what a hooker actually did during a game and how difficult it was. As scrums were refereed properly at international level when I played, I knew the necessary skills could not be gained in a couple of seasons, no matter how intense the training. Secondly, they had not thought through the conundrum as to how their recruits would acquire the requisite experience of first-team and then representative rugby. A perfect example was the case of Martin Pepper. Martin was a very good openside flanker, but barring his path to full honours were a number of established players such as Peter Winterbottom, Gary Rees and Neil Back. Martin joined Quins and was chosen for the scheme. He worked diligently and made decent progress. He was selected for the second team, much to the chagrin of the incumbent, but then he, and all like him, hit the same problem. No senior club was going to risk playing an inexperienced hooker in important games just because the RFU had this scheme in place. A catch-22 problem existed: they were not selected because they had not the right experience; they could not get the right experience because they were not selected.

Returning to Mr Ubogu: sure enough, when Victor faced the rigours of scrummaging in Test matches, he struggled; he was under pressure in the scrums and because of the energy taken out of him he could then not carry the ball effectively. In addition, it increased the strain on the rest of the pack. Hooking the ball in a retreating scrum is a scary business and during Victor's first cap against South Africa at Twickenham, that is what I found myself doing on more than one occasion. At one scrum, in the final fifteen minutes of the game, we formed for a scrum and Victor turned to Peter Winterbottom, who was moving to pack down behind him. In a polite, public-school voice Victor said, 'I'm very sorry, Peter, but my legs have gone.' Winterbottom's response would not be capable of being broadcast, no matter how late the watershed.

After the game, I went to Will Carling and told him that I wanted Probyn back in the team. By this point my relationship with him was, at best, one of armed neutrality. We clashed over matters concerning the off-field activities of the team; in addition, his support of the muddled thinking of the management angered me because it was I and my fellow forwards who had to live with the consequences. He said that he thought Victor had played well, apart from in the scrums. At this I let forth a volley of invective, which included the observation that his saying that was like saying that, apart from the shooting, Mrs Abraham Lincoln enjoyed the play.

The conversation ended when I was told that I and the rest of the pack would just have to work harder. This left me seething because it confirmed what I had suspected, namely that my influence within the team was resented. I am sure Will thought my complaint was purely the result of my friendship with Probyn, and in part it was. However, I was not so sentimental that I would ignore a new player who was Probyn's equal or better. Above everything, I wanted to win, and nothing, my friends and family included, came before that. Probyn was reinstated but it was not because of my representations. When Carling raised the same question with other members of the pack, he got similar answers to mine. Most of all, the direct utterings of PC Dooley left him in no doubt as to what we thought.

Shortly thereafter, Jason took me to one side and said, 'I'm telling you 'cos you're a mate. They're thinking of asking Victor to switch to hooker.' My first response was predictable: rage. But I also felt betrayed. I knew that I had always put England first, and in so doing, had sometimes upset people close to me. Given my circumstances, I did not think it was possible to show more commitment: I bordered on the obsessive as it was. I had put my head above the parapet on the issue of amateurism and spent hundreds of hours in meetings and on planning the players' commercial campaign, most of which had gone unseen.

I now must admit that I had no right to expect my tenure to be favoured ahead of England's requirements but I knew the scramble to manufacture bigger hookers was nonsense. That nobody seemed inclined to listen to my reasoned and ultimately accurate comments on the matter was frustrating in the extreme.

Looking back, I think that the pressure of work and my insecurity about my future in the team triggered minor depression. I once looked up the symptoms of clinical depression and was shocked by how many of the physical and mental symptoms I was able to apply to the way I felt and acted at the time. It would be wrong to say that the following applied constantly, but there was a good number of times when I felt anxious, inattentive, unconfident and that all I did ended in failure. In typical fashion, I focused my attention on my mistakes in a manner more extreme than usual and I often found myself asking, 'What is the point?' In a childlike way I felt that life was unfair. My wife noticed this, but what most concerned her was the physical symptom of early-morning waking. I would often lie awake from five o'clock, unable to go back to sleep, even though I felt exhausted. Whenever she raised the subject, I would angrily dismiss her observations. I did not know what to do. The only response I knew was to try harder, which often made things worse.

My fitness levels dropped and I found this inexplicable because I was putting in the hours; to compensate, on the field I played with more than my customary belligerence. None of this was positive and I feared that I might go from a certainty to tour with the Lions to missing out altogether. England's form that season did not help because collectively we played without control, and whereas we usually dominated up front, we were outfought in some games.

Our opening game in the 1993 Five Nations was against France at Twickenham, and it is recorded as a 16–15 win. We were very fortunate to come out on top. In a tale of two crossbars, our winger

Ian Hunter chased a penalty kick by Jonathan Webb that struck their crossbar, and gathered the rebound to score under the posts. In the dying minutes, a drop kick from Jean-Baptiste Lafond cannoned off our crossbar and we scrambled the ball to safety.

Owing to an injury to Wade Dooley, a young second-row was given his debut for England. I remember him walking into the room in which the forwards' meeting was to be held on the morning of the game: firstly because he was early (I liked that) and secondly because he was a huge man. I remembered how anxious I had been in similar circumstances and thought about how to say a few words of comfort without taking the 'old git' approach. I simply started to tell him how I had felt, what I had worried about and the reasons why I need not have done. When I looked back, I told him, I had been chosen because I had the ability to compete at this level; all that was required of me was to focus on my own job; this was simple, though it also required total concentration, not because international rugby was hugely quicker, more physical or more skilful, but because the combination of a small step-up in each area meant that, unlike what happened in club games, a player could not afford momentary inattention.

Whether it helped I do not know, but he played a good solid game that afternoon and it was obvious that his future in international rugby would be lengthy. His name? Martin Johnson.

Our attempt to gain an unprecedented third successive Grand Slam unravelled in Cardiff the following week. Wales had appointed Alan Davies as their head coach once the RFU had made it plain that he would not have a chance of being given a similar position with the England team. Wales had been in steady decline for the past five years, but the change under Davies, with no new talent available, was almost instantaneous and showed how badly the Welsh had been organised during that period. I do not think Alan brought anything revolutionary to the Welsh but he was always thorough and well organised. Given this framework, the players of quality that Wales possessed were able to flourish and stop the slide.

When we played them, they were still at the beginning of their recovery, and although they showed moments of what they might be able to achieve, we dominated most of the game. However, we could not finish any of the many chances we created and the Welsh defended heroically. We lost as a result of a freak try scored by the Welsh winger, Ieuan Evans. Emyr Lewis broke from their back row and chipped ahead; Ieuan hacked the rolling ball forwards, but as Rory Underwood was about fifteen yards from him, there looked to be no danger. As the ball rolled into our in-goal area, Rory sauntered back, admiring the views and probably thinking how tedious it was to have to defend. Ieuan sped past him to touch down. Jonathan Webb, our fullback, was also covering Ieuan's kick but left the ball as it appeared that Rory had ample time to get back and touch the ball down. When he saw what had happened, the mild-mannered prospective orthopaedic surgeon angrily kicked the ball into the enraptured crowd.

After the game, I started across the dressing room, intending to give Rory the benefit of my advice, but his crestfallen face showed that he knew the gravity of his mistake and it would have been wrong to make any more of it. Every player makes mistakes, but not all happen in such exposed areas. Anyway, in response, he could point to the many tries he had scored where he had shown fantastic skill and no little bravery. In the modern-day penchant for diving over the line chest first, a few wingers ought to study Rory's way of stretching with his outside arm, riding the despairing cover tackles and touching the ball down a fraction of a second before he was bundled into the corner flag or over the touchline.

The game was my forty-third cap, and with it I took the record from John Pullin for being England's most-capped hooker of all time. The pleasure I should have felt at this was marred by a particularly complex and vicious attack from Gollum, my *alter ego*, who framed his persuasive arguments thus: 'So you're England's most capped hooker of all time. Do you really think you're anywhere near players like Pullin and Wheeler? How can this be right when they're trying to get you out of the team? And not even for another hooker; any old player who happens to be big. What are you going to do, go on a rack? You don't count any more, and I'm surprised it's taken them this long to see through you. You fraud. If only they knew you can't even concentrate on the game any more – we both know you're not playing well. You can fool them, but not me. If only they knew what a fucked-up individual you really are, there wouldn't be all this sycophantic praise, you'd be ridiculed and don't pretend you would not know it was deserved.'

Many will find the above bizarre; some will find it resonates painfully. But for me, it is real, though I wish it was not so.

I did not, even in my most extreme fantasies, picture my name being bracketed with the like of Pullin and Wheeler, two men whom I admired whilst growing up. The forty-third cap was not as relevant to me as being now associated with men of stature. At the time of writing, my record is still intact. Fourteen years it has stood, whilst many records set by players from my era have been broken. Given that more recent international players play significantly more games per season and get capped when they invariably come on as a substitute, the preservation of this record is something that even Gollum has found difficult to ridicule.

When I broke the record, I did allow myself a smirk at the thought that I had proved many critics wrong, particularly those who had insisted I was too small. I had played through what, at that point, was the most successful period in England rugby history and proved my argument about size and technique was correct.

The narrow and unusual loss to Wales was England's first defeat in nine games in the Five Nations tournament. Reading the resultant press would have given the impression that the world was about to end. The press, having had nothing but England victories to write about for over two years, savaged us and demanded the removal of half the team, which they said had become too comfortable because players were certain of selection. The last point produced a grim smile from me, as I thought about the fact that I was having to contend with not only the attentions of Jon Olver and Graham Dawe for my position but also, potentially, those of Victor Ubogu and – if the RFU got their way – anybody else who was bigger than me.

It was inevitable that there would be changes but they did not occur in anything like the expected numbers. The replacement of Rob Andrew with Stuart Barnes brought back into the squad a figure who divided opinion throughout England because of his attacking abilities as well as his weaknesses, and who still divides viewers and readers due to his analytical, if romantic, views on the game. His advocates claimed that had he played more often the England team would have won more games and done so by playing more attractive rugby.

Barnes was the fulcrum of the very successful Bath side of the late 1980s and early 1990s. Though his kicking was average and his defence less than that, his vision and surprising pace over thirty yards set him apart from all the other fly halves in the Home Union countries. Barnes and Andrew each had their advocates, and naught would persuade people to switch. As with most debates, the longer it ran, the more stereotypical became the positions of both factions. In the end, the gross generalisation was that Andrew could not attack, and Barnes could not tackle. Neither description was true: both players could perform all the tasks required by a number ten. The difference was in outlook. Barnes was a risk-taker; Andrew more conservative (which makes his aberrant decision-making in the 1991 World Cup final all the more difficult to explain).

Barnes's return was covered as would be the Second Coming. When we ripped Scotland apart 26–12 at Twickenham the following week, many doubting Thomases were ready to convert and do penance for denying the Messiah. After an audacious feint to kick in our twenty-two, Barnes dashed through the hole left by Scotland's back row, who were still in the air trying to charge down an imagined touch-finder. Familiar with Barnes's play, Jerry Guscott appeared on his shoulder a fraction later, and the brilliant attack went the remaining length of the field, finished by Rory

Underwood. The speed of Barnes's reaction and Guscott's acceleration were breathtaking.

Barnes's inspirational break was the focus of incredible media praise the day after the match, with pundits asserting that, had Barnes been England's fly half in the games played by Andrew, we would have won the World Cup, been a more attractive team, and so on. What happened in our final game in Dublin proved the acclamation was premature, and that even a player with talent like Barnes cannot single-handedly win games if his pack did not first win its battle.

Ireland tore into us and at no point did we control the game. The 17–3 defeat was one of the heaviest we sustained whilst I played in the Five Nations, and as it was the final game before the Lions squad was chosen, it influenced the make-up of that squad. Behind a beaten pack and under pressure from a rampant Irish back row, Barnes was powerless to prevent defeat and was unable to perform as he had against Scotland the previous week.

On Friday 7 June 1993, I sat alone in my tatty hotel room in Invercargill, South Island, New Zealand. I was 4,803km from the South Pole, in a place with more inbreeding than the Forest of Dean. I was cold, damp and utterly miserable.

The training session from which I had just returned had included a twenty-minute stoppage, during which every tour-party member, our hosts and any animal close by, sought sanctuary from hailstones so large they dented car and factory roofs. Following the news that I had not been chosen in the British Lions Test team for the opening Test against the All Blacks, this divine mockery had reduced me to a state where, for the only time in my rugby career, I considered feigning injury. I shared this moment of crisis with Stuart Barnes who, like me, had been labouring in a midweek team that was gradually being undermined by the poor performances and bad attitude of its Scottish and Irish forwards. We agreed that the abject and cowardly refusal to fight and play like Lions had denied us a proper opportunity to challenge for a Test jersey. It was the lowest of the low points I reached in my rugby career.

This contrasted with the relief I had felt, a few weeks earlier, when told I had been chosen for my second Lions tour. Sixteen other England players were also selected. The significant absentee was Jeff Probyn, who was comfortably the best tight-head in the northern hemisphere. In spite of the fact that the coach, Ian McGeechan, and the captain, Gavin Hastings, came from Scotland, the number of England players provoked the jibe that this was an England development tour. Subsequent events proved those choices were correct, unlike the selection of the entire Scottish front five.

The reason for selecting the Scottish forwards *en masse* was never divulged. It must have been thought that whilst individually the players might not be the equal of others, as a unit they were better than the sum of their parts. The alternative explanation is that usually astute men had temporarily taken leave of their senses. That the best players in a particular position should be chosen and then combined is an important Lions tradition. Time and again, it has delivered surprise combinations that have worked brilliantly. Players like Neil Francis and Peter Clohessy of Ireland must have been as disappointed as Probyn not to see their names on the list.

The major difference between the Scottish and Irish forwards chosen for the Lions squad of 1989 and those in the 1993 squad was that the former, unlike the latter, were seasoned players and had demonstrated their mettle in many internationals. Kenny Milne and Nick Popplewell were honourable exceptions on the 1993 tour, whilst their fellow Scottish and Irish players refused to play and fight, unlike their counterparts in 1989.

My relationship with Kenny Milne was more cordial than the one I had with Steve Smith in 1989. We had been adversaries for a few years, and technically Kenny was one of the best hookers in international rugby. His tour moniker of 'Village' (as in village idiot) was given by his Scottish compatriots and he was a good tourist who knew all the words to 'Bohemian Rhapsody'. Though

I disagreed with his selection as the Test hooker, it was not his choice and I congratulated him with as much grace as I could summon; which was not much. He was generous enough to say that he thought the choice was marginal; but he did not realise that, when he also said it had probably been made because he was bigger, this nearly triggered a lecture about the 'big hooker versus small hooker' debate. It was Kenny's candidness that removed any lingering thoughts about leaving the tour, even though my anger over his selection remained. He deserved my support and I was a Lion; real Lions did not quit.

Our form was reflected by the judgement of most rugby pundits and every New Zealander that we would get nowhere near the All Blacks. The first Test was lost with the All Blacks being awarded a dubious try when their centre, Frank Bunce, and our winger, Ieuan Evans, contested a high kick from Grant Fox. Without the aid of video replays, the Australian referee, Brian Kinsey, decided Bunce alone had control of the ball as it touched the ground in our in-goal, even though the arms of both players were wrapped around the ball. Recovering from this dubious decision we fought back to lead 18–17. The final play of the game saw one of the worst refereeing decisions in Lions history. Kinsey penalised Dean Richards for playing the ball in a ruck when it was actually handled by an All Black forward. A superb pressure kick from Fox robbed us of victory.

My selection for the midweek game against Taranaki suggested that Milne would keep the Test berth for the second Test, but I played well in our 49–25 win, the only decent performance by the midweek team in the entire tour. My mood was improved considerably when I was included in the team to play against Auckland only three days later. The XV for the second Test was not yet announced, but my elevation into the Saturday team strongly hinted that I was in pole position to claim the jersey. We lost narrowly to the provincial champions and I did not know if I had done enough to replace Milne. When Ian McGeechan approached me after the game I knew I was in: his demeanour indicated good news, and he simply said, 'You're in for the second Test because you're a competitor and we need competitors.'

New Zealand is the hardest tour in world rugby. South Africa comes a close second and both countries have a similarly claustrophobic atmosphere caused by the fact that everybody knows about rugby, and they all have opinions that they share with you whether or not you want to hear them. The difference between the two countries is simply the weather. Hard grounds are not as much of a trial as constant rain. Damp seems to seep into your bones and kit does not dry. When you play badly you cannot hide, and when a tour party fractures as ours had done by the time the second Test arrived, we had to be self-sufficient.

Many of my England colleagues and friends had been in the Test squad from the start of the tour. From our many discussions about every facet of the tour, I knew that the attitude of the Test squad contrasted starkly with the façade of dedication shown by the midweek squad. Even so, I was startled by the extent of the difference in attitude which led to a difference in quality. There was a determination to show our detractors that their sweeping judgements concerning us were wrong. Paul Burnell of Scotland could not make an impression on the All Black scrum and outside the set piece did not offer much. The choice of Peter Wright as a tight-head in front of Jeff Probyn was a travesty. Wright was so poor technically that I found myself showing him how to pack at an angle and twist his opposite number to alleviate pressure. As I did this I was thinking about Jeff and the fact that, had he been on tour, we would at least have posed questions of the All Black front row. I could have forgiven Wright's lack of scrummaging ability had he fought his corner but, when outclassed, his reaction was to retreat into nights on the piss akin to those on a club tour. Lest this be seized upon as another example of my anti-Scottishness, the poverty of the above-mentioned players disappointed Ian McGeechan greatly. When asked at the end of the tour by an Irish journalist what he thought of the Scottish contribution to the tour, he pointedly replied, 'I thought Gavin captained very well.'

Like Wright, others who were similarly outclassed reacted in similar fashion. This split the party, and given the stresses of a Lions tour, a disjointed group is almost certainly not going to succeed. The management became aware of the problem before it got out of hand. A group of senior players, of which I was one, discussed the behaviour and we were each asked how we would sort it out. The other players said their piece and they broadly agreed that the best solution would be for them to make it quietly known to the whole squad that the management was aware of what was going on and would not tolerate it. The management, particularly Geoff Cooke, the manager, agreed with this subtle action.

When it came to me, I knew that my alternative strategy was unlikely to find favour as I was in a minority of one. Nevertheless, I was playing in the midweek team at the time and had experienced the frustration felt by the players who were trying their best to win promotion to the Test team. I knew what being a British Lion should mean to a player and how jealously the accolade of selection should be guarded. I said that in a team meeting the finger should be publicly pointed at the wastrels, who should be reminded of the Lions' history, and their betrayal of it should be forcefully enunciated. Anybody who showed himself incapable of or unwilling to give his all should be on the next flight out of the country. A few wry smiles met my advice and it was ignored in pretty much the same way as the deserters ignored the softly, softly approach.

The Lions' second Test win in Wellington was one of the memorable events that sustain the Lions aura. We were given scant regard before the game but the winning margin of 20–7 was the largest recorded by the Lions in a Test match in New Zealand. Our forwards outplayed the All Black pack, and I had another out-of-the-ordinary moment as I celebrated Rory Underwood's touchline run from the halfway line that sealed the win: cans of beer started raining down on me from the stands. This is a practice that even football has stopped but, on this occasion, I noticed that one of the cans that landed near me was unopened. I picked it up, opened it and drank it, toasting the crowd. This resulted in a hail of cans being lobbed at me, but I couldn't drink them all.

As in the final Test of the 1989 series, the most important moment in our win happened in a scrum. In the second half, the Kiwis forced a five-yard scrum during a period in which they threatened to reverse the momentum of the game and before we had put space between the sides on the scoreboard. Having hooked the ball, their pack set for a pushover try. I felt the tremendous pressure come through their front row, and momentarily I feared that Jason Leonard, who had only played a few times at tight-head, was too high. However, we absorbed the drive, and as front-row players will attest, there is a moment when you sense the other pack is vulnerable to a counter-drive. I did not call our shove, but we slowly edged their pack backwards, and Zinzan Brooke, their number eight, knocked the ball on as a result of it getting tangled with the foot of one of their retreating second-rows.

There are legions of players who play international rugby and never beat the All Blacks. Though New Zealand have something of a mental block when it comes to the World Cup, statistically they are the most successful international side by a distance, and any win against them is special. Winning on their turf and being unarguably superior was even more satisfying.

I now wonder whether, within the satisfaction of our win, lay the root of our downfall in the final Test in Auckland. I did not think so either before, during or after we lost the deciding game by 30–13, but something that Sean Fitzpatrick said whilst we were interviewed on the field, shortly after the final whistle, has stayed with me. His answer, when asked to explain the difference between the Kiwi performances in Wellington and Auckland, was simple, but telling: 'I just think we needed it a bit more today.'

That comment, unwittingly or not, referred to the tremendous pressure to win that every All Black side faces as the result of public expectation. The legacy of great All Blacks of yesteryear is something that has no equivalent in English rugby. Football is our national game, and even that does not occupy the dominant position in English life that rugby does in New Zealand. Faced with the ignominy of losing a series at home, there was an edge of determined desperation about their play in that game. I do not believe any Lion gave less than his all, but a loss would not have been greeted with the shame and period of national introspection that would have followed an All Black defeat.

As I walked from the field after our defeat, the rest of the Lions started a lap of honour. I couldn't face this. Fuelled by the taunts from my *alter ego*, I felt that I had let our thousands of supporters down, and I did not want to be involved in something that I thought would be derided by the Kiwis as an example of losers losing well. 'I told you that you weren't good enough' rang in my head. I waited in the tunnel, out of sight, to complete the customary shaking of the hand of each opposition player. My absence from the Lions on the pitch was noted and attracted two kinds of comment. The first, that I refused to shake the hands of the All Black team and thus demonstrated my lack of sportsmanship, was untrue. The second, that I refused to thank the Lions fans for their support was, I suppose, technically true, but not out of any lack of respect; I felt that I did not deserve that support and felt it would have been fraudulent to accept it. This reaction is mine to own and I should have swallowed any self-induced embarrassment and registered the gratefulness I felt for the efforts made by thousands of people over thousands of miles. I cannot now rectify my omission, and it joins many similar acts in the column marked 'Things I wish I had done'.

# 17

## All Change

### 1995 Five Nations and Rugby World Cup

On Wednesday 24 November 1993, England trained at the Quins ground. After training, we returned to the Petersham Hotel. I had brought to the hotel, not only my kit and clothes but several large boxes full of lever arch files. These related to a £20m damages claim being made by a client against his former firm of solicitors. This complex professional-negligence claim had been run by a fellow partner but for various reasons I had been asked to step in. I knew that we were having a problem getting the necessary witness statements to support the claim but, while reading late into the night to familiarise myself with the case, I learned that unless we exchanged them by the coming Monday we faced being debarred from calling such evidence.

In between training and meetings on Thursday, I arranged to see three important witnesses the following afternoon. The problem was that they were in Glasgow. I went to see Geoff Cooke and explained my dilemma. He was not thrilled when I said I had to be allowed to go to Glasgow, as that was not how he wanted his players preparing for such a big game. Had he not agreed, I would have gone anyway because for all that I got out of playing for England, it was impossible to live on pats on the back.

I flew to Scotland at Friday lunchtime, took the details for the statements, and flew back early evening. I went to the team meeting, ate dinner whilst I worked and finished dictating the final witness statement just before midnight. A courier came to take some files and tapes to the office, where the statements would be finalised and faxed for signature the following day. I went to the bathroom and fell into bed exhausted. The next day I got up, had breakfast, and casually beat the All Blacks.

The above account illustrates the increasing impossibility of players combining their need to have a roof over their heads with the escalating demands made by the RFU in terms of time and effort. The All Blacks had smashed everybody on their short tour: the week before our game they had beaten Scotland 51–15 and were heavy favourites to win at Twickenham.

It was undoubtedly because I was struggling with legal matters that I felt little of the usual pressure that came with a game against New Zealand, but this was also partly because the Lions tour a few months earlier had allowed me to play against their players several times. They no longer held mystique for any of the English Lions and we were in no doubt that we could beat them.

The build-up included a preposterous meeting solely about the Haka. The Maori challenge 'Ka Mate' had been performed before games by All Black sides for many years, but only over the most recent thirty or so has it become an overt and intimidating ritual. If you look at old footage, it looks more like a Morris dance.

Some Kiwis have a precious attitude to the Haka. They insist they have a right to perform it; which they do, but only at home. Elsewhere, the host union has discretion as to whether it is performed. This sensitivity has reached the stage where some Kiwis claim that no non-Kiwi has a right to have an opinion on, or to speak about, the Haka. Further, the slightest indication of dissent, such as where on the field it is performed, the time it is performed, and even the proposal that the host country reply in similar fashion or with songs or verse, draws allegations of disrespect.

To face this moment of pure theatre in sport is a unique experience and whether or not it intimidates is down to the psyche of the players who face it. It used to inspire me and it should stay. However, the recent introduction of other hakas by the All Blacks before games, and which seemingly get more theatrically staged, should not be condoned. The alternatives may be traditional in the sense that they are as old as 'Ka Mate', but they are self-evidently not traditionally associated with the All Blacks. In our meeting, we discussed turning our backs, going down to the other end of the field and so on, but my view was that we should stand and face the challenge, because what did it say about us if we did not?

In the end, when the Haka had finished there was a natural break whilst we took off our tracksuit tops. During this pause the Twickenham crowd belted out 'Swing Low, Sweet Chariot' and it was game on. We deserved our 15–9 win and it should have been more. There was no luck involved, and we should have faced only fourteen men for seventy-five minutes of the game. Fortunately for New Zealand, the officials missed the cynical and cowardly stamp by Jamie Joseph, the Kiwi flanker, on the ankle of the prone and defenceless Kyran Bracken. To his great credit, Bracken, who was winning his first cap, carried on with his ankle heavily bandaged and enjoyed the celebrations afterwards to the full.

Unfortunately that win, and the fact that England won the International Sevens title, meant we were again named BBC Sport's Team of the Year in 1993. As before, we did not deserve it and, when the time came to go on to the stage to receive the award, I wanted to stay in my seat. I did not, because my feelings did not deserve to be inflicted on everybody else, but I could not wait to get off the stage and hated every second of the applause we received.

We struggled badly during most of the 1994 Five Nations, Geoff Cooke's final Championship, trying to define a style that suited a team not yet established and with insufficient knowledge.

The lack of understanding extended beyond tactical issues: it related to what was required mentally, how to prepare, how to handle pressure, and what to learn from victory and defeat. When we lost to Ireland and struggled to beat Scotland, I remember saying that too many of the new faces were happy to have gained caps and did not feel the pain of losing sufficiently personally. I now think that, although I was right, most players have to go through ordeals and painfully learn these lessons, especially the public nature thereof, and that there is no convenient short cut.

At least they were spared the ignominy of losing at Murrayfield. As I stood on the halfway line watching Jon Callard prepare for a last-second penalty kick – wrongly awarded to us, by the way – I received fearful abuse. When the kick went over from fifty metres, I turned to my detractors, bowed, stuck two fingers up and turned and jogged to the tunnel. Even when I showed such wit and diplomacy I could not attract any members to my Scottish fan club; there's no pleasing some people.

Fortunately we had the French to galvanise our efforts, plus the extra spice of playing in Paris. The likes of Johnson, Ojomo, Rodber, Clarke and Back had replaced the stalwarts of our pack and some went on to become equally good if not better players. Our 18–14 win looked close on paper but we were good value for the away win, England's seventh in succession against France. Paris was still a difficult place to play, but the newcomers gave an indication that they had taken to heart some of the stick that the press had dealt out after our first two games.

The final game was an oddity. Wales, under Alan Davies, came to Twickenham, knowing that a win or defeat by fewer than fifteen points would secure them the Five Nations trophy. If we won by sixteen points or more, the trophy would be ours. We did win, but the 15–8 scoreline gave Wales the prize. In just two seasons, Alan Davies had lifted Welsh rugby out of the depths to the point where it had won the Five Nations. A rather bashful-looking Ieuan Evans accepted the trophy from our rather bemused-looking sovereign; it all felt flat, as neither side had got what it really wanted.

The game marked my entry into the 50 club, a select body for those players gaining fifty or more caps for England. It was not the number that was important but the fellow members. Whatever my *alter ego* had to say about it, my name could not be erased from alongside the greats of the English game, even if part of me felt I should not be there.

Geoff Cooke was never universally popular with the RFU, despite delivering the longest and most successful period of rugby in their history. The RFU saw him as a players' man, and he was; he was the bloody coach, for God's sake. During our arguments over professionalism Cooke refused to drop players as demanded by the RFU, and he was never forgiven for this treachery. He was a brave man and deserves recognition for that.

I did not have much, if any, of a relationship with Geoff. This will probably surprise most readers, and considering that we fought for the same goals for about six years, it amazes me. Yet that was how it was. I can count on the fingers of one hand the number of times we were in each other's company and chatted freely about anything. He had far closer relationships with some of our backs, and I feel sad that I could not have been closer to the man responsible for building the base from whence came England's later triumphs. Few remember how awful England were when he took the position of coach, and some, like Clive Woodward, subsequently doubted his achievements and claimed he produced dull rugby. I and the rest of English rugby should be grateful for what he did.

The end of the 1994 season marked the decisive break between the side that Geoff built and the one Jack was to build.

Cooke's replacement was the man who had guided Bath in their years of hegemony in English rugby. He was one of the best rugby brains I met, but his style did not suit all. Jack Rowell and his longtime assistant Brian Ashton were used to working with a squad of extraordinary players. Within the Bath set-up, there was the ideal mixture of brains, aggression, sincerity and rugby knowhow that allowed Rowell to delegate much of the preparation to the players. He believed that this mirrored what had to happen on the field, where a coach could not accompany his team, barking instructions and determining tactics. When he introduced this *laissez-faire* approach to England, I was immediately comfortable, as were the senior players who always demanded a say anyway. Most of those players had reached positions in their outside jobs that required accountability.

However, with Rowell came the break-up of a team that had been settled for the best part of four seasons. In came many younger and relatively inexperienced players who were not familiar with his style. The fact that these players were not very familiar with responsibility either on the field or in their careers, where they were also junior, meant that they sometimes looked lost. On occasion, Rowell's unusual intellect and sense of humour resulted in some players being unable to understand what he said or wanted from them. This foreshadowed Brian Ashton's problems in the 2007 World Cup when players basically complained they were not told how to play.

Rowell's first challenge was the England summer tour to South Africa, which was the ideal tour because the following year the third World Cup would be held there. It was a tour that gave a fair indication of which players were likely to be included in our World Cup squad; it also saw the start of a chart, divided into weeks, that was given to each player, detailing their expected training, diet and time commitments from that point until the flight to South Africa the following year.

It was the first time I had been to South Africa. As I got on the plane, I thought wistfully about the fact that I had turned down the opportunity to play there five years earlier and the £40,000 that had gone by the board as a result. Nineteen ninety-four saw South Africa host the first tour since they had been allowed back into international rugby. Nelson Mandela had been released and it was a time of flux, with hopes high but expectations reserved, and the atmosphere was alive with speculation about Mandela's chances of peacefully integrating the various factions that, only months before, had been engaged in armed conflict.

I had played against the Springboks only once before, but the memory of huge men trying to shove my head through my spine in the scrums was one that had, surprisingly, not left me. I thought it would be physical and I was not wrong. If there was one thing that distinguished my games against South Africa from the games against the Aussies and Kiwis, it is the Springbok flirtation with casual violence. Bar the odd incident, no game in which I faced Australia or New Zealand was marked by excessive use of the boot off the ball, indiscriminate punching, gouging or biting. True enough, if you were near the ball and, worse, if you were blocking its release, you got mercilessly rucked, but if not they left you alone, as they were only intent on winning the ball.

We did not play well in our opening game, against Natal in Durban, and lost to Transvaal the following Saturday at altitude at Ellis Park, Johannesburg. However, the 21–24 loss on the veldt was a game we could have won, had the referee, Ian Rogers, been watching as Will Carling touched the ball down, rather than running back to their twenty-two, having already ordered a drop-out. It was a fantastic game played at blinding pace and one in which Transvaal made very few mistakes. The fact that we got so close should have alerted rugby pundits to the fact that we were nowhere near the underdogs they made us for the first Test the following week.

The game also contained an incident that, in spite of my loud protests, our management refused to highlight. Had they done so, they would have saved the rest of the rugby world a good deal of unnecessary violence. The Transvaal prop, Johan le Roux, bit the ear of our fullback Paul Hull whilst they were in a maul and Hull had hold of the ball. The wound was plain to see afterwards and I was incensed. That sort of thing, like gouging, has no part in rugby, which is a sport of violent collisions and carries inherent risks anyway. On this occasion, the old English fear of being labelled whingers prevailed, but by saying nothing, we tacitly condoned such an obscenity. It came as no surprise that the madman le Roux was banned eighteen months later for taking a chunk out of the ear of Sean Fitzpatrick. On reflection, maybe we were right to keep quiet.

The first Test at Loftus Versfeld, Pretoria, was a strange occasion. In a way, it felt as though we were bystanders to a series of events held by South Africans for South Africans. Rightly, the presence of President Mandela was significant and much celebrated. This was a game of rugby, the province of white South Africans hitherto, at the home of the Blue Bulls, in the heartland of the Afrikaners. As we ran on to the field, we were greeted by the hurling of oranges and a pair of scissors. We watched as South African army helicopters swooped over the stadium, and some of the crowd booed the new national anthem. Yet the feeling of being thought incidental to all this, allied to the pre-match rubbishing of our team by the South African media, so angered us that we tore into the Springboks at the kickoff.

The next twenty minutes were amongst the finest ever played by an England team in the modern era. For me, they matched the period in 1992 when we ripped the French apart on the way to our second Grand Slam. Two moments stood out for me. I caught their scrum half, Joost van der Westhuizen, as he tried to deal with a poorly tapped ball from the lineout. We recovered possession and the backs worked the ball along the line and scored. Later the Springbok captain François Pienaar tried to drive the ball forward and was hit by Ben Clarke and in quick succession Dean Richards and Tim Rodber. The rest of our pack joined in to drive Pienaar several yards backwards and win us a scrum.

Rugby's place in the South African psyche was demonstrated in the reaction to their crushing 15–32 defeat. As well as every paper carrying the normal sporting reports, their main editorials also commented, with most agreeing that the Springboks had been taught a lesson in humility.

The re-match was played the following weekend at Newlands in Cape Town. I cannot decide whether the game was lost because we were too happy with the first Test win or whether South Africa reacted to their savage criticism, as had the All Blacks in the third

Test of the Lions series in 1993. Certainly, also, the monumental party we had after the initial win could not have helped physically. Perhaps it was a little of all three.

The changes to the Springbok team made it plain that they were not going to have their forwards outplayed two weeks in a row. The maniac le Roux came into their front row, and throughout the second Test ran about the field putting his boot on any white shirt he could see. This approach and the fact that he had wild eyes and occasionally bellowed 'I love it!' made me think his play was not entirely normal. Without the titanic presence of the injured Dean Richards we, as a pack, did not front up and, though we had chances in the game, we did not deserve to win.

I have little doubt that my earlier mention of South African casual violence will have drawn howls of protest from some, but had they seen the intentional violence of the Eastern Province side in the final match of the tour they might modify their objections. Graham Dawe was outstandingly brave in the face of unacceptable kicks and punches that were delivered at more or less every breakdown. When the referee refused to take a strong hand, I understood why Lions teams in the past had felt it necessary to get their retaliation in first.

The brutality of the above tour speeded up the maturation of all the recent caps, and the 1995 Five Nations saw England win a third Grand Slam in five years. It was an indication of how much English rugby had improved that we were made heavy favourites to achieve the feat. When I came into the side, the public were happy if we played well; if we won, then so much the better. There were a few survivors from the team that had won the 1991 Grand Slam, mostly backs, but the team had now made a successful transition from old to new.

The first game in Dublin was played in the most difficult conditions I ever experienced as an international. The wind that blew straight down the Lansdowne Road pitch was so strong that, if you threw a ball into the air, it was immediately carried ten yards by the gale. When I put a ball down, it would not stay still and began rolling quickly with the wind. It was also bitterly cold. Rain and mud are essentially neutral because they do not favour one side. The team that played with this wind at their backs could kick a ball seventy yards without too much trouble.

Martin Johnson betrayed his forward roots when he cited this game as one of his favourites, as there was virtually no move that went along either backline. We played against the storm in the first half and had no option but to continually drive the ball with our forwards. Passes were snatched by the wind and propelled several yards behind their intended recipients, and fifteen yards was about the limit on any kick against the wind. It was a masterful forward display that prevented the Irish from capitalising on their advantage.

Time and again, our back row started drives that were carried on by our front five, but after twenty minutes Tim Rodber had to leave the field with an injury. A player's worth is often best judged by the reaction he provokes from opponents. I studied the body language of the Irish pack that greeted the sight of a lumbering Dean Richards, who replaced Rodber. To a man they slumped, as if to say, 'This isn't fair – not him.' Deano did not disappoint, setting the platform for drives that often went thirty or forty yards.

The most important thing to remember when playing with the advantage of a strong wind is to understand that it alone will not guarantee victory. We still had to work in the second half but won well in the end. I must also mention that we totally outscrummaged their front row of Nick Popplewell, Keith Wood and Peter Clohessy. Before the game, the team had wound me up in a meeting by referring to them as the best in the world, a point made in a number of papers. Our response was the best answer to such drivel.

France came to Twickenham for the second round of games and fancied their chances, having won their summer series against the All Blacks. In the pre-match jousting, I created a quote that has stood the test of time. 'The French,' I told the media, 'are like fifteen Eric Cantonas: brilliant but brutal.' Paul Ackford, who by then had become a rugby journalist, called it the most irresponsible comment he had heard that year. I thought it was rather apt. Instead of their usual rabid reaction to my comments, the French went out of their way to show they were unconcerned and totally relaxed about this statement.

They were right, they were laid back; so much so that they played like a girls' school on the Saturday, and we hammered them 31–10. That was eight in a row.

We beat Wales in our next game with some ease. They had lost Scott Gibbs and Scott Quinnell to rugby league, but I was upset that my old friend Alan Davies was fired at the end of the Championship, having won it only the year before. The England game was used by his critics as one of the reasons he should go.

This set up another Grand Slam decider with Scotland, but this time we were at home. It is from that game that my unpopularity with the Scots burgeoned to ridiculous proportions. It is now forgotten that the tone for the game was set in the week before by ridiculous comments from John Jeffrey, their former flanker. Labelling the English 'Barboured yobs', he claimed the Scottish team were regularly subjected to abuse when they drove through the Twickenham car park before games. I doubt whether most of the Home Counties set could drag themselves away from their lavish hampers or unstuff their mouths long enough to shout abuse.

The game was entirely unsatisfactory, with Scotland having one objective, to kill as much ball as they could and see if they could win on penalties. We won 24–12 but it was a poor game. Straight after the game, I was pulled to one side by Nigel Starmer-Smith of the BBC. He asked me whether I was happy with a third Grand Slam, and I told him what I thought: I was very unhappy with Scotland's negativity and they had contributed almost nothing to the game. People have since said that I should have been gracious in victory, but when I am asked a question I give a straight answer, and my description was accurate. From the reaction to these game-related comments, you would have thought I had advocated the murder of every Scottish firstborn.

In the BBC studio, an apoplectic John Jeffrey, conveniently ignoring his earlier anti-English slurs, attacked me whilst Mickey Skinner could be seen in the background trying not to laugh. Complaints about my remarks flooded the BBC switchboard, though interestingly many of the written complaints included quotes ascribed to me of things I had not said. I know this because I reviewed the interview carefully two days later. I received scores of abusive letters, and in one, the author was still swearing on the ninth page.

I took a phone call two days later and the caller announced, 'Hello, this is your only Scottish friend.' It was Finlay Calder. I was tempted to say, 'And your point is?' but he continued by saying, 'You were right, but what did you expect us to do?' He rounded off his call by saying, 'When you next come up, we'll go out and do some missionary work. You're in dire need of a better image up here.' After this incident, whenever I visited Scotland or was near a group of Scottish people, I got all manner of stick, but on the few occasions I challenged the person who made the comments, they could not accurately quote anything I had said that day. Once I knew this was the sort of reaction I would invariably face, I just said the first ridiculously provocative thing that came into my head.

The best backhanded compliment I received, and an amusing one at that, was in the form of a website set up by someone from the Scottish rugby club, Annan. 'Is Brian Moore the Anti-Christ' invited viewers to vote on whether I was Beelzebub or an angel sent from above, whilst the demonic music of *Carmina Burana*, by Orff, plays in the background. I voted hundreds of times and am still voted as Satan by a heavy majority.

England's preparation for the 1995 World Cup was as intense as was possible for a team composed almost fully of genuinely part-time players. It was also the most uneven tournament because several sides – Australia, New Zealand, South Africa and France amongst them – were semi-professional in all but name. Considering this fact, we did well to get the team into the position where we and France could legitimately claim to have a chance of winning the Cup, together with the big three southern-hemisphere teams.

For the last eighteen months of my England career, my life had largely had the same pattern. Go to work; train at lunchtime; work; train in the evening; go home; eat supper watching *Newsnight*; go to bed. In contrast, many of the players in the teams that had a realistic shot at lifting the Webb Ellis Trophy worked part time and were given all the time they wanted to train and play.

There were many differences between the 1995 and 1991 tournaments. England's preparation was significantly more detailed. The event had a much higher media profile and when I got into the games in South Africa, I realised that the ferocity of and power in the tackles, rucks and mauls had increased substantially. England introduced little that was revolutionary; by that time, the mechanics of fitness and nutrition were widely known, but the degree to which each received attention increased each year. The only thing that was totally new was a neoprene one-piece training suit for each player. The theory behind training in the suit was that it raised body temperature and, in doing so, would replicate the heat in which we would play our games.

I trained with the suit but as I ran around Wimbledon Common, looking like a cross between an SAS stormtrooper and a character from *Blake's 7*, there was always a lingering fear of arrest. The suit was unbearable at times, and when I told a medical friend that the aim was to raise my core body temperature by one degree, he shook his head. He then told me that, to get some idea of how significant this seemingly small alteration was, I should consider the fact that if I suffered a similar drop in my core body heat, I would be entering the first stages of hypothermia. I didn't use it too much after that.

The other event of note in England's countdown to the Cup was the decision by the RFU to sack its captain only six weeks before the team left for South Africa. Officially they said it was because of Carling's description of the RFU as 'fifty-seven old farts'. Even if that remark was offensive, it was hardly grossly so. In reality, I believe it was the secretary Dudley Wood's payback for the team's continuing refusal to kowtow in the amateurism debate, and Carling's part therein. That Wood was prepared to destabilise his own team so close to a World Cup illustrates his priorities. There was no tactic he would not use, no depth to which he would not sink, in a battle that, by that stage, he knew had been lost. It was unadulterated spite.

In the end, the RFU were humiliated by every player's refusal to take the captaincy. All my career I had envied Carling; I would have sacrificed even more to have had the honour of the captaincy, but not under those circumstances. After a weekend of media frenzy, the then RFU president, Dennis Easby, came to one of our evening training sessions in Marlow to announce that, as Carling had apologised, he had been reinstated. Easby was brave to face our hostility and mockery, but it was his own fault for not standing up to Wood, who was only an employee, whatever his title. Wood did not have the courage to face us himself.

Things in South Africa opened with a welcome lunch at the Constantia winery in Stellenbosch. Unfortunately, this was a perfect demonstration of administrators not having a clue about modern-day preparation for rugby. All the teams had to travel to the venue from the hotels that they had only checked into a few days previously. We were unhappy about this unnecessary event, but at least we did not have the ridiculous trip suffered by the Welsh team that had to get up at 5 a.m. to arrive on time. Whilst the multitude of administrators mixed freely, the teams stayed together and glared at opponents they would shortly have to engage in battle.

Our pool in the first-stage games did not contain any of the other favoured teams, but it could have been tricky because we had both Argentina and Western Samoa to beat, along with Italy. Our wins against the Argentinians and Italians were a struggle. In neither game did we look impressive, but they were won and another victory would mean we played the runner-up and not the winner of another pool. We did beat the Samoans, but it was an attritional game in which they repeatedly hit our players late or with their infamous 'tackles', which were actually shoulder charges, as they made no attempt to wrap their swinging arms around the player. It got to the point where we considered telling the referee that if he did not stop these dangerous and illegal challenges, we would leave the pitch. Due to several injuries during the game we finished with our back row containing Kyran Bracken and me on either flank.

Next, was a chance for revenge: our quarter-final against Australia, the team that had beaten us in the 1991 final. With under two minutes remaining of the game, I stood on our 22-metre line and watched Australia's David Campese line up to try a drop kick that would break the 22–22 deadlock and win the game.

Not him, of all people, not him. As I waited and tried to get into a position to make an attempt to charge down the kick, I thought of the sub-editors' headlines that might accompany a successful Campese drop-goal: 'Campese kicks Carling's cohorts out of Cup.' The ball went to him, he swung his boot – and missed. The large English contingent in the crowd roared and I took a few moments to commiserate with the great man as I jogged across the field for the resultant twenty-two drop-out.

From the re-start, we forced a lineout near the halfway line. I had the ball in my hands and was thinking about the call and which jumper to use. I did not find out until later that our poor performance in the lineouts that day was down to the fact that the Aussies cracked our codes early in the game. I decided to throw to our middle jumper, Martin Bayfield, reasoning that if the timing was good on a fast flat throw, Bayfield would get to the ball first. I threw and Bayfield caught the ball two-handed.

As there was less than a minute to go, I wanted the ball passed to our scrum half Dewi Morris. We knew that Rob Andrew, our fly half, was going to try and go one better than Campese. Dewi screamed that we were not close enough and he wanted the maul driven ten yards closer to their line. As we drove the Aussies back I was afraid the ball would be spilled, and was relieved when Dewi called for it. I stood up in time to see the ball soar between the Australian posts. We led 25–22.

I was about to celebrate when the referee indicated there was time for the re-start. The Aussies stole the ball and there was a series of rucks and at each one I screamed, 'Let them have it. Don't give them a penalty.' We stole the ball and it was driven twice more by our back row; Dewi took it and shaped to kick. Instead of hoofing it anywhere off the field to bring forth the final whistle, he put in a delicate rolling kick which looked as if it would not go out of play. I willed the ball over the touchline with each revolution and it finally crossed the chalk. The whistle went and the Aussies went with it.

Our confidence was high after that win and we did not fear playing the All Blacks in the next stage. That confidence led us to believe that their new sensation, winger Jonah Lomu, could be marked by only Tony Underwood. Lomu's subsequent demolition of the unfortunate Underwood demonstrated the difference between preparing from detailed video analysis and planning after having actually played against the players and team in question.

The semi-final against the Kiwis took place at Newlands in Cape Town, and it was the only game I played for England in which, after the first twenty minutes, I knew we could not win. To the immense disappointment of the millions of watching England fans, Lomu ran over and round all would-be tacklers. Inside five minutes they scored two tries, and when Zinzan Brooke dropped a goal from forty metres, I knew it was over. When that kick went over, I caught the eye of my old adversary, Sean Fitzpatrick. I expected the usual sledging but he just shrugged his shoulders. It did not matter that we scored four tries in the second half because we lost 45–29. In normal circumstances, our total would have been enough to win, but on that day we were well beaten.

South Africa won the final, amidst allegations of food poisoning, and they learned from our game by immediately surrounding

Lomu with at least two players whenever he got the ball. By so doing, they prevented him dominating the game, and the world witnessed the iconic sight of Nelson Mandela, dressed in a Springbok shirt, raising the World Cup alongside François Pienaar. It was a victory that had huge meaning in terms of the stability of the winning country, if not the whole of Africa.

Before the final, we had to play the French in the dreaded third place playoff. This game is pointless because nobody cares which team comes third and the players, having lost in the semi-finals, just want to go home. France ended a run of eight successive defeats in a match that was one of the worst in the whole tournament.

After the game, my number was again drawn out of the bag for a drug test. Out of England's five previous games, my number had randomly been chosen four times, including the game played only five days earlier. I refused to take the test, which naturally caused a row. Don Rutherford, the RFU technical director, told me that if I did not take the test there would be a public furore. I said I did not care and I would tell the press that I did not believe the tests were random, given the frequency with which I was chosen. I also reminded him that, in the 1991 World Cup, my number had been the first out of the bag in all six games I played; the odds on this were 85,766,121 to 1. If I took the test, as demanded by Rutherford, the odds on the 1995 tests were 4,084,101 to 1. He told me that I would be banned but I told him that, as I was retiring, that really didn't matter to me. They wrongly put my number back in the bag and chose another player.

It was a suitably contentious note on which to end my eight-year, 64-game England career. Would I change any of it? Only the 1990 Murrayfield game and the 1991 World Cup final; and all the mistakes I made. Those apart, I could not have done much more. I played at many different levels: schoolboy, junior club, senior club, university, student, under 23, B team, divisional, full international, Barbarians, Hong Kong Sevens and British Lions. It was a career that I could not have thought of achieving when I was young. At times, even now, it feels like another life, lived by another person. Intellectually, I appreciate the magnitude of what I did. However, because of the constant battles I have with Gollum to repel negative thoughts and to stop dwelling on my mistakes, it means my memories bring feelings of pride and sadness in equal measure.

# 18

## Rugby Becomes Professional

The benefit of hindsight usually leads me to see past events differently, but not in the case of the amateurism/professionalism debate. What I thought about the issues then, I still believe now. My impressions of the people and the events are the same. Further, things have turned out much as I expected: professionalism, with its good and bad points, is here to stay. Even though that debate is over, the way the game moved from amateur to professional is important because its consequences are still being felt.

In 1895, the breakaway Northern Rugby Union (which later became Rugby League) was formed by clubs which intended to repay the money their players lost by playing rugby and missing work on Saturdays to play rugby. The same principle was behind the vicious battle that took place in rugby union from the mid 1980s onwards, until the game turned professional, shortly before the 1995 Rugby World Cup.

Not only did the changes affect players and team officials, it radically altered the RFU and its influence over English rugby. Had loss of control been the principle that opponents of professionalism said they were defending, I might have had some sympathy with their cause; but it was not. No, what they wanted to save was the cult of the amateur; that and their own privileges, although they were never so vulgar as to admit to the latter.

The post of RFU secretary used to be an honorary post. Naturally, this drastically restricted the type of person that was chosen; not only because he had to be the 'right sort of chap', but he either had to be so wealthy he did not need an income, or he had retired; with most secretaries, it was both. At that time, the attitude of the RFU was, in a way, similar to that of the Civil Service regarding government: players, teams and coaches came and went; the Committee remained. This longevity guaranteed power and continuity. To be an England player was and is a great honour; but, in the minds of many of the Committee, players were not of prime importance. They could always pick another fifteen, and a fifteen who would be bloody glad to step on to the field without complaint. This was all about to change.

By the mid 1980s, it was well known, but not admitted, that players in France, Wales and South Africa were paid for playing. In Australia and New Zealand, the players' careers were being organised so that they could have whatever leave was required to enable them to train and play. In England, meanwhile, players were not paid, and the stories of exaggerated expenses were largely urban myths. In 1985, the RFU voted against establishing a World Cup because they said it would lead to a professional game, and because players would meet and discuss what they were and were not allowed to earn.

I came back from the 1987 World Cup knowing which players had their own companies, through which they channelled payments. When asked about the schemes run by players in other countries, the RFU, through its staunchly amateur secretary Dudley Wood, said that they had raised this with the relevant union's IRB representative and had been assured this did not happen.

During this so-called amateur era the following happened whilst I was on the Lions tour to Australia in 1989. An offer was made to me and other players to tour South Africa in an invitation President's XV. The naming of the touring side was deliberate so that it could not be identified as coming from one specific country, thereby causing a particular union embarrassment. Nevertheless, the invitations were sent via each player's relevant union to ensure the tour had legitimacy within the IRB.

I remember the initial meeting because it was held behind closed doors. Given its clandestine nature, it was actually begun by Finlay Calder in a hushed voice. Indeed the first few players to comment also spoke quietly, until we all realised what we were doing and laughter broke the tension.

When first mentioned, the proposal was for the whole squad to tour *en masse*. Finlay outlined the tour, saying it would last three weeks and we had been promised payment – proper payment, not inflated expenses. The offer was genuine and the subject of money had been raised without embarrassment by the South Africans, but it was up to us to discuss both the principle and the terms.

The political antipathy towards South Africa had intensified since the England tour of 1984. South Africa was still under apartheid and banned from world rugby, so it was no longer involved in formal Test matches, and those sportsmen who toured in any of the major sports faced a difficult reception back home. I have never subscribed to boycotting sports events unless they are accompanied by a total breaking of trade and diplomatic relations. I do not accept that sport should pay the political price when governments and business do not do likewise. Sport is an easy target, one that can be, and is, bullied by those who will not take similarly difficult decisions. Nevertheless, were we to go at that point, it would be in the face of strident protest. There was, we thought at the time, a possibility that some people would have to give up their jobs, and even face suspension from playing or a permanent ban.

At the time, we did not realise that the invitations to go on this tour had actually been formally passed from the SARFU to the RFU and other home unions – without mention of the cash aspect, of course. The formal approach was for players to go and play within the current laws of amateurism. When we found out about this later, the unanimous view was that the contrasting unofficial offer had to have been made with the knowledge of the South African rugby authorities. The logistics of sponsorship rights, player appearances, kit and so on could never have been organised to the satisfaction of all the commercial partners without this being so.

The first figure mentioned was £20,000, but as always happens when group discussions take place, things soon escalated. When we got up to £100,000 per man, a lone voice with a Gloucester brogue piped up from the back. 'Now, hold on a minute.' Iron Man Teague pointed out, rightly, that the £100,000 sum was 'fanciful'. I think this was the word he used, or it might have been 'bollocks'. He further pointed out that £12,000 was about the average annual wage for an average worker and even were the sum on offer to be this low, it would be earned in three weeks not fifty-two, and was still a decent whack.

It was left up to representatives to go and see the lie of the land. Four of us – me, Finlay, Bob Norster and Donal Lenihan, our own home unions committee – went to meet Barney Oosterhuizen, an agent for the First National Bank, which was putting up the cash. He was keen to stress he had no official connection with the SARFU; however, it was inconceivable that they did not know what was going on.

Whilst we were considering this offer, John Kendall-Carpenter, a former RFU president, whose views on amateurism matched those of the RFU secretary Dudley Wood, flew out to meet us in Australia to broker some kind of official deal. It was at this point we realised that official invitations had been received by our respective unions. He told us that we would not be penalised by our unions if we went, as the tour had now been sanctioned by the IRB. In addition he mentioned that the official tour allowance would also be available. At the time, it was £12 per day.

Trying not to snigger at that paltry figure, I and a few others asked questions of no consequence to be polite, as well as seeking reassurance that players accepting these now-official invitations could not be penalised, which he confirmed. I have often wondered if Kendall-Carpenter was simply a fool, unaware of any of the political realities surrounding such a tour. The more interesting supposition, infinitely more sinister and Machiavellian, was that he knew full well what was going on behind the scenes, but had to be seen to use the official line as a cover because South Africa had made it plain that, if they got no players, they would simply blow wide the world of rugby and establish a professional game. In doing so, whatever they might claim to the contrary, they would have been supported by the Anzac unions and probably the French.

Details were eventually thrashed out, such as which offshore account would be used and the fact that the players would be responsible for their own tax when they brought the money back into the country. Shortly thereafter, I received a call from Sandy Sanders, the then president of the RFU. I disliked Sanders for his adherence to amateurism and for being oblivious to the evidence that, all around him, it was being ignored. But I do give him enormous credit for being one of those who resigned from the RFU Committee over the issue; hardly anybody else had the honesty to do so.

Sanders told me that he had heard rumours of big sums of money being made available to players and that, in his opinion, anybody who even talked about money would have professionalised themselves. I told him that his point of view was unlikely to be upheld in a court of law, reminding him that, although the RFU liked to pretend its laws were real, they were subject to the proper statutes of our land. 'Are you being offered money?' he asked. 'I can't say,' I replied, knowing it is always wiser not to lie when you do not have to.

I then spoke to Will Carling, who was not on tour, and he told me that the RFU had assured him that anybody who toured would never play for England again. By this time, I had a full grasp of the political dimensions to this matter and was very confident about what could and could not be done; and thus what could and could not be threatened. I told him that that was nonsense because the RFU had passed on the official invitations without demur or caveat and had therefore sanctioned it. Moreover, unless they could prove a player had taken the cash, they could do nothing about it. The usual procedure was to make a player swear an affidavit confirming he had not received money; he was guilty unless he did so, even if the RFU had no evidence of payment. I was sure this was contrary to natural justice and would not be upheld before the courts. More importantly, if a player called their bluff and swore that he had not taken any money, what could they do without any other evidence? Say 'Liar, liar, pants on fire'?

Would I have lied for such a sum? Yes, given the duplicity of everyone else in the amateurism debate. I would have done so without a twang of conscience. In any other circumstance, I would have a great deal of difficulty lying on oath.

No final group deal was done, as Finlay rightly wanted this supreme distraction to be out of the way whilst we grappled with the not inconsiderable task of beating Australia. It was left up to individuals to discuss their own deals and, from that point on, differential sums were offered. The final offer made to me was £40,000 for three weeks' work – a large sum even today. In 1989, it was almost three times my annual salary. I had a difficult decision to make.

I had just got back from Australia, having won the Test series with the Lions, and had been away for almost ten weeks. I wanted to go to South Africa both for the money and for the fact that I fancied testing myself against the Springboks who, by reason of their exclusion, retained the mystique that had gone with the advent of the first World Cup, when all teams had been open to scrutiny by other countries.

I approached Neville Radcliffe, the senior partner of the Nottingham law firm I worked for at the time, and with whom I got on very well. I said that I sought unpaid leave, but obviously didn't mention the payment offered. He came back to me and said that some partners were firmly for me, others staunchly against. Of those against, there were two factions. The first simply said it was too much time off and it would send out the wrong signal to the rest of the firm. He felt that these could be overruled by the fact that more of the senior partners were in favour than not. However, the second group had strong political objections, and given this, were they to be overruled, he felt that at best there would be considerable resentment against me and the senior partners; at worst there might be more direct protests. Finally, that if and when it came to discussing a possible partnership in the future, those who had been overruled could and would make it very difficult for me to be elected.

I eventually decided not to go. I did not want to be the cause of internal strife and reasoned that over the course of a long career, particularly if I became an equity partner, the sum offered would be small. Ironically, eighteen months later, in 1990, I left Nottingham for a different life in London. I now wish I had taken the money.

The Lions who did go were augmented by internationals such as Jeff Probyn and Paul Rendall from England. Their fellow forwards Mike Teague and Peter Winterbottom now have their own special handshake: conventional, followed by gripping the other hand by crooked fingers and then the general hand gesture for cash, rubbing the thumb and two fingers together.

Sure enough, the RFU made no protest at all. No player was banned: all threat and no action. What the RFU did not realise was that their hypocrisy and empty threats meant that when the England squad got into later battles over amateurism, they had no credibility because we knew they didn't have the balls for a public scrap.

In the two years that had followed the inaugural 1987 World Cup, the time demanded from players by their countries had grown markedly. This, together with the now-open flouting of the amateur laws, created so much pressure that, in 1990, the IRB announced that a vote would be taken on a proposed relaxation of the amateur laws, allowing 'communication for reward' but not payment for playing. A small group of players began to take the lead in discussing these matters with the RFU, and eventually I ended up taking a leading role because of my legal experience. I worked closely with Rob Andrew and Will Carling, but all the players helped when they could.

The RFU knew that the change would happen but tried to prevent it. In 1990, I sat in a hotel in Horsham with a senior committeeman called Cliff Brittle. He said that he and several others were considering resigning if this change was allowed. I told him that I did not believe he or his mates would resign and I was right because they did not. Ironically, a few years into the professional era, Brittle would stand for election as chief executive, on the platform that he knew what was best for the future of the professional game.

During this meeting, I made a number of points to him that would turn out to be significant. I told him that the best plan was for the RFU to manage the inevitable change to professionalism, so that they were in charge. Further, that it was a chance to restructure the English game by contracting all the top players and by organising it into four geographical divisions, just as they did in Australia and New Zealand. Not only did they not listen, they tried not to implement the law changes passed by the IRB later that year.

One man in particular was responsible for leading the RFU's disastrous and always doomed campaign to keep rugby amateur: Dudley Wood. As he was fond of telling people, Wood had a background in big business. He was subject to the instructions given by the RFU's executive committee, irrespective of whether he agreed with them. However, Wood was a rarity in that he was full-time and the committeemen were not. He had continuity of tenure whilst presidents, committeemen and players came and went. Wood had access to all the information, plus the time and resources to co-ordinate willing plotters and divide opponents.

Given his personal views, Wood should have resigned and continued his fight openly. He did not do this, and waged a campaign of obstruction and delay that at times disrupted the England team and created an irretrievable breakdown of trust between the players and the RFU. He also organised his acolytes to stop the RFU discussing and preparing for the change to professionalism, whilst remaining aware that the rest of the world was doing so.

Most unions took the alterations to mean that as long as they did not pay players for playing, anything else was fair game. They concentrated on more important matters such as developing structures that would improve the standard of their coaching and training at international level. Their representative on the IRB put in hand changes to the laws of the game that would suit them. They seamlessly managed their transition to professional rugby. The RFU simply buried its collective head in the sand and pretended it was all a bad dream.

At one meeting, Wood stood before us and said that, as far as the RFU was concerned, the changes allowed players to earn money for communication, provided that communication did not have a rugby connotation. Since the only reason anyone would want to use the services of players was because they were rugby players, anything those players did would not be sanctioned.

When I pointed out that this rendered the clause meaningless, he simply smirked like a fourth-former and said, 'Yes, it rather does, doesn't it?' I wanted to punch his stupid grinning face. A bad-tempered meeting ended with the following exchange: I had shown the changes to a senior contracts lawyer and received advice that they were so ambiguous they authorised almost anything short of actual payment to step on the field. I told Wood that the RFU's interpretation was wrong. He replied by telling me that 'I think you will find the RFU can do pretty much what it likes'. As I left, I said, 'I think you will find that they are not above corporate law.'

I am now not even sure that the RFU's stance was as it was presented by Wood, because the full committee voted by a large majority to endorse our commercial campaign; further, Mike Coley, the then marketing manager of the RFU, approached us to manage our commercial affairs.

We did not trust the RFU and we had already organised ourselves for the expected IRB changes by forming our own company and engaging Bob Willis, the former England cricketer, as our agent. When the proposals went through at the end of 1990, we thought we were clear to earn money from off-the-field activities, and Willis began approaching possible sponsors. Without our agreement, the RFU publicised a pitch for agencies to look after the England team's commercial rights. Three companies and Willis's duly made their presentations, notwithstanding the fact that we had already signed a contract with the latter. The charade was played through without the other companies being told of this fact.

From the outset, Willis was plagued by calls from Wood about what the Committee would and would not allow. We parted company with Willis under circumstances that were not fair to him or to us, due to articles that were run in the popular press. To this day I regret not being more belligerent and taking the whole matter to court. Another lesson we learned was that, of all things, the RFU was most afraid of bad publicity. Given the behaviour of Wood and the like, there would have been plenty of that and it would have prevented most of the attempts to derail our commercial activities over the next five years.

We then enlisted the help of a company called Parallel Media whose director, Robert Dodds, was the son of a Surrey Committeeman. Between us, we planned a strategy called 'Run with the Ball' and managed to present it to the then president, Mike Peary. A former serviceman, Peary was a throwback to more honourable times. Although his personal preference was clearly towards amateurism, he was fair and tried to see what could be achieved within the changed rules. The presentation was slick and compelling. Afterwards, Peary agreed to, and got, full-committee approval for us to go ahead with the campaign. Wood stayed behind to give his thoughts to the company and to me.

The sleights that came from Wood were disgraceful. He began with a long and pompous diatribe about his years of experience in business, after which he said he would give the presentation two out of ten for presentation, and less for content. Given that Dodds managed a number of large global accounts for high-profile businesses, including Coca-Cola, Wood's comments were deliberately insulting and an attempt to draw an abusive response. Wood could then go back to the Committee and complain. Dodds kept his cool and calmly dismantled the comments, whilst I was gripping the table to prevent myself leaping across it and ramming the written notes down Wood's throat.

Having full approval, we went round a number of receptive companies and made presentations. All expressed interest, but were concerned about whether this was allowed. Peary attended some meetings and, as president, gave his assurance that this had indeed been authorised. To our consternation we then had calls after every presentation from the companies saying that they had been called by Wood, who had told them that, despite whatever we, or Peary, had said, the campaign would not be allowed.

Naturally, I railed at Peary and asked how a secretary of the RFU could flout Committee decisions. I asked why he was not sacked. Although Peary agreed, he simply could not find a way to discipline Wood. That is how much power was ceded to Wood at the time.

Against this background, progress was patchy and we again made the mistake of playing by the rules and honouring our commitments. Under our 'Run with the Ball' campaign, we promised to spend large sums on promoting the game. We paid for a whole week's coaching course at the Richmond Athletic Ground for hundreds of kids, and provided coaches, equipment and other things. It cost tens of thousands of pounds. This took place during the World Cup of 1991, and even though we spent our own money, the RFU were still challenging everything we did. As a result, we could not finalise deals and could not exploit our growing popularity. It took two years for the RFU to stop directly calling our potential partner companies, and their campaign against us only finally stopped in 1995, when the game went professional, just before the World Cup.

Our refusal to speak to the press after our historic win in Cardiff in 1991 was a protest at Wood's duplicitous acts. The press, encouraged by Wood, chose to portray this as a fit of pique on our part over our refused request to the BBC for £500 to cover all interviews for that season. I was portrayed as a militant, but several of the forwards were in favour of staying in the changing rooms and not taking the field until assurances were received that Wood ceased to undermine our commercial efforts. Eventually, players each earned something like £7,000 for each of the two years before the game went professional. For me, it was the principle, not the money, that counted.

Meanwhile, the situation with many of the other main unions had changed so markedly that the pretence of amateurism was farcical. Even those within the game had to admit that a formal adoption of professionalism was necessary to stop the growing accusations of hypocrisy over what had become known as 'shamateurism'. Players were doing almost anything they wanted, and the off-the-field earnings became, in all but name, a wage for playing. For example, a player would write a small article or make a limited number of appearances for a sponsor and get a sum that was out of all proportion to the normal commercial rate for the activity. Moreover, these payments were often paid monthly, with no correlation to the things to which they supposedly related.

The summer of 1992 was unusual as I did not have to prepare for a tour. It was my first full break and first free summer for eleven years. It was also the summer I married my long-term girlfriend, Penny. When people asked how I spent my holidays when not touring, I used to reply, 'I don't know; I've only ever had one.' That, plus the honeymoon, which we spent in Venezuela, were the only two holidays we ever had together. In retrospect, I find this fact appalling and I am amazed I did not refer to it during my arguments with the RFU over amateurism. Their insistence that players became fitter and gave more and more time to England had real consequences for players. It was not right for a player not to have holidays, both from a personal and a playing perspective, and though the RFU knew of the difficulties, over the next few years they flatly refused to reduce the burdens, whilst continuing to prevent us from profiting from our sacrifices.

A few months before the IRB vote in May 1995, there was an audacious attempt by the Australian millionaire, Kerry Packer, to replicate his World Series Cricket by contracting the top rugby players from both hemispheres. That attempt is now forgotten, but it came much closer to succeeding than was admitted. I and a few other players obtained the signatures of about thirty of England's top players for the Packer initiative. Similar numbers from Wales, New Zealand, Australia, France and South Africa signed, and I had several meetings with Packer's intermediary, Ross Turnbull. On one occasion, Packer's son, James, flew to London to reassure us that the plans were genuine and showed me details of the players who had signed and whose contracts he had in a safe in Australia.

The world's leading players were already earning money from off-the-field activities but the sums involved were small compared to those promised by Packer. Not one player had any doubt that the forthcoming vote would declare the game professional, and they wanted to be rewarded properly for their efforts, as they were professional in all but name.

The support from the world's leading players for the Packer plan was solid until the South African players broke rank and took details of the proposals to their union. Afraid of losing control of the game at the highest level just before the start of the World Cup they were hosting, the South African Rugby Union agreed to pay their players more than they had been promised by Packer. What must be borne in mind is that this deal was made before the IRB vote had even taken place. Its very existence demonstrates that, as we alleged, other unions were aware of their players being paid for playing. When the situation had reached this acute stage, only a fool or someone wilfully blind could not see that the imminent vote to adopt professionalism was a foregone conclusion.

By way of stark contrast, Wood succeeded in preventing English rugby from having any sort of plan to deal with the seismic changes that would accompany a 'yes' vote by the IRB. Above anything, that was Wood's worst crime. Using a business example, a chief operating officer in a large company might fight against a major change in law that he personally believed was wrong. However, if he knew the law had even a reasonable chance of being introduced, he would put together a plan to deal with what might occur, rather than favour his own view and thus be in breach of his duty to shareholders to act at all times in the company's best interests.

I remember clearly the carnage that took place in the months after the change to professionalism. With no idea what players were worth or how the clubs would be run as businesses, there was a free-for-all, with players changing clubs for ever-bigger transfer fees and wages. Some clubs had benefactors, but others borrowed money and went out of business as they chased success. Every newly professional club lost money heavily when their books did not balance, but to be fair to the owners, they could not accurately have predicted their income without the co-operation of the RFU.

Eventually, wages and transfer fees settled down but almost £150m was wasted in the first years, a large proportion of which was due to the RFU's failure to plan. It was a supremely ironic moment when, years later, the RFU raised the issues of centrally contracted players and the possibility of reorganising the professional game from clubs to divisions. I had recommended both of these fifteen years earlier.

The continuing club-v.-country rows that sporadically break out between the RFU and the English Premiership clubs have their origins in the RFU's failure to manage the change from amateur to professional. Had they done as some people, including me, suggested, they would control the top players. There would not be continual arguments about clubs releasing players, nor about who has to insure players, and so on. The talent in the northern hemisphere would be organised, with England's four divisions playing against the three Irish provinces, the four Welsh regional clubs, the two Scottish franchises and whatever four teams the French decided to put forward. This Super 17 would equal the standards of its southern-hemisphere counterpart, and the success of the Heineken Cup suggests it would generate far larger crowds than the present Guinness Premiership and Magners League.

As it is, the men who have invested huge sums to finance the professional game rightly resist any attempt to centrally contract players without adequate compensation. They continue to underwrite the losses of the clubs and have borne the scandalous claims by the RFU that they are 'Johnny-come-latelys'. If they had left it to Dudley Wood and the RFU, England would not have a professional game.

# 19

## 'Wanking and Dyeing One's Hair'

### Richmond RFC and Retirement

I sometimes get asked, 'Do you still play for fun?' I always reply, 'I didn't play for fun when I did play.' This glib response is nevertheless an accurate description of my approach to the game during my international career. It all meant too much to me, and I put in so much time, energy and thought that it became a serious business. It would be only a slight exaggeration to describe the way I conducted myself as pathological.

I did have fun, but it was an adjunct to, and not because of, what I did. The physical battles during games brought satisfaction for having successfully gone through them, not whilst they were being waged. Training to a point where you are gasping for breath and feel sick is not fun, and the satisfaction comes, perversely, when you stop. It is all highly addictive and, as with all addictions, the thoughts and feelings connected to it are not always rational, but are always extreme. Add to this the adrenalin surge that comes every time you run on to the field in a packed stadium, and you have something that is as strong as any drug.

Rugby was perfect for working out my frustrations and rage during training sessions and games. As a game of violent collisions, it allowed me to fire into rucks and mauls quite legally and yet with as much force as I could muster. In addition, playing in the front row guaranteed me direct confrontation for eighty minutes. Some positions allow a player to manufacture a way to stay out of the way of his opposite number; the front rows are going to be head to head whether they like it or not. To survive, I had to be in the right mood every time I took the field, and to be honest I did not find this difficult. But what would happen to me when that belligerence no longer had an outlet? Some of it was manufactured for the game but most was innate, and I never bothered to think why or from where inside me it came.

Retirement raised all kinds of spectres for me, and had I not had to deal with this at the same time as my first marriage ran into trouble, there is an even chance I would not have got divorced. Neither rugby nor retirement caused my marriage to fail, but I had so many issues about retiring and they were so powerful that I could not disentangle them from my personal issues. The two sets of problems produced one incoherent mass of thoughts and a general dissatisfaction with my life: I felt wretched. As I could not differentiate one from the other, I tried to deal with them collectively. What I should have done, but could not do, was approach them separately and deal with them in different ways.

Most people's lives progress to a point in their fifties or sixties where they have reached the peak of their career, they have brought up their children, secured their social standing and have established interests and a group of friends. I had to deal with a fact that is common to all sportsmen: in my mid thirties, I had reached my peak, I had lived my dream, and nothing I did would ever match it. Yet I had virtually the whole of my adult life still ahead of me. Although the birth of my children was highly emotional, it did not give me the same emotional high.

As I approached retirement, I had bouts of terror that I could only control by firmly closing my mind to thinking about the subject. Whenever my thoughts drifted to it, Gollum appeared to remind me that 'all this will soon be over', often adding 'and about time, you fraud'. What would I do then? Rugby had dominated all else in my life, and although it demanded so much, it gave me the security of status and purpose. I was almost institutionalised.

In the eyes of the public I was Brian Moore, Harlequins and England, rugby player. When I walked down the street, people would say, 'Look, there's that rugby player,' and I began to define myself in the same way. What would they say when I no longer played or appeared in the media? Who would I be when it was all over? Yes, I would be Brian Moore, the lawyer, but so what? What was special about being a lawyer? Anybody could be a lawyer. My life in rugby had been so far out of the ordinary that I assumed everything thereafter could not be anything but mundane in comparison. My life would be boring; *ergo*, I would be boring.

I wish that there had been specialist help available to talk me through retirement and the problems it raises for all players. It would have been so helpful if there had been somebody who understood the fear of retirement and had been willing to spend some time discussing what I imagined were insane thoughts with which nobody else had to struggle.

My thoughts were so disjointed that I did not think through all the consequences of retirement. I clung to the 1995 World Cup as a chance to get away from everything and concentrate on rugby, hoping that in a different country I might find space to gather my thoughts. This was always doomed to fail as the only thing that changed was the setting; the problems remained unsolved.

As I touched down at Heathrow airport after the World Cup, along with the rest of the England squad, I turned to Dean Richards and said quietly that I was now going to look at flats, as I was divorcing and needed somewhere to live. Poor Dean, what was he supposed to say that was of any comfort? Wisely, he quietly wished me all the best and offered his support if needed.

If you are in a long-term relationship, you will know that there are enough problems created by just getting on with it. Each person's family and work put a lot of pressure on the union. In the case of sportsmen, you have to add the external pressure of the media and the fact that the sport, something which is outside the partnership, demands that all things therein are subservient to it. For example, in the ten years that we were together, honeymoon excepted, we went on only one holiday together that was more than a long weekend. All my vacation time from work was absorbed within the time I was given off to attend training sessions, pre-match gatherings, games and tours.

Penny supported me throughout the many times I was truculent and unreasonable because something had not gone as I wished concerning one or another thing connected with training, playing, selection, or something that had been written about me. The surges of emotion and adrenalin that accompanied games, especially internationals, must have made living with me a trial at times, made more difficult because of the underlying consequences of the events during childhood.

The spouses of successful sportsmen get little commendation. If everybody knew what part they played in the success, this would not be so. Imagine having constantly to have your life dictated by the demands, at times unreasonable, of your partner's sport. Weekends, dinners, parties, birthdays, weddings – nearly all social meetings are affected. Many times, Penny went alone to events at which she was the only single married person. Moreover, the times when I was available, my mind was often not on what was at hand, but was drifting and thinking about rugby.

These drawbacks are more easily borne if the family's livelihood comes from the sport, but at the time I played this was not the case. The last three years of my England career, we were asked to achieve standards that were professional in all but name, and yet not allowed to earn from these efforts. When I could not justify all the time and effort I spent on what was essentially still a hobby, it must have been difficult to bear. Though she understood the reasons why I pursued my rugby goals in the way that I did, there must have been times when she cursed the game, and the fact that she was forced to deal with its fallout.

The catalyst for our break-up was not rugby's but my fault.

However, the strains exerted by rugby made things far worse. When I left, because of all the time I had spent away from home, Penny returned to the separate life that she had had to construct during the frequent times that I simply was not there.

During the months after I drifted away from Harlequins in the first half of 1996, some of the aggression that I had previously channelled into rugby fuelled bouts of heavy drinking night after night around London's Parson's Green, where I rented a flat after my divorce. Things didn't get any better, and although I enjoyed some of the parties and sessions, it got to the point where I went because I had to, not because I wanted to. I was certainly drink-dependent, if not worse.

I do not know if there is such a thing as a sporting-retirement consultant, but there is a huge need for players to be taken through the likely effects of ending their playing careers. The divorce counsellor I had seen during the turmoil of my break-up the previous year helped a little. If nothing else, she made me understand that I had little chance of sorting myself out if I did not deal with the way I left rugby. Given its central role in my life, it was the most powerful force and would continue to be so unless I found a way to say goodbye to playing, on my own terms.

As in my youth, when I was in danger of going badly off the rails, sport, rugby, would help me out of what had become a desperate situation. I decided that I would play one or, possibly, two more seasons; and that, having set the time of my retirement, and with some knowledge of how it would affect me, I would not leave with regrets – at least none relating to the end of my career.

I toyed with the idea of joining a junior club or a semi-professional outfit where my experience would be valuable, and where I could make a valuable contribution on and off the field. I even made enquiries with Rob Andrew, who had moved to Newcastle to become director of rugby, but his tone throughout the conversation made it plain that he was not keen. Bizarrely, it was as a result of yet another late evening with Joe and Margi Clarke, the owners of the renowned Sun Inn in Richmond, that I realised

Richmond Rugby Club was also gearing up to attempt to break into the first division of what was now professional rugby.

I do not know why I had not thought of them previously, but as my enquiries into their set-up went deeper, so did the conviction that it was the right club for me. They had assembled by far the strongest squad in what was then called the Second Division. Richmond's head coach was John Kingston, whom I had known for many years as a fellow front-row player, and whom I respected for his honesty and intelligence. Under his charge, he had players like Ben Clarke, Scott and Craig Quinnell, Alan Bateman, Jim Fallon, Andy Moore, Adrian Davies, Richard West and Darren Crompton. I knew I would have to fight hard to prove I still retained the desire for what was a serious campaign to win promotion, but I have not walked away from many fights.

I trained very hard that summer, and whilst I was past the peak of my rugby prowess, I was fitter than most of the squad. It was also obvious that I was serious about the forthcoming season. Most of the squad were either fully or semi-professional. I agreed a salary and also made sure that the time commitments would allow me to continue to work in my law partnership. However, when it came down to it, I did not want to be beholden contractually to any club, and I did not cash the cheque they sent me at the start of the season.

I knew from the first training session that I was going to enjoy whatever time I spent at Richmond, and I was right: I had more fun and enjoyment in the one year I played there than in the five I had had with Quins. This is not a direct criticism of Quins, because undoubtedly the extra strain of playing for England and the British Lions took its toll, but I liked nearly all the people in the Richmond set-up. I could not say the same about the Quins one. It was fascinating to see the interaction between the various players who played on a different basis. Within two years of the start of the professional era, all players in the First Division/Premiership were fully professional, but when I joined Richmond in autumn 1996, there were a number of semi-professional players and one or two amateurs. That year gave me an insight into the lot of professional players, and though it has changed markedly, it is only the degree and not the principle that has altered. For example, there were various issues: how players spent their time away from the club; what educational qualifications they had; how could options be made available to them after their careers were over; these issues were as relevant then as they are now.

Richmond had a number of good club players who had been responsible for its rise to the top of the second tier of English rugby. They were nowhere near as talented as the professionals and they made up most of the semi-professional group. But they brought a balance to the atmosphere within the club, as they had lives outside rugby and a different perspective from that of the professionals. One such player was a prop called Matthew Yeldham. Matt worked in the City, and hailed from Dulwich College, one of the country's top private schools. He was described by Craig Quinnell as 'the poshest bloke what I have ever met'. Yeldham was so splendidly, effortlessly superior that he amused continually, and he made two stellar comments that still draw a smile from me when they are remembered.

The non-full-time players were invited to the club one afternoon to see how the professionals spent their day. I could not attend but Yeldham did and I was interested to hear about his experience. When I asked him about his impressions of the lot of the professional rugby player, he announced to me in his patrician tone: 'Do you know, Brian, I have concluded that being a professional rugby forward for Richmond RFC mainly involves wanking and dyeing one's hair.' Perceptive as well.

One Friday evening, we caught the train to Newcastle for the first of two games against our main rivals that season. During the journey, I played quizmaster, posing questions from a quiz published by the *Daily Telegraph*. Yeldham correctly answered any question put to him or his team; Craig Quinnell was slightly less impressive. As we disembarked, I chatted to Yeldham and praised his general knowledge, to which he replied, again in an aristocratic manner, that he would have expected anybody with even a modicum of decent education and schooling to know the answers. As an aside, he added, 'Good Lord, one saw tonight the dross now turned out by state comprehensives and sink council estates.' Like I said, perceptive.

We went to Agen, in France, for a pre-season tour and the squad's sports psychologist was a little taken aback at my answer to the stock question, 'What do you want to get out of this?' I said that I wanted the respect of my fellow players. I explained that most of them knew me by reputation, but that was not enough for me. I wanted to demonstrate that it was deserved and that my presence was down to my contribution to their efforts, not down to past glories. I would play as well as I could and help as much as I was able to.

I didn't pass on my knowledge of French props to our tighthead in one 'friendly' because sometimes things have to be learned first-hand. After I struck a ball against the head, there was the usual fracas and the French loose-head was taunted by our number three, who kept saying 'Monsieur, Un–Nul', referring to the strike. He continued as both stood face to face at the front of the subsequent lineout. The Agen hooker threw the ball to the back of the lineout and our prop looked up to follow its flight. As he did so, the French prop dropped him with a short jab, and as he lay prone and insensible leaned over him and said, 'Monsieur, Un–Un.'

We played well that season, and what I found most enjoyable was to play with players from different countries. It is now normal for Premiership teams to have cosmopolitan squads, but my previous clubs had been almost exclusively filled with English players. Training took place as it had always done in the early evenings, and even though I had come from a more senior club, I could see the difference made by a team of professional coaches working with professional players. Sessions were sharper and ran smoothly. As players now had all day to devote to rugby, things like calls, set moves and other tactical matters were discussed and absorbed before training. I had to do my homework in the evenings. Previously, most training sessions were interrupted to discuss such things, and on a cold wintry evening we had to waste time warming up again.

I looked with envy at the systemised weight-training programmes planned for each player because it was this aspect of fitness that had largely been absent in the amateur days. Although I had always trained with weights, the programmes were general, whereas those given to the Richmond players were far superior. I also envied the time the professionals had to rest properly. The necessity of resting is not commonly understood. Any athlete will tell you that to get the maximum benefit from training, the body has to be allowed to absorb the work. It is self-defeating and possibly destructive to keep piling session on top of session with insufficient intervals of rest. Although I worked at my desk, sitting down, between my training sessions at lunchtime and those in the evenings, that was not the equivalent of sleeping or relaxing without the pressure and stress of work. Another thing that they did not have to contend with was commuting. I do not need to explain to commuters how draining and unpleasant are the daily journeys in overcrowded trains or buses and especially in the Tube. On hot days, when the temperature on the Central Line could top 100 degrees, my journey from work to training meant that I arrived already tired. From that starting point, I could not get the full benefit of the work I put in during the next two hours.

Our league had three unofficial groups. Richmond and Newcastle, in the first group, were comfortably apart from the clubs that had money to spend on players, but not the virtual blank cheques provided by Ashley Levett and Sir John Hall respectively. In turn, this second group sat above the teams that had quite limited funds and employed only semi-professional and amateur players.

We beat the bottom-tier clubs easily, but playing against the middle-tier teams was not as easy as it looked on paper. Playing against us drew extra effort from all the other clubs, but those in the middle tier were sufficiently good to beat us if we did not play well. However, given the commitment of our players, we did not allow ourselves to fail, and lost only once, to Newcastle on their patch. We got our revenge in the return match at Richmond, and our points difference compared to theirs meant they had to settle for promotion as runners-up. We were the champions.

It was announced towards the end of the season that training the following season would be moved to the mornings and afternoons. This was correct for all sorts of reasons but it meant that players who were not fully professional would struggle to train unless they could secure time off. I could have taken whatever time I wanted because by then I was an equity partner and only my billing at the end of the year counted, not when or how I billed. The season had been wonderful and I would have liked to have played with Richmond against teams with which I was more than familiar, but I knew I could not realistically devote the time. In addition, something happened during my visit to see the English National Opera at the London Coliseum near the end of the season. I do not know where it came from, but I suddenly thought, 'Would I rather be here listening to the soaring arias of *Die Zauberflöte* or banking into a scrummaging machine?' When I realised I wanted to be embraced by Mozart rather than by two seventeen-stone men, I knew it was time to finish.

I prepared for my final game, which thankfully was at home. I knew it would be a difficult experience but I also knew, deep down, that I could not pretend I had the will to play a season in the Premiership. We won the match, and in the dressing room afterwards the champagne flowed and the rest of the squad were naturally euphoric. I joined in at first, but as I started to take the tape off various joints and from around my head, I knew I would not do this again. I started to weep quietly, already grieving for a life ending, and then started sobbing fully. Some of the younger players wondered what had produced sorrow amidst joy. A few senior players, who knew what I was feeling and who shortly would face a similar day, whispered an explanation to them. They left me to go through things uninterrupted, while I thought about the many outstanding events of twenty-four years of playing rugby, the good and the bad. In the end I was left all alone, staring down at a floor filled with the usual detritus and a few smatterings of blood. I breathed in the heady mixture of aftershave, deodorant, liniment and sweat. Scott Quinnell came in from the medical area, put one of his massive arms around my shoulders, kissed me and said, 'Don't worry; we love you.' That he had the sensitivity to understand what I felt and the compassion to make that gesture says much about the man. I met many like him whilst I played, and I miss them all.

# 20

## Soho, Politics and Transsexuals

My fears about retiring were assuaged partly by being able to finish on my terms with Richmond, and partly by the disappearance of one of the biggest terrors I had associated with retirement. For so many years, all my private life had been second to rugby. I had had very little time to do anything else, to the extent that I feared I would not be able to fill the evenings and weekends that I would now have to myself. Within a couple of months, however, my diary was full and I wondered why on earth this issue had caused me so much anxiety.

It will be difficult for most people to believe how amazed I was at having the simple luxury of a whole weekend to do whatever I wanted. Most people take this for granted, but the third weekend after retiring, I had a weekend in Paris and I found myself giggling at the novelty whilst boarding the Eurostar at Waterloo. The year following retirement turned out to be a hugely enjoyable time. I revelled in my new-found freedom and was able to re-establish friendships that had faded because I had simply not been around. I was able to indulge my interests in opera and wine, and in addition, two sports helped me to dissipate some of my competitive energy.

During my year at Richmond, I had been sent off (this only happened twice in my eighteen-year career) and banned for nine weeks. I was, not unnaturally, aggrieved by the severity of the sentence. I must be the only player to be suspended for trampling on an opponent whilst I was in possession of the ball. During my unexpectedly spare weekends, a friend had taken me to Stamford Bridge, the home of Chelsea FC, and I reconnected with the first sport I had ever played. Having performed every Saturday for nearly two decades, I was never able to go to any football games, but I retained my interest and avidly followed football on TV. I promised myself when I retired that I would not watch rugby for a whole season because I did not want to encourage thoughts of playing again. I enjoyed myself so much at Stamford Bridge that I bought the first of eleven years of season tickets, followed the Blues' rise under Gianluca Vialli, and have continued to support them right through to the present day.

I did not ski when I played rugby. Not because I was banned from doing so; rather, I wrongly assumed there was a good chance of injury. On the third day of my first ever skiing holiday, I knew I had found a pastime that would become a passion. It was by accident that I started skiing in Argentière, near Chamonix, France. My secretary had been a chalet girl there in her youth, and I booked my first week without knowing that the Grand Montets is recognised as one of the most challenging ski areas in the world. I just followed my French instructor, Olivier Rosenberg, and because I was very fit and used to being coached, I made rapid progress. At the end of my first week, I did the unpisted black run which starts adjacent to the Argentière glacier. I was hooked.

Oli is now a firm friend and my approach to skiing showed that the driven side of my nature was alive and well. While I sat berating myself for my poor carving turns, my friends enjoyed the après-ski in the bar. By starting another sport from scratch, I was able to see how my personality affected my sport and, more importantly, how participating in sport affected my personality.

I drove Oli mad with my constant questions during lessons, but

I need to understand why I am asked to do something so that I can think about how and why a particular technique works. Once I can do that, I am able to recognise mistakes and how to correct them. As we were discussing my performance after one run, I noticed that Oli was highlighting good things and skirting round the errors that I knew I had made. I semi-jokingly said to him, 'It's OK, get on to the bad things, I'm not a back.'

It is true that I respond to criticism far better than to praise, but I wondered what this said about my character, and I came to realise that my competitive character is driven by two distinct elements. Firstly, there is the positive element where I want to better myself, to reach out for a goal for the team, for my friends and so on. But this is dwarfed by the second element, represented by Gollum and his many insults, and I will go to almost any length in my attempts to silence him and prove him wrong. 'How many times are you going to fuck that up, you half-wit?' 'Stop wasting everybody's time and go back to the children's home where you should have been put in the first place.' These are just two examples from Gollum's lexicon of negative phrases. If at times my behaviour seems extreme and intense, it is purely as a response to that sort of taunt.

I realised that rugby was the perfect game to play for someone like me. Its physical nature allowed me to hide, not intentionally, the destructive side of my character. That side was not always characterised by physical aggression. More often than not, it just went on in my head. What made this all the more confusing was that it brought me success. My dedication to training was praised; yet, had I demonstrated the same attachment to say, collecting train numbers, I would have been thought strange and obsessive. Eventually, I found a better balance for things that should be fun, such as skiing and, recently, motorbike-track days. They attract me because with both there is an element of danger, which means I have to face the ensuing fear and overcome it; in this, I find an echo of my playing days.

During my playing career, I had been chillingly disciplined for over a decade in pursuit of my rugby ambitions. I had not had the sort of early adult life lived by countless young professionals, the likes of whom can be seen all over London. Carefree and flush with money, they live it up with their mates for five or six years before their careers and relationships become more serious and they eventually decide to move on.

My life of irresponsible cavorting took place over the five mad years following retirement when I lived in Soho's Beak Street. I bought a stunning flat and partied like there was no tomorrow. My first four years in Soho were fantastic. Although I continued partying, it was not like the depressing year after my divorce and after leaving Harlequins. My legal career was going well, I was saving money in spite of what I spent, and I had some extraordinary times.

I hate name-droppers – though I will mention that I have met the last seven British prime ministers and been to a Buckingham Palace garden party – so I won't list all the individuals I met in my short Soho life. A surprisingly large number of people live in Soho, of all ages and ethnicities, gay, straight and just curious. I got to know the barrow boys on Berwick Street market, and although I was recognised in most of the bars, people left me alone. There were so many recognisable faces in Soho that I was way down the scale anyway.

I went to nearly every establishment in Soho over four years and got to know a Kiwi, Bruce, and an ex-Saracens second-team player, Ross, who between them ran twenty-five of the doors to London's happening places. As a result, I got into places without being a member and often without queuing, but this was because I never made a fuss. If I didn't recognise the doorman, I queued and politely asked if so-and-so was about. If they said no and required a membership card, I asked them to pass on my regards and went somewhere else. Later, Bruce would say, 'Why didn't you get him to call me or tell them who you are?' I didn't do this because I don't think I am anybody special; in fact, at times I feel a whole lot less than most people. Moreover, 'Don't you know who I am?' is possibly the stupidest question to pose anywhere, because either they don't, or they do and don't care; both of which mean 'You're not getting in'.

I did become a member of Soho House, a private members' club, and spent a lot of time there. 'The House' had a policy of not giving memberships to sportsmen, particularly footballers, not because of the individuals themselves, but because they did not want their inevitable entourage. After my first few visits, I got used to the strange standoff that occurs between people from totally different areas of life. I believe that you revere people who can do what you always wanted to do but had not the talent for. Like everyone else, I have actors and musicians whom I admire – to me, Peter Gabriel is a god – and I was lucky enough to meet some of them and became friends with a few.

Conversely, sport fascinates people from the arts and I think it's because of its adversarial nature. Sport passes definitive judgements on its participants: you score more points, run faster, throw further. There is no argument about who wins. Actors and musicians, on the other hand, live in a subjective world. They may be technically limited but wildly popular. Whereas I could always point to the scoreboard, their success can depend on the tastes of a critic. Because of this, we had a mutual respect for each other's space and only chatted when a third party made an introduction. In any case, I was never sufficiently confident to go over and introduce myself. However, when we did talk, they were far more candid than normal. I think my most memorable experience in Soho House was of a very late night spent around the piano, when I and several other miscreants accompanied some old Welsh bloke whose surname was, I think, Jones.

It was also there that my schoolboy love of politics was rekindled. I met Fraser Kemp, a Labour MP, and told him I was thinking of one day standing for Parliament. I had spoken at a Halifax town council meeting when I was thirteen, so I knew I was odd (something of a necessary condition for a politician), but I also knew that my political leanings were long-standing and genuine. After meeting Fraser, I visited the House of Commons several times and got to know a number of MPs. I also worked for Labour before the 1997 election, delivering leaflets and helping with constituency visits.

Election night 1997 was a fantastic evening. About twenty left-of-centre wine writers met at Oz Clarke's house in Fulham. We toasted the Portillo, Hamilton and Mellor moments (when all three Tory grandees lost their seats in spectacular fashion) but at around 3 a.m. I went off to the Party's celebrations at the Royal Festival Hall. I arrived as D:Ream's anthem 'Things Can Only Get Better' was being played, and I saw Blair arrive by helicopter and give his speech.

The celebrations ended at around 6 a.m. but we wanted to carry on. The Hope and Anchor pub welcomed four of us with frosty glares: they rightly resented outsiders invading what was supposed to be a pub for Smithfield Market workers. The landlord refused to serve us, but as we walked to the door, his wife said, 'Ere, you're that farkin' rugby player, 'ave a drink.' We drank, had breakfast and the others went off to Downing Street whilst I went straight to work. When my secretary saw the state of me she said, 'I don't wish to be rude, Mr Moore, but do you really think you should be advising clients in your state?' I left, got a coffee on the way home, and leaned unsteadily in a Soho doorway to drink it. I had drunk half of it when a woman walked briskly past me and dropped a pound coin into the cup. Things could only get better, couldn't they?

Two years later, I took a call from Fraser whilst skiing in Lake Tahoe. He told me that there was a by-election in Newark because the MP had had to stand down after allegations of electoral fraud, and did I want to be a candidate? I said I did, thinking it would go no further. He rang back and told me I was now the Labour candidate and could they announce this? I had worked in Newark and knew that the massive swing to Labour was temporary in what was a natural Tory seat, so I asked for more time. I frantically rang people I knew in the political arena, and then called him to decline. We arranged to get together when I returned. We met in a pub in Whitehall and I explained that I really wanted to try for my home seat of Halifax. He then said we should pop across the road to meet Gordon.

As I followed him, I realised we were heading for HM Treasury. I met Gordon Brown in a huge room, and he was sitting behind a massive desk that was raised by being on a dais. The chairs we were to occupy were much lower, and I thought, 'I'm not falling for that old trick.' I asked to move to the opposite end of the room where there was a small fireplace and four ordinary chairs. Due to my surroundings, and because I had not expected to meet the Chancellor of the Exchequer, I was nervous and rehashed an old joke, saying, 'Nice to meet you, Gordon. This is the closest I have been to a Scotsman for five years without having a fight.' Fortunately, he laughed and then pressured me, in the right way, to do something I had always wanted to do. I knew Newark was not right but the temptation was so great I almost went back on my decision.

In the end, I was able to resist and to restate my decision. I went on to say that I realised I could not chose a seat but that, if I did enter politics, I wanted to do it for the right reasons and for people and a place I knew. There were too many MPs who had no life outside politics and this lobby-fodder was unhealthy. I also said that I knew I would be marked down for my refusal but that I should get some credit for having the balls to withstand what, by any standards, was extraordinary pressure.

In Labour's second term I was offered the chance to stand in another by-election for the seat of Leicester South. This was, more or less, what I said to the party chairman, Ian McCartney: 'To summarise, you want me to stand in a by-election, which is always difficult for the party in power; in a seat that has a 30 per cent Muslim population; and the election is the day after the Butler Report on the arms-to-Iraq scandal is published.' When he said yes, I replied, 'Ian, I'm sorry, but do think I am a complete cunt?'

Considering that in all my time at Nottingham, Harlequins and Richmond I never made a single claim for expenses, I would have been a crap MP.

The Soho lifestyle made my law career appear mundane and I convinced myself that I was bored. The arguments that began between my partners, caused by poor management, were sufficient reasons for me to resign. I had saved some money, and a few months before leaving law had financed the set-up of a digital media company that worked for BT and similar clients. Initially, it went very well and the company was shortlisted for the 'New Media Company of the Year' award given by one of the top industry publications. I entered a joint venture with Ten Alps, owned by Sir Bob Geldof, to develop content of the then new WAP phones. Unfortunately, this did not work because the technology was so new it could only handle what was a glorified text service.

I also opened a nail salon in Soho that was run by my girlfriend and soon-to-be second wife Lucy. It lost money but I comfort myself by remembering that several companies opened similar salons. The New York Nail Company has scores of salons in Manhattan and thought, like me, that the time had come when women in Britain would emulate their Big Apple counterparts and want beautiful nails. Some did, but most, with limited budget, felt nails were something they could do themselves.

I decided I should know a bit about the business and enrolled to do a manicurist's course. The first day I attended training in Luton, the supervisor said, 'Have you come to drop somebody off?' She was staggered when I told her I was taking the exams. When the theory paper was marked, she told me mine was the highest mark she had seen. I said that I didn't want to be rude but that the paper was set for sixteen-year-old school leavers and, as I had a law degree, I would have killed myself had I not passed. Part of the practical involved doing two sets of nails, and ending by painting them in a dark, rich colour. When I did mine properly, Lucy said, 'You bastard, you've never done a set properly before today,' to which I replied, 'Well, some people just like pressure.'

I worked in the salon occasionally and saw all parts of the Soho community. As it was next to the cabaret club Madame JoJo's on Brewer Street, we used to do the nails of their transsexual performers. When one stunning six-feet-four lady swayed out of the salon, showing off legs that went on for ever, she left to whispers of 'Bitch!' from the various nail technicians.

It was too good to last, and as before, I lost the plot. I didn't want just to be a party-goer; I wanted to be an international-standard party-goer and, in my attempts to reach the top, I forgot that I was forty years old and not a student. I married Lucy in the Scottish church in Knightsbridge, and when she became pregnant she wisely said that she could not live with a man whose sense of responsibility extended only to ensuring he had enough money to last until 5 a.m. the following morning.

When she went into labour at around 3 a.m. one Sunday morning, I dashed out to hail a cab, forgetting that it was still rush hour in Soho. After five desperate minutes of unsuccessful flagging-down, I ran to nearby Regent Street and saw an empty cab with its light turned off. Virtually throwing myself in front of it, I started to try and explain the situation, but the cabbie interrupted, saying, 'Aw wite, Brian, 'ar yer dowin', me owd cocker.' We picked up Lucy and drove to the University College Hospital in Fitzrovia. On the way, Lucy was panting with pain and he said, 'Ar yer dowin?' I said, 'Well, I'm a bit nervous actually and I . . .' 'I'm not farkin' tawkin' to you,' he bellowed, and then roared with laughter. He would not take a fare and, as he left, he gave me a 50p coin and told me to put it in the baby's hand for luck. What a blinding geezer.

On 9 December 2001, our daughter Imogen May was born. It was time to put away childish things.

# 21

## 'You Talk Rubbish'

### Commentating and the BBC

Training should be compulsory for everyone before they broadcast live to eight million viewers; I mean, without it, they could just spout any old crap.

The BBC first approached me to co-commentate with Ian Robertson on Radio Five Live. I was very keen to work with Ian because of his iconic status in radio broadcasting. Also, the job was something I could do in conjunction with my other professional commitments at the time.

The radio commentary job was viewed as a long-term appointment but lasted just one season. Robertson is a master of his art, but when he indulged in his anti-English asides, I refused to let any go by without challenge. At the time, I was angry because I was convinced that Robertson had knifed me. It also fed the insecurity about whether I could do the job in the first place. Years later, I challenged Robertson and he denied any responsibility but said that the producers thought the dynamic between us was wrong for radio. It was acceptable for commentators to disagree on TV, thank God, but on radio it came across badly. Listeners did not have pictures to look at and decide which of us was right.

Fortunately, BBC TV Sport asked me to take up a role as a pundit for their coverage of the following season's Six Nations Championship. Although many do not know it, the TV and radio sections of the BBC are demarcated strongly and few people work heavily with both sections. At first, I found being live on camera quite thrilling, giving my views on the prospects for both teams and then analysing how they were doing during the game. However, after a few games, I was frustrated because the tight schedules of the BBC meant that every minute was jealously guarded. Consequently, the pundits did not have fifteen minutes in which to deconstruct the game. I had to give my views in 'tabloid speak', and was given about one minute to do so before, during and after a game.

When I was asked to try co-commentary, I jumped at the chance. After my first game, I told the BBC I would prefer to pursue a commentating career. Although nerve-wracking, being a co-commentator meant involvement for the whole game – added to which, performing live gave me a certain *frisson*. Although it is nowhere near akin to playing, it still gives me the thrill of per-forming live. Knowing that so many people are listening to what I say is simultaneously exhilarating and terrifying. I am aware that I can say anything I want and occasionally I have to fight the destructive urge to say something especially outrageous or rude. On the morning of a broadcast I get a mild dose of the nerves that I used to feel before a game because I know that my mistakes will be highlighted by viewers and even by TV critics and writers.

Some people think that commentary is an easy job; it is not. I do not pretend it has the stresses faced by a policeman or the intel-lectual challenges faced by a nuclear physicist, but what makes my job uncommon is that I do it live and with an audience of mil-lions. Many people who are very good at their jobs hate having to speak in public, even if they have only a small audience. When I talk, I am acutely aware that what I say is heard and scrutinised by millions of people in their front rooms, and in clubs and pubs all over the world. Moreover, what I say will be the subject of comment in the media, on websites, not to mention the BBC complaints log.

Before I even get to a ground, I will read about the game, read the sub-editor's notes regarding the players and the teams, and make sure I have in my pocket a copy of the laws of the game. An hour or so before kickoff, I do a technical check of the equipment, and make sure that the levels for crowd noise relative to my own and that of my fellow commentator are right. I make sure that the link between me and both the programme director and the video replay team works, and I then tape the team lists to the desk in front of me so that they don't blow away during the match. Just before the game starts, I turn on the link to the referee's microphone.

My job is to augment the commentary provided by my partner but not to rehash what he has already said or what viewers can see. I try to explain what has happened and why, and to give an opinion on the play, the referee's decisions and anything else I think is interesting. Whilst doing this, I am simultaneously listening to three voices, all often talking at the same time. Firstly, I have to take in what is being said by the referee (and when Lawrence Dallaglio was playing I had to listen to him and the referee). Secondly, I am also taking note of what the programme director is saying as he talks to the cameramen, describes what shots are coming up, and sometimes comments directly to me. Finally, I am sometimes communicating with VT, the replay team, about what edits they should make and what footage I want replayed.

I could turn off one or all of these voices, but I don't because I need the information to know what is going on and what I am going to see on screen. Listening and talking at the same time is not easy. Viewers can tell when I am distracted. I sometimes begin a sentence and, because I'm trying to take in what is being said, I lose track of where I meant the sentence to go and have to continue speaking whilst I scramble to find a suitable ending.

There are probably only two absolutes in my job. The first is: do not swear. In everyday life I swear far too often, so before every single broadcast I say to myself, 'Whatever happens, don't swear.' It is the one thing that will get a broadcaster sacked immediately. The second certainty is that, whatever I say, someone will complain, say I talk crap, or try to get me sacked.

The fact that I cannot please everyone was no better demonstrated to me than when I looked at the complaints made to the BBC after a game between England and Scotland several years back. There were equal numbers of complaints alleging that I had been biased against one or other country. When I saw this, I thought about the fact that the two positions were irreconcilable and, given that all the complainants were convinced they were right, I decided from that point on that I would please myself. By this, I mean that I would try to ensure that no point I made could not be defended. That does not mean I am always correct, but I can at least point to the reasons behind the comment.

A very small number of comments are constructive, but most are purely critical. Every broadcaster gets complaints, and over the years, those against me have alleged everything from racism to stupidity. It frustrates me that complainants will not specify the source of their discontent because I could then answer them properly. Unfortunately, assessments of how I speak, whether I provide insight and so on, are purely subjective. Many assert that because they disagree with something I said, this means I am no good at my job. Yet the very fact that they get sufficiently worked up to complain means I have fulfilled my prime role of delivering explanations and opinions. People are free to disagree, but it is infuriating that they fail to recognise this simple premiss.

Fortunately there are people who take the time to answer some of the critics online and to them I give thanks. Their balancing comments are important because if, for example, the BBC makes an issue of something that I have said and refer to their chatrooms on Radio 606, I can at least point out the positive messages. I also remind them that it is in the nature of things that people are far more motivated to make negative comments than write in and praise any broadcaster.

The standard criticism against me is that I am biased towards England. This is untrue and cannot be supported by any proper review of my commentary. I always go back through my commentaries and I am viciously self-critical. When I inevitably find mistakes, I cringe and try not to repeat them. Yet it seems that some viewers cannot dissociate my commentary from my performances for England as a player. In the latter, I was unashamedly English and admit that to opposing fans I must have been a hateful figure. Unable to forget that image, some viewers only single out criticism I make of their team and ignore any positive comments. They are not reacting to anything I actually say, but rather revealing their own preconceived prejudices.

The England players certainly do not support the above view and, if anything, I am harder on England than on any other team because I expect more of them. It may be unfair that I assess them from the perspective of an experienced international, but decisions and their execution are either good enough or they are not. What is the point of equivocation when everybody has seen the incident? My comments are not personal, and when players occasionally confront me, I ask them whether my comment was accurate and whether in the debriefing meeting after the game they accepted their mistake. Invariably they have to say 'yes', because they, more than anyone, know whether they made an error. It is my job to call it as I see it and to ignore the fact that it will bring them discomfort. I hated criticism when I played, but I never shirked responsibility for my mistakes. Anyway, I tell them, the best way to shut me up is to play well, and when they do so I will highlight the fact.

I pass comment on the scrums far more often than most other commentators do, and to the accusations of obsession I can say only this: of all the areas that viewers find puzzling, this is the number one. Most players, ex-players and referees did not play in the front row and need as much help in understanding what goes on as does the ordinary viewer.

Some people complain that I explain the bleeding obvious, but given the size of the audience for Six Nations games, and the fact that rugby is a minority sport, the vast majority of those viewers have only a casual acquaintance with the laws of rugby. If experienced viewers have to suffer what they think are simplistic comments, so be it; that is preferable to far more people being left in ignorance.

Probably my most persistent critics are referees. By their nature, referees are strange people. Theirs is a difficult and often thankless task, and the game cannot be played without them. At the highest level, they have fractions of a second to make decisions under incredible pressure. They are not helped by the ambiguity of the laws they apply, nor by the fact that those laws are often needlessly and frequently altered. However, as a group, they do not help themselves. Innate defensiveness is not the right attitude to take when discussions take place about the performance of one of their brethren. The reason the BBC and Sky do not have referees in the commentary box is that the latter start from the position that the referee has made the right call, and then work to justify the decision; rarely will they directly criticise a referee, because to do so breaks an unwritten rule within their cabal. I look at the incident, then the decision, and then give my view on whether I think the referee is right. I am not always correct, but I am one of very few broadcasters who will admit to my mistakes and apologise on air.

I agree with referees that factual mistakes about the laws are not acceptable, and if I make such a mistake I am more critical than them. However, given the vagueness of some laws, I can legitimately see an incident in a way they do not like without being wrong. A discussion I once had with a group of junior officials shows why these laws can be so difficult to interpret. I had criticised a penalty given at a scrum, and when I gave my reasons for the comment, the group came out with four different interpretations of the relevant law. I simply commented that if they could not agree amongst themselves what that law meant, how could they definitively say that I was wrong?

Although referees will dispute this, I try not to criticise decisions that are arguable, but when I see a call that I believe to be entirely incorrect, I will not shy away from commenting simply because it might upset somebody or is against some unwritten protocol. Players are criticised; coaches are criticised; I am criticised; why should referees be the only group immune from such scrutiny, particularly when, at the Elite level, they are paid?

I have to put my hand up about my tendency to be mischievous. I do not set out to cause controversy and 95 per cent of what I say is not contentious, but I do use descriptions that are also used by spectators. This may, or may not, be unprofessional, but it mirrors – without the swearing – the way I speak ordinarily, which is a combination of vernacular and formal language. Some love it; some hate it; but it will not change and I am sure that the BBC will be the first to tell me if it is unacceptable.

I am sure that this quirky style proves as irritating as it does entertaining for my partner commentators. I seem to have struck up an 'Odd Couple' relationship with Welshman Eddie Butler. The question people ask me most often, though not framed as politely, is 'What do you really think of Eddie Butler?' The fact is that I like and get on well with him. Our arguments are never manufactured, they come as a result of us both believing we are right. Contrary to popular impression, they do not happen that often. To some they are refreshingly different; to others unprofessional and grounds for summary dismissal. Like I said, you cannot please everybody.

In fact, in my relatively short commentary career, the BBC has indeed found some of my observations unpalatable. Some of their admonishments have been deserved and others reflect their sensitivity to increasing political correctness, to which, as a public-service broadcaster, they are subject.

My first run-in was over a comment made in an Edinburgh Reivers game. The referee was a policeman, and the Reivers number eight a former policeman. The number eight was tackled short of the line and, whilst still held by the tackler, proceeded to crawl forward and put the ball down. It was plainly a penalty for not releasing the ball, but the referee awarded a try. When Eddie Butler turned to me and asked why the referee had made that decision, I replied, 'Well, they're probably both Masons.' Just a joke – or so I thought. On the Tuesday after the game, the BBC legal department called me to say that the Police Federation solicitors had sent a letter before action, saying my comment was libellous and demanding an apology, damages and costs. The legal department said the BBC wanted to apologise but needed my agreement as they would effectively be doing so on my behalf.

At the time, I was a litigation partner in a London law firm and had run a number of defamation cases. In a blistering bout of invective, which contained some words that were not strictly legal expressions, I told them why I would not say sorry; principally because they had no case. I also said, in more reasonable terms, that what upset me more than the demand was the lack of protection they had given me. I knew, as a result of litigating against newspapers, that press lawyers made a complainant crawl over broken glass before they even considered an apology. Sometimes newspapers made a complainant issue proceedings, even when they knew they were liable, just to test the complainant's resolve. Yet at the first sign of trouble, the BBC wanted to surrender. As a broadcaster and journalist, I had responsibilities, but I should also have protection from speculative or vexatious claims. I drafted my own letter of response and they sent it on my behalf. Sure enough, we heard nothing further.

I had to publicly apologise a few years ago after commenting on the way a French player was rucked by an English forward. To be fair to me, I did explain that the action was illegal. I was possibly pushing my luck to add that I thought players should be able to stand on each other, but I was reminiscing about the days when players were allowed to use their feet to clear players who obstructed the ball. In retrospect, and bearing in mind that some people cannot recognise an attempt at humour, maybe it wasn't wise to then add, 'And anyway he's French and I don't care.'

The comment that drew a formal reprimand came in a Calcutta

Cup game. A Scottish centre objected to the way the English second-row forward Danny Grewcock tackled the Scottish scrum half. To exact retribution, the centre delivered the most ineffectual footballer's attempt at a punch. When Eddie Butler asked me to comment, I described the punch as a 'gay slap'. At that point, I understand the BBC switchboard went mad with people indignant on behalf of the gay community and alleging homophobia. Interestingly, I understand that few of the callers were gay. Those who believe the comment proves I am homophobic will have to square their allegation against the contrary evidence that a few years ago I sponsored a solo West End show starring a friend of mine, Alana Pallay, who happens to be a transsexual from Hull.

As a form of penitence, I was sent by BBC *Rugby Special* to do a report about the Kings Cross Steelers in London, the only gay rugby club in England. Their players were no different from those of any other junior club, and I had not expected otherwise. What the politically correct zealots fail to consider is that, having lived in the heart of Soho for six years, I know the gay community well, and it has a very dry, savage, often outrageous sense of humour, and no subject is off limits. Some of the players from the Steelers told me they had laughed out loud at my remark and that, if that comment was the worst of their problems, they would be well pleased. They added they were sick of straight people complaining on their behalf and presupposing what their reactions would be to such comments. Not one of them thought it was anything other than a joke; they didn't all think it was funny, but that was not the point.

The BBC meeting at which my reprimand was given was short. I walked in and was asked to explain my comment. The following response has to be considered against the circumstances in which it was said and the fact that I kept a perfectly straight face when I said it. Verbatim: 'I think you will find that the correct *Oxford English Dictionary* definition of the word "gay" is "light-hearted", and that is what I meant. If you and other people want to misuse the true meaning of the word, it says a lot more about you than me.' Pause. 'And you can't prove otherwise, can you?' The senior manager thought for several seconds, looked straight at me, and said, 'Look, just fuck off. But please don't do it again.'

In conclusion, good news for fans, bad news for my critics: I have no intention of changing.

# 22

## Writing, Wine and World Cup Finals

After the madness of Soho, I needed to get my life back on track, so returned to law by joining a small but highly regarded commercial firm, Memery Crystal, as a salaried partner, and worked in commercial litigation. Though my practice grew, it was very slow and I was not certain that it would achieve the critical mass required to be made an equity partner.

I was in the difficult position of being paid well but not very well, and I earned extra money from outside work, such as after-dinner and motivational speaking, but this often meant leaving work early, travelling to another part of the country, and not returning home until the middle of the night. A second divorce gave me significant maintenance obligations and I had no choice but to continue to juggle the various jobs. However, almost concurrently, three openings presented themselves. Firstly, an offer of a fixed freelance contract with the BBC as a co-commentator; secondly, a column for the *Sun* newspaper, resurrecting my role as wine writer that I had fulfilled years earlier for the defunct newspaper, *Today*; and finally a rugby column in the Monday sports supplement of the *Daily Telegraph*.

It was obvious to me that things could not continue as they were, but if I had to give up one of the jobs, which should I choose, given that I had to ensure a regular income? Law would give me a good, regular income, whereas the other jobs, apart from the BBC one (which incidentally does not pay much), were not guaranteed to provide that. Furthermore, the newspaper columns could be stopped without much notice.

I thought hard about what to do and I was terrified of leaving a job in which I had seventeen years' experience in favour of jobs in which I had little experience and at which I was far from sure I would succeed.

When I was considering my options, I tried to take into account what I call my 'grass is greener' trait. Ever since I was a teenager, I have become restless when I feel I have mastered a subject or completed a task. This has happened even when I have been doing well, and at times it feels as if I have a self-destruct button inside me. It is true that I am driven, but, as a result, whatever I achieve, and however many boxes I tick, there is always something I have not done. It is sad, but I am more or less permanently dissatisfied.

When making a decision, I sometimes find it useful to try and view my life in reverse, meaning that I look back at it from my theoretical retirement. By doing just that on this occasion, I was given the answer to my employment conundrum: I thought that if I remained a lawyer, even a successful and wealthy one, I would always be left wondering once I retired what my life might have been like if I had taken up the other roles. I was also well aware that offers to broadcast for the BBC and to write for national newspapers are not made more than once. I decided to take a chance and to leave law only when I was content that this was not another case of me not recognising that what I had was good. I am pleased I took that gamble.

My chance to write for the *Sun* came when I went to dinner with the editor and her then husband, who is a friend of mine. Discussion turned to the success of the Richard and Judy Wine

Club and I said it was no surprise to me. When asked why, I said that about 70 per cent of wine is bought by women as part of the weekly shopping. It was these same women who stayed at home to raise a family and who were consequently more likely to watch daytime TV. Sensing an opportunity, I wondered out loud why the *Sun*, given its demographic, did not have a regular wine column. When told the idea was being considered, I said that I had written such a column for the *Today* paper; and that was that. Tasting wines each week, solely for my readers, I now have the great fortune to taste good wines and to get paid for it; not exactly the dream job, but far better than most.

The chance to write for the *Telegraph* came out of nowhere. Although I had started writing weekly columns for the *Sun*, and a few one-off rugby columns for the various national papers, I had not actively looked for the opportunity to write regularly.

I received a call from the then Sports Editor, Keith Perry. He told me that their previous rugby columnist, Stuart Barnes, had left for the *Sunday Times*. Incidentally, although I disagree with Barnes on much of his writing, he is an excellent writer. Keith told me that the Telegraph Group was making many changes in the face of tightening economic conditions. Their idea was to have me write a bi-weekly column with Keith Wood, though this was later changed to Will Greenwood.

At first, I struggled with my style. Although I did not think I had done much writing as a lawyer, this was because I did not recognise that I was 'writing' all that time. My writing just happened to be stylised and formal. The vocabulary I have developed as a lawyer is wide but only tangentially useful for writing articles and things such as this book. This is because, as a lawyer, I quickly had to learn to speak and draft very formally. Unfortunately, after years of dictating in this fashion, on occasion I unintentionally slip into that mode when I speak, and it sounds stiff and pompous. So nowadays I have to refrain from thinking and writing as a lawyer and stop myself from qualifying every point I make.

I have had to eschew the practice of trying to think my way

through writer's block. I used to try and focus as I had done when wrestling with a case file, blotting out all else and picking my way slowly through the problem, linking things logically until I got out the other side. But this approach is worse than useless when it comes to writing an article. The fact is that creativity is not logical, and when I struggle, I now simply get up from my desk and do something completely different. Trying not to think about the subject clears my mind until something presents itself. I then have to exploit the idea, even though I have no idea where it came from and, for me at least it cannot be summoned up by will.

Before I started my *Telegraph* column, I discussed what they wanted, with whom I would liaise, and so on. I thought very hard about the first few pieces, and many of my initial efforts were quickly consigned to the recycle bin, accompanied by the thought, 'Jesus, you sound like a fucking barrister addressing the High Court.'

When a piece is going to be good, it just pours out on to the page. But some can take hours. I cannot deny that part of the satisfaction I derive from writing is the public platform it gives me to sound off. Looked at from a different perspective, it is also part of my need for recognition of my efforts, my need to feel appreciated. Whatever the basis for this feeling, there is no denying it. Any journalist who says differently is a liar.

One occasion when I had the satisfaction of seeing someone read and react to a piece of mine occurred on a morning train into Waterloo. I was standing looking over the shoulder of a man who was reading my column. His mate sat across from him, facing me. At various points, the reader, who was Scottish, 'tutted', then started voicing his disagreements by intermittently exclaiming 'rubbish'. As he read on, he started reading bits out to his friend, each time choosing a different way to describe what he thought of the passage and/or its author. 'The bitter little twat' was one of the more polite descriptions.

His mate, who had recognised me as soon as I had got on the train, was desperately trying not to laugh, but was finding it ever more difficult as his companion continued. That he did not alert his friend to my presence showed a fine sense of restraint; he also clearly wanted to make sure that, when he later embarrassed his mate by repeating the story, he had as much ammunition as possible.

As the train pulled into Waterloo, the Scottish bloke got up and turned directly to face me. An initial blank look of incomprehension turned to recognition, then to discomfiture and finally, so as not to lose face, to aggression. 'I don't know why you read such rubbish,' I said. 'Neither do I,' he replied, 'you talk crap.' 'I notice you felt compelled to read every word of it, though; which is what I want anyway' was my response. At which point I left, to the sound of his companion's guffaws. It was going to be a good day.

In the middle of 2008, the *Telegraph* gave me the chance to write a full page on general sporting matters. It took me some time to consider whether to accept because I was not sure I had sufficient knowledge. However, I have been interested in many sports other than the one with which I am usually associated, since I was young. I am also able to comment and view other sports from the perspective of an international sportsman, and because I am not part of the cliques which develop in some sports, I do not swallow some of the fallacious claims made by its participants.

When I started the general sport page I used to get criticism along the lines of 'I think you've had too many bangs on the head' or 'What do you know about such and such sport?' Almost all the critics used general assertions such as 'You talk crap' but did not deconstruct my comments using other facts to refute my points. These are further examples of people wrongly assuming that because they do not agree with me, I cannot do the job. I am pleased that these comments have largely stopped appearing because it is a sign that people have accepted I have the right to comment on sports other than my own.

At one time, such was my absolute need to be proved right that I would trawl through every webpage and every comments section, seeking out the critics and arguing my point, even if it took hours of research to strengthen my position. I still cannot fully break this fetish: after all, it is important for a writer to be in touch with public opinion (he states unconvincingly). At least now I can accept that somebody is allowed to have a different point of view. But in situations where critics are factually incorrect, I still cannot let it pass without comment; I need more help!

Harking back to the invaluable advice of my English teacher all those years ago, I am always aware that it is easier to stand on the outside and snigger, rather than risk mockery by doing something. Having been a player who played regularly in games that were reported on, I also know that what is written about a person always, no matter how much that person disagrees, has some effect. As such, I try to be fair and to make sure that I write nothing that I would not be prepared to say to a person's face. They still might not like what is written, but I will be able to give the reasons for my comments.

My writing appears to offend some sports journalists, who have gone out of their way to mention me in their columns. I do not know why they have taken this attitude towards me, but their hostility is not a figment of my imagination. In 2009, therefore, I was utterly thrilled to be nominated and shortlisted for the most prestigious award a sportswriter can win, the British Press Award of sports journalist of the year. As I had only been writing my general sports column for six months and they only have this single award for sport, my recognition was a great honour.

Having a press platform can be abused, either by dwelling on the scurrilous or petty, or by obtaining content by persuading people to break their duties of confidentiality. But it can also be used positively to tackle important issues and attempt to change things that are wrong. I recently campaigned successfully to stop the 'rain tax' being imposed by Ofwat on all volunteer-run, non-profit-making bodies including small sports clubs. Being able to help in this way gives my natural campaigning zeal a worthwhile outlet and, when I'm successful, I gain far more satisfaction than I would even from winning awards, because I have made a difference.

I will continue to do this, not just because of my needs but because I constantly receive communications from people saying that they have tried but nobody will listen to them because they are a small group and/or do not have money or political influence. I sometimes get accused of self-importance or self-promotion in these instances and I do get angry about this. But if I didn't grit my teeth and put up with these accusations, it would mean allowing the continued bullying of those people who feel they have no other means of protest.

There are times when my writing has resonance because I cover a particular sporting moment or issue and it brings into focus personal issues; sometimes painful and long-standing ones.

For several hours after the 2007 Rugby World Cup final, I sat in my Paris hotel room trying to fashion my thoughts on England's brave loss to a much better South African team. My highly emotional state arose because of two previous finals. I knew that, at that moment in time, I was one of very few people who knew exactly how the England players felt. Losing narrowly in the biggest challenge of all can distort your perception of your rugby life for years afterwards; possibly irretrievably. I knew how each mistake would now be playing in the back of the maker's mind and how hollow would sound the comments that they had exceeded everyone's expectations. Some would be wishing it had not been so narrow a loss, because the pain produced by the possibility of victory can be worse than that of a sound defeat.

Alongside my contemplation of their lot, there was also part of me that was reflecting on my own inability to deal with my defeat in the corresponding game sixteen years earlier, and recalling the way I saw the 2003 triumph of Martin Johnson's England team.

I did not see the 2003 final live in the stadium. As I could not get time off work to go to Sydney, I watched it at a friend's house in Parson's Green with about twenty other people. I always thought we would win the Cup because we were the best team in the world at the time and we had the best pack. I cheered with everybody else when England scored and launched myself into a jumping frenzy when Johnny drop-kicked the last-minute winner.

I felt euphoric as each player received his medal, but the instant Jason Leonard had the sash put over his head, something inside me just broke and I started crying. No, I did not just cry, I sobbed and sobbed and sobbed.

Naturally, this was odd for all the others celebrating this fantastic feat, and after about ten minutes one of my friends came and asked why I was crying and why I couldn't stop. The fact that I lied was because I was thoroughly ashamed of the ignobility of the sentiment that had triggered this outpouring of long-held grief: jealousy. I have recounted my pathological reaction to losing to Australia in 1991, but at that moment in 2003 I knew that Jason alone had been given a chance to resolve any issues he may have had from playing in the losing team. For me and every other England player from that team, there is no assuagement.

I still would give almost anything, and for several years after the defeat would indeed have given anything, to put right the tactical errors made and not to have to bear the taunts of Gollum that have been thrown remorselessly concerning my own failures within that failure. But I cannot, and therein lies one of the cruellest beauties of sport and that is why it absorbs me and so many millions of others. It is also why I relish the opportunity I have been given to write about it.

# 23

## The Demise of the Scrum and a Testament to Daniel James

I apologise to those of you who gamely stay with the next few paragraphs in good faith, only to find you are nearly losing the will to live. I decided to do a chapter on the scrum because the way in which it has been altered demonstrates the way in which the IRB has seemingly moved away from the majority of its traditional public when it comes to the way rugby is played.

Rugby has always been run for the benefit of its players. Recently the views of marketing men and their puppets on the IRB have begun to introduce impossibly subjective concepts such as 'attractiveness' as factors to be considered when law changes are discussed. Eschewing its traditions, the IRB has raised from secondary to primary the goals of attracting crowds and viewers. In doing so, it forgets what has sustained rugby for the past hundred years and why the vast majority of us love the game.

Elite referees have unilaterally decided that they have better things to do than referee scrums properly by ensuring the ball is put in straight and packs do not push before the put-in. In failing to do what their predecessors found perfectly straightforward, they have given credence to the principally southern-hemisphere view that the scrum is merely a means of re-starting the game. They have unwittingly altered the nature of the scrum and the players involved, particularly hookers. The game is now blighted by endless resetting of scrums and arbitrary penalties. The engaging of the front rows is becoming a safety issue, and laughably the very problems created by Elite referees are now erroneously being cited by them as reasons why they have too many things to deal with to referee properly the put-in and shoving laws.

Are they really saying that they cannot see whether the ball is put in according to a law? If not, why not? Referees used to be able to do this for nearly 100 years. Scrums have not become more technical; the sequences in the scrum happen at the same speed. Actually they are more controlled now because the referee is in charge of when the front rows come together. In fact, there are no reasonable excuses for this deliberate avoidance.

I am a small man; at five-feet-eight and weighing just under fifteen stone when I played, I was nearly always smaller than my opposite number. However, the front rows in which I played were never outscrummaged because scrummaging used to be a technical discipline. It may not have been quantum physics, but it was nevertheless an art and required an apprenticeship.

When my side had the put-in, the prime aim was for a steady platform so that I could strike the ball. Transferring all my weight on to my left leg, the non-striking leg, and then sweeping my right leg forward and round to hook a straight-fed ball was dangerous and/or impossible if the scrum moved. I then used a 'tap' signal. When I used to bind around my props, I did so by gripping their shirts just below their shoulders. When it was my team's put-in, my scrum half stood to my left and waited for me to very quickly release my left-hand grip and 'tap' by moving it up and then down quickly. This signalled I was ready and the scrum half should feed the ball into the scrum immediately. This gave me the advantage of knowing the ball would be fed; whilst my opposite number had to guess.

Conversely, when it was the other side's put-in, my job was

either to strike the ball against the head or to make life as uncomfortable as possible for my opposite number.

The non-striking options were to go for an eight-man shove and try to push them off the ball; or I called a wheel, whereby one side of the scrum pushed and the other either stayed still or pushed less hard. The resulting imbalance 'wheeled' the scrum. Usually we, and everyone else, achieved a wheel by one side driving forward and the other side pulling back. This meant the scrum turned quickly. All of these options made playing the ball from the scrum more difficult.

Sometimes I called a 'drop-wheel'. Totally illegal, this was what we called a 'disciplinary' measure where we whip-wheeled the scrum, but one prop dropped his opposite number on the floor and we drove over the top of their front row. I still have the scar from the six stitches given to me by Daniel Dubroca in Paris in 1988 when the French did this to us.

My most popular way of winning a ball against the head was to put pressure on their hooker, driving him into a position where he could not lift up his foot to strike because his body was crunched up due to the pressure. Another benefit of this was that it prevented the hooker from seeing the ball before or during his strike, which made the strike itself more difficult and certainly more difficult to control and direct.

If I decided to strike for the ball, I got my feet as near to the put-in side of the tunnel as possible, tried to anticipate when the put-in might be and get my foot to the ball first, hooking it back into my side of the scrum – happy days.

The double strike was invented by Jon Olver, then of Harlequins. He would strike once, whereupon his opposing hooker would think he had struck too soon and tap for the ball to be put in. However, after striking, Olver would immediately strike again and nick the ball. If this was not penalised, you sometimes had a rugby version of the Tiller Girls with both hookers darting out their legs willy-nilly.

When the other hooker used the 'tap' system – and most did –

I sometimes placed my hand next to his and then tapped, hoping his scrum half would mistake my hand for his own hooker's. He would then think his hooker had tapped and put the ball in. When this came off, it left the other hooker screaming at his hapless scrum half.

A favourite ruse of mine was to place a finger on top of the other hooker's tapping hand. If undetected, this meant that as soon as he lifted his hand to tap, I knew the ball was coming in and could dive across the tunnel and strike just before he did, leaving him dumbfounded.

I or my tight-head could simply grab the other hooker's tapping hand and hold it down so that he could not move it. Not receiving the signal to put in the ball, his scrum would be left with the ball presented and I and the tight-head shouting, 'Put it in, make him put it in!' If he did not, the referee would often penalise him. The drawback, possibly, with this one, is that it usually caused a fight.

When my tight-head dominated his opposite number, he could try and strike the ball with his outside leg. Few tight-heads were good enough to do this, though Jeff Probyn and Gary Pearce, two of the most effective/illegal tight-heads to have played, could both manage this on a good day. There was nothing I could do as a hooker if a tight-head did this because he was nearer to the ball than me, so he got to the ball first. I usually remonstrated with my loose-head for giving him such an easy ride.

Two inventive ways to win a ball against the head did not involve the front row. The first was invented by Pierre Berbizier, the former France scrum half. When the opposition scrum half presented the ball he looked to see if the referee had gone round to the other side of the scrum to watch the two props; when he did, Berbizier slapped the ball out of the scrum half's hands into his own side of the scrum. England refined this and had a specific call of 'Berbizier'. Jason Leonard would collapse the scrum before the ball came in, thus drawing the referee to his side, leaving the way open for Dewi Morris to do the slapping.

A variation of this is 'the hand of Back', used by the Leicester flanker Neil Back to help his team win the Heineken Cup against Munster. Quite simply, instead of the scrum half, it was Back who slapped the ball out of the scrum half's hands.

Because referees do not make scrum halves put the ball in straight, all of the above techniques, save the eight-man shove or wheel, are now redundant. It doesn't matter what a front row or hooker does on an opposition put-in, they will not win the ball unless it is kicked back to them because it is fed so crookedly that there is no way they can reach it with their feet.

As a result, packs have stopped trying to strike for the ball. Now they just use what is termed power scrummaging. They hit as hard as they can when the front rows come together and keep pushing, which is illegal. It is now attritional, not technical, and moreover, because both packs drive as soon as the front rows engage, the scrum is inherently unstable. This is potentially dangerous, as players slip or catch their feet on the legs of other players. It makes a collapsed scrum more likely, and the dangers of that are well known. Further, the force of the impact has increased, which is bad for the spines of the front-row players. These issues are no longer matters of style; I believe that they will be the subject of legal action at some future point when a player is injured as a result.

Another inadvertent consequence of referees copping out has been the change in physique of the hooker. Where once being too large meant you were too inflexible to strike for the ball when under pressure, now it does not matter because you don't have to strike. We have a generation of players who are big and powerful but not ball players. Previously they would not have been picked because they would not have been able to do the primary role. See the connection? Well, that's more than the IRB and the Elite referees did.

I was at the Elite Referees' Conference in 2006, where the then IRB president Dr Syd Millar disavowed all responsibility for this failure to referee. With utter disingenuousness he claimed that it had never been condoned by the IRB. I was only there as an observer, but I couldn't keep quiet. I explained how the practice had changed entirely the way the scrummage was approached. I pointed out the developing safety risks and reiterated the question as to why referees were able simply to ignore this law because they felt it was too much trouble to referee.

The response was a promise that on 1 January 2007 there would be 'zero tolerance' for scrum halves who did not comply with the letter of the law. Did this happen? Did it, Hell. If they want rugby-league scrummaging or no scrums at all, then fine, but do it by conscious decision, not by omission.

Finally, as a reminder that the risks taken by front-row players are not theoretical, there is the story of Daniel James. I reproduce here in full my *Telegraph* article on Daniel, from 23 October 2008. The article and readers' comments can be found online at:

http://www.telegraph.co.uk/sport/rugbyunion/3242030/It-took-courage-for-the-parents-of-Daniel-James-to-say-goodbye-Rugby-Union.html.

I believe that the time and trouble you take to find the page will be more than repaid by the eloquence and compassion to be found in the expressions of support in the readers' comments. I will probably never write anything as satisfying and powerful, and my description of the James family's extraordinary love and courage drew comments from all over the world. That other people make different decisions does not diminish their bravery; it is a personal decision and that is the only comment I or anyone else is qualified to make.

The best consequence of success in sport is the opportunity to enrich the life of someone else. This is a feeling nobody, however rich, can buy. As a former international hooker, I know that it also brings other things – equally moving, of greater import and some-times inspirational, but never a pleasure.

I vividly recall my first visit to a rugby player who was in one of the country's acute centres having suffered serious spinal injury. As I write, I can feel the tears welling up and, as then, I cannot stop them.

I was not prepared for the experience, not understanding what might be my reaction. More importantly, what it needed to be to help the unfortunate boy who, either side of a collapsed scrum, had looked forward to his degree at university, but now contemplated a lifetime of manual evacuation of his bowels, assisted feeding and knowing he would never be independent.

Though rugby is not the most dangerous of sports, there are serious injuries, and those pertaining to the front row, particularly hookers, resonate keenly. The uniquely vulnerable world of the hooker within the scrum is one in which I dwelt for years without serious injury.

However, I also remember the times I got the engagement, the 'hit', wrong, suffering a 'stinger', a neurological shock like a lightning bolt down my spine; when I was driven upwards, my neck being slowly bent, close to hyper-extension, before I managed to pop my head out of the scrum; when the front rows collapsed and all I could do was turn my head a little to minimise the chance of my neck taking all the weight of the collapse and fracturing.

Daniel James, son of Julie and Mark, represented England at under-sixteen, university and student level at hooker. In playing for the last two teams he was following the same path which years earlier had led me to that which also cannot be bought: the honour of representing my country at full international level.

I know how Daniel felt pulling on the no.2 jersey; the mixture of fierce determination and pride, edged with fear and the pressure of carrying not only his dreams, but those of his friends and especially his parents. I know that Julie and Mark were so very proud.

I am sure that in a quiet moment before he played, he thought of his mother and father. How much he owed them for driving him to training, coping with his mood swings according to how he played – and just how much he loved them. I hoped he told them at the time, because too few of us do.

Unfortunately, I know exactly how, in March last year, Daniel dislocated his spine when a scrum collapsed during a training session at Nuneaton RFC.

Colleague Mick Cleary, in his earlier column, chose precisely the phrase which is more apposite to me than most, given the similarities with Daniel. 'There but for . . .'

I cannot dwell on that collapse as it reminds me too much of my mortality and that someone else was chosen by fate to suffer. I cannot know the workings of Daniel's mind as he struggled with his catastrophic injury and, if I'm honest, I do not want to because in those thoughts lies madness.

I can make an educated guess at how his mum and dad felt when they were told of his accident and with what they battled thereafter. If the following sounds patronising, so be it: only a parent can come remotely near to understanding what it must have been like for Julie and Mark.

If you have not had a child, your perception of this is intellectual. That is what makes parenthood special, it is emotional. You may hypothesise that Julie and Mark would gladly have swapped places with their son; but you cannot feel that or the guilt they probably feel for encouraging him to play the game that, at times, they will feel killed their son.

All this is secondary to the astonishing courage they showed in accompanying Daniel to the Dignitas clinic in Berne, where Daniel was assisted to take a life which to him had become unbearable, particularly given the contradiction of rude health and near total incapacity.

I do not know how they faced the conflicting emotions of saying goodbye to the little boy they saw score his first try and the desperate wish to keep him with them. If they get counselling, which they must, they may have to face admitting something I felt while watching my father struggle through the last hours of his life, gasping for breath – that when I cried, 'Please don't struggle any more,' part of this was because I selfishly wanted him to spare me any more pain.

My father was elderly, but still the walk from his death bed was a searing experience. No parent should have to bury a child and I do not have the ability to suppose what that walk felt like for Julie and Mark.

It is still an offence under the Suicide Act 1961 to 'aid, counsel or procure the suicide of another'; the penalty is up to fourteen years' imprisonment. Julie and Mark now face the ordeal of investigation by the West Mercia police following notification of their act of love by a 'concerned' individual.

Of that person, I say concerned is the last thing you were, other than in an intellectual exercise of morality, a concept incapable of standard definition by two people, never mind entire organised groups – however concerned they, in their delusion, may be.

Among the many letters Julie and Mark will receive, there will be a handful which will say they will be punished on the final day. Yes, some people are that pitiful. To such authors I put this – if you reserve judgment for God, why then usurp this by presupposing the conclusion?

If there is a God I believe he will understand what was done and why.

Headlines have stated that Julie and Mark have defended their actions. Mr and Mrs James, you have to do no such thing. If there is a final reckoning, it is between you and your God – no one else.

# 24

## Letting Go

The excesses of Soho gave way to the comfortable middle-class surroundings of Wimbledon. I had run round Wimbledon Common many years earlier in my *Blake's 7* rubber suit when everybody had given me a wide berth. Even so, I thought it was a nice place. Sufficiently far from London's thrusting centre but with rapid transport links to get back if I was driven mad by the incessant talk about house prices and Harry fucking Potter: 'My Emily is only four and she's read the entire series. It's so clever; grown-ups can read it too.' Of course they can – it's a bloody book.

It may have been outbursts like the above that caused the break-up of my second marriage. There is little point in speculating about degrees of culpability because in the end the same point is reached: divorce. All I would say is that, if ever a man wants to extend his working life by twenty years, he should get divorced for the second time. As with my first divorce, the second was very painful and I, like everyone else in that situation, had to try and make decisions that required the greatest altruism, in circum-stances that were almost guaranteed to ensure that quality was in short supply. When I met Lucy I was beguiled by her sense of fun and attractiveness and I cannot explain how we drifted apart so badly. Even so, for bearing, giving birth to and mothering my first daughter, Imogen, I will always thank her.

The truth is that the nearest I got to positively wanting children was indifference, but when the everyday miracle of birth took place, my life, like that of all parents, was transformed. Nothing in all the preceding years had managed to shake my self-centredness: I could only see things in terms of how they would affect me. The greatest thing about parenthood is that it is emotional; unfettered by concerns such as logic and intellectual consistency. You need no academic achievements to feel the unadulterated joy of holding your child and hearing them say that they love you. A young child's words are the only ones a person can hear and be sure that they are genuine, and unaffected by cynicism or influenced by ulterior motive. After years of existing in a world of political manoeuvring at work, scheming committees and stress-inducing conflict on the rugby field, the first years with my offspring have been the only times when I have come close to feeling whole.

That fatherhood threatened to make me properly happy should have signalled to me that something would occur to mar this joy. This time it was not behaviour, such as excessive drinking. It was the way in which my thoughts and emotions about being a parent became linked to another issue from my very earliest days that had lain hidden but not dormant: in my first book I wrote that my adoption had had few consequences. I was wrong.

It has been so difficult to disentangle the multiple strands of thoughts and feelings surrounding this issue. Sometimes I wish I had not felt compelled to search for my birth mother, Rina; but I know that that is not true. It is rather that I wish I did not have to experience the confusion and emotions that it brought and still brings. Even writing about the topic brings feelings of guilt and disloyalty to both my mothers; and I do not need any more guilt or regret that can be turned against me by my *alter ego*.

My comments on adoption were legitimate according to my knowledge at the time my first book was published. I received letters, and had more than a few discussions with strangers who approached me because they had read my words. Some people wanted to share their experiences of meeting their birth parents, but more often, people asked whether I thought they should trace their birth parents.

There are few certainties with adoption, but I would not offer the following two if I did not believe they were almost universally applicable. The first thing I told all those seeking guidance from me was that the tracing of a birth parent should not be done without feeling almost physically compelled to take that step. Curiosity, even strong curiosity, is not a good enough reason to seek information about, or make contact with, a birth parent. I say this because once a fact is known, it cannot be unknown. It may be forgotten or suppressed for a period, but it will always be there, and its effects cannot be predicted and can work so subtly that it appears to have had no influence. Some people told me they only wanted to know a few basic facts, such as their mother's nationality, what she looked like, where she lived, and so on. The problem was that with each bit of information, I was able to prompt them to admit that they would then like the next small scrap that logically followed. They would almost certainly not be content once they succeeded in finding the information they did not yet possess. And however successful they were, the end result would be the same: they would always want more. This Jack can never be put back in his box.

The second absolute for me concerning adoption is that, in so far as it is humanly possible, tracers must rid themselves of all expectations about what they will find. My parents would not help me when I raised the possibility of tracing my birth mother until they judged that I was sufficiently equipped to handle the consequences. Their reticence was as a result of the experiences of several adopted children who had successfully traced their birth parents. In some cases, the consequences had been disastrous: a few had been positive, but none had been unproblematic. Of those consequences that had been negative, the most painful were the instances where children had found out sufficient details to know where a parent – almost always the mother – now lived and had turned up unannounced. The brilliant and amusing Mike Leigh film *Secrets and Lies* deals with this matter when Hortense, the searching daughter, knocks on the door of her birth mother unannounced. Whilst Leigh manages to find humour from this meeting, nobody should ever take that action. There are many reasons for this and not just for the shock that it would give the parent. All manner of things could occur that are undesirable and they too cannot be undone.

My parents knew of cases where the parent had refused to acknowledge the child, even when shown proof that they had given birth to the person standing before them. Another had been so embarrassed about the episode that had led to conception that she had told nobody about the adoption and, although she had subsequently admitted the fact, she had angrily thrown the child off her doorstep. In other cases, after a first meeting that promised a relationship, subsequent attempts had gone badly wrong. In one case of which I am aware, this was enough to induce the offspring's depression and then suicide.

As I stated earlier, I was always aware that I was adopted shortly after birth. I was curious about this but not in any meaningful way until I was about to go to university. I cannot account for my increased interest but it went no further when my opening questions were met with terse replies. In fact, my mother made a statement that was so out of character that I was shocked. 'We chose you and brought you up, and in one way we were the winners.' I ascribed this to her being upset and fearful that I would no longer think of her as my mother. I could understand that and it sufficed as a reason for me not to make any similar enquires until I was married and in my thirties.

When I raised the subject again and more than once, my parents explained their previous reluctance and told me of the above episodes. They gave me all the information they had, and amongst the papers they gave to me was, crucially, my birth certificate. My father's name was not on the document but my mother's name, Rina, and my original surname of Kirk were detailed, as was the fact that I was called Brian at birth. Armed with this information, and knowing the parish in which the registration had taken place, I contacted a firm of enquiry agents that provided a range of services to my law firm, including tracing people. Within two days they came back with information that included my birth mother's address and phone number. She had not moved from the city of my birth, Birmingham, and lived in the district established by the Quaker and chocolate-maker Joseph Cadbury.

The details sat in my drawer at work and the temptation to call the number was difficult to resist, but I did the right thing. I contacted the social-services department at Richmond upon Thames London Borough Council and explained my situation. They agreed to write to Rina, saying only that somebody from her past had asked them to make it known that he would like to call her. That way, if she had not told anyone else, she could pretend the reference was to somebody else. As it was, she knew straight away that the letter referred to her decision of many years past and she replied saying she wanted me to make contact.

After all the many hours I had spent thinking about what words I would say to her, I decided on a few, but when it came to the call I forgot them all. The conversation was brief, as what we had to speak about needed to be done in person. Nevertheless, just speaking to her altered me. I had done something that nearly everyone else takes for granted: spoken to the person who had brought me into this world. We arranged for her to visit me in London, and one Sunday morning in 1995 I stared out of the bay windows of my house in Twickenham, waiting for her to walk to my front door. When I saw her, the first thing I thought was how attractive she was.

We hugged each other and through initial tears talked for the next few hours in a strangely incoherent way. Rushes of conversation were punctuated by long periods of silence during which neither of us knew what to say. As we talked about such deep and moving subjects, it did not seem right to interject with some banality just to keep the conversation going. She had a peculiar accent that was a mixture of Brummie and Yorkshire, and as it turned out she hailed from Sheffield, so my natural family was from Yorkshire all along. She told me that I had a full sister and brother, which was a shock, even though I had considered it likely that I might have had half-siblings.

She had only ever told her then husband John, now sadly deceased, about me, and the account of her revealing my existence to Natasha and Gary shortly after I had made contact was also unusual. Sat at a family lunch, she began to tell them about the fact that before they were born she had given birth to, and put up for adoption, a boy who, she continued in a matter-of-fact way, had been in touch with her. And, she carried on, it seemed he was rather good at sport and in some circles was quite well known. When she told them my name, my brother refused to believe her; but then, as she replied, why would she make that up? Gary's reaction was partly dictated by the fact that he is a rugby fan, had played hooker at his Birmingham school, and the school had had fixtures with my school. He and Rina had also watched Five Nations games on TV in which I had played.

Rina told them, as she had me, that she had begun a relationship with the man who was the father of all three of us whilst he had been a student. This Malaysian man now seems to have sired three families and is or was a dentist in Crickhowell in Wales, the same place as my England teammate Dewi Morris grew up. Small world. Indeed, you couldn't make it up. When she left studying to find a teaching post, he made it plain that he was not going to stay around. The early 1960s were not the liberal times of today and the difficulties of being a single mother with no decent prospects of looking after her child had led her to the difficult decision. When we first met, Rina asked me to forgive her for her act and I told her that I did not think it was my place to judge her, but, in so far as it was within my remit, I forgave her.

I have since met Gary and Natasha a few times; both look more oriental than me, and Natasha is quite striking; both went to university, in London and Sheffield respectively. I have seen Rina more often, though in total even my meetings with her have not been numerous. You may think this strange, but as I alluded to earlier in this chapter, I think that very few matters concerning adoption are straightforward and even fewer are without problems. As soon as I met Rina I knew where my innate aggression and competitiveness came from. She will say that some of her own aggression and combativeness have been imbued by her circumstances and by the fact that she had two further children by the same man who returned, did not marry her and then deserted her again. She is considerably left of me in political terms and in truth she is not somebody I would cross without need. Therein lies one of my difficulties in maintaining a relationship with Rina: we are too alike in the aspects of my character that need smoothing, not sharpening. With all my natural family, I have no shared history and, given that they all live in different places, that is unlikely to change.

Being a parent forced me to reconsider Rina's decision in ways that had not occurred to me previously for a number of reasons. I had always assumed that the circumstances surrounding my adoption must have been so dire that they gave my natural mother no choice other than that taken. In fact, I had never allowed myself for an instant to think otherwise. Why was this, particularly given my years of legal training whereby I was taught to try and consider a matter from many positions?

Not until I held my daughters did I understand the fact that adoption necessarily includes rejection. By insisting to myself that there were good reasons for this when it came to my adoption, I shielded myself from having to consider the almost unbearable alternative that it might not have been an act of pure compulsion. I know I could kill anyone who tried to take my children from me. For the first time, I had to consider that this is what had happened to me: Rina had allowed me to be taken from her. Possibly worse, it might not have been forced. Knowing the strength of Rina's will,

I could not make sense of her decision. As with other things in my life, I was able to accept it on an intellectual basis; but for a long time, and sometimes even now, I cannot justify the decision emotionally. Thoughts and feelings are two very different things.

I can argue that her decision was an act of strength, because in possessing similarly protective emotions she had had the courage to think about my best interests. Then again, how could she have known that my adoption would bring a better life? How could she have been sure I would be adopted and not spend my childhood in a children's home? Until I had my own children, I had not asked myself or her that sort of question because the answers are so dreadful, if they are not convincing, that I could not be sure I could deal with them. Since then, however, I have still not been able to summon up the courage to ask her. Not asking, not considering, has been a defence mechanism, but one that has been only partly successful. It stopped the acute and immediate pain that came when I first touched the issues, but when I consider my actions and thoughts at different times in my life, the unresolved angst caused by this and by the childhood abuse have been working their nasty little ways unseen, but not unfelt.

The warped chain of logic in my head goes like this: if her decision was reasonable, her rejection of me was also reasonable; since being rejected is a hurtful experience, I must therefore be a bad person and deserve this pain.

Another problem I have with trying to make my way through all this is that any approach I take brings with it incredible guilt. My mother will be hurt by these words because of the implicit challenge to the role she has lovingly fulfilled for over forty-eight years. I do not believe that I think any differently of my mother than I would had I not traced Rina, but as this has now occurred, I have no way of judging this in any event. Fear of disloyalty to my mother has limited my developing any relationship with Rina, but this also makes me confused because I feel guilty for not being in contact with or seeing Rina more than occasionally.

Rina will be unhappy that I harbour any suspicions of her

motives for having me adopted because she did what she thought best at the time and could not reverse her decision, which she told me she subsequently regretted. When I was adopted, there was not the legislation and assistance to help children trace parents that now exists. As she did not expect to be contacted, my approach has foisted a relationship on her.

As for tracing my natural father, I have no desire to see him. Because I could not voluntarily absent myself from my daughters' lives, I cannot feel anything for a man who has done this not just to me, but to several of his other children. What kind of man does this? Not one that I respect. My obligations to my girls will never go away; but more importantly I want to help them, guide them, love them, as far as I am able. I cannot imagine any situation that would change this. I feel the bond with them so deeply that I could not blithely leave. It would wound me to my very soul and I am not sure I would want to live with the guilt I would feel by abandoning them.

I am constantly thinking about the conflicting issues that face me surrounding my adoption, and in truth I have no idea what to do about them. Some people will say that I should not ask questions that I know might upset my mother and Rina; but not to do so means I have to bear all the uncertainties and all the upset that comes from not finding some resolution to my situation. Although they did not want or ask for any of these problems, neither did I.

The Hollywood-style ending of a tripartite meeting, one without rancour or accusation, where we walk off into the distance holding each other, has entered my dreams, but it is not going to happen. I did not start this journey wanting or expecting such an outcome, but the fact that it has even entered my head gives credence to my earlier advice that a person seeking contact with a birth parent should not exacerbate inevitable difficulties by imposing unrealistic goals. There are no precedents to guide me along this complicated path and it is a case of doing what I think is best in the circumstances. However, I think I owe it to my mother and to Rina to carry on trying to balance the conflicting demands of maintaining a relationship with each of them. In the end, we are all part of the same story, and it need not have an unhappy ending.

Having had to consider my adoption in detail and its effects on my life, the thought of doing the same in respect of the abuse I suffered as a child filled me with dread. The effects have been much harder to pin down, and so much of my thinking seemed to be so conceptual that many times when I tried to link something to it I found a number of alternative reasons for an incident or a piece of my behaviour. I wrote pages and pages on the subject for the purposes of this book, but none of them made much sense when I reread them the following day. They seemed to me to amount only to a morass of confused stories, interspersed with pop-psychology. As a result, they were thrown in the bin.

As I continued to struggle, I had a moment of insight in which the following thought came forward: the fact that I cannot find clarity concerning this subject means that the consequences of the abuse, even though undefined, have been dramatic but in an all-pervasive way.

The secret me, the bit I kept for myself, the bit that nobody could touch, was my defence mechanism against being harmed again. If there was something that was internal, whatever that something was, then it couldn't be taken away, could not be abused. In so far as it may have protected me, it also led to a crippling fear of intimacy. Although this did not prevent physical intimacy, it still marred sex as a complete act. Both the mental and physical sides have to coincide to create total satisfaction and because I would not risk being vulnerable and kept something for myself, that could not happen. Instead I mistook intensity for intimacy. Anything edgy, tending to the extreme, seemed more exciting, but when experienced was invariably unsatisfactory.

In a similar fashion, my relationships, at all levels, have been imperfect. It is not just the very close relationships that have suffered. This fear has also caused me to have difficulty in social gatherings of any kind. And at the very times when I might have been expected to be happiest or most content, I have all too often felt detached and unable to fully share a moment of victory or a moment of joy. Added to this, because I did not have any insight into why this happened, I would also be angry; all of which provided Gollum with potent new ammunition with which to hurt me.

This fear is also principally responsible for the self-destructive behaviour that occurred in my past. At times, when a situation or a relationship threatened to become sufficiently comfortable that I was able to consider taking the last stride towards contentment, I would do something to wreck it, thus preventing any chance of putting my happiness in the control of another person. You will immediately have spotted the inherent irony of doing this: it made me unhappy anyway.

I believe that the abandonment issue was also at work in the above sort of behaviour. Having previously been abandoned, there was no way I could risk this happening again, and I would leave before I could be left. Though this too made me desperately unhappy, I would console myself with the thought that it would have happened sooner or later, and at least this way, I was in control.

Even now that I have some understanding of these issues, it is not as simple as switching from uninformed and unhappy to informed and full of the joys of spring. There is no guide to risking intimacy that is universally applicable. All the theories and treatises that exist can never deal with the infinite variations that make up an individual's life and circumstances. Little by little I am trying to trust more, invest more emotionally in things, and open myself up. With this, inevitably I suppose, there has come hurt. People let you down; they act in a disloyal way. But what is the alternative?

Either of the two issues, abandonment and abuse, would have posed more than enough problems for me. In unison they have been an ordeal, and continue to be so on an almost daily basis, even though their influence has diminished. I am now much more aware of my moods and motives, and of what might lie behind a certain feeling or proposed action. As such, I have started to have some success in recognising and dealing with these twin monsters.

# 25

## The View from
## Wimbledon Common

'What is the similarity between marriage and a tornado? They both start with lots of sucking and blowing but in the end you wind up losing your house.'

'I'm not going to get married again; next time I'm just going to find a woman I dislike and buy her a house.'

There are hundreds of jokes about divorce and most would have captured my bitterly cynical mood after I had seen two marriages fail. Strangely, those experiences did not lessen my belief in marriage as the best basis for a lifelong relationship and certainly for raising children. However, after my second divorce, I vowed that I would be objective and take a lot of care about any future serious relationship, and that I would not enter into one for two years.

I didn't manage to keep either of those promises because, not long after, at an after-show party at the BBC's *Sports Personality of the Year* programme, I met a girl who, according to her, was 'working the room', making sure her BBC guests were being looked after in her role as the BBC's MotoGP producer. I liked her immediately and knew within a very short time that my vows would be broken. I reasoned that they had been as generalised as the advice that you should not buy the first house you see. What if that one is the right one? Do you eschew it because of vernacular wisdom?

I am not sure the title of Mrs Moore III was especially attractive but Belinda overcame any misgivings and we married in December 2008, a year after she gave birth to our daughter, Larissa Holly. We are getting on with the most important task of all: raising a decent, healthy and happy family. I try to give the benefit of my experience to my two girls and worry about their future, as do all parents. I try not to resurrect my former life through them and am always mindful that, whilst they have part of me in their persona, that persona is not mine to control. One of the most difficult things about parenting is knowing when to keep quiet and not interfere, and realising that some lessons have to be personally learned. Both my daughters seem to have my argumentative and spirited nature; I just hope that it can be tempered or at least directed in positive ways.

That this book ends on a relatively mundane note might not be ideal for the reader, but for me it is a sign that, after so many years, I am at last beginning to understand my thoughts and actions, which at times still border on the pathological. I have had to accept that my extraordinary experiences gained through rugby were exactly that, and they were not meant to last in perpetuity. In fact, one of the things that made them special was their transient nature. The most common question I get asked at dinners and so on is, 'Do you miss playing?' I used to trot out a stock answer, saying I did not because I realised that I could no longer play due to the passage of time, and anyway my life had many different strands, all of which kept me busy.

I no longer say this, because it isn't true. And pretending that I do not miss my playing days is not to face the consequences of retirement. I miss that life more than I usually admit. It is not just the crowds or the acclamation; I miss the thrill of direct physical confrontation. I wish I could still enjoy the fantastic repartee and solidarity generated by competitive matches and the banter outside those moments of stress. And I miss my mates. Whenever I meet any former teammate, it is as if our past glories occurred only last week, and I get twangs of nostalgia. I wish there were more events or occasions at which I could meet the boys, but we all have to get on with leading busy lives that have too little time for enjoyment anyway. I now try not to yearn for those days, and instead to be grateful that I have had them. Not many other people have had the chance to experience something similar.

My working life today is very different from when I was a City lawyer. This book was written in my garden shed; well, actually it is my office. Although it is unbearably hot in summer and freezing cold in winter, I had to distance myself from my house, even by a few yards, in order to work properly. There are good and bad points about working from home. No commuting is the major plus, as is not having to take time off to wait for workmen. One of the biggest downsides is that I did not realise how much I would miss the office atmosphere. Working from home can be lonely, and some days I would not leave the house unless I forced myself to do so. It would be perfect to have one or two days a week when I could join in the repartee that goes on in every office, and I may actively seek some role in the future that would give me this.

Another aspect of working alone, which can be positive or negative depending on how it is approached, is the time it provides for uncluttered thinking. When I am trying to develop an idea, it helps not having anybody around. However, with my personality, it also gives me the opportunity for introspection and for unhealthily dwelling on matters. Although I never manage to stick to a routine, I try to be disciplined and to establish one because otherwise I waste time; also, the structure brings me some semblance of order.

I am in the process of establishing and setting down my personal and professional goals for one, five and ten years hence. It occurs to me that this document should also include plans for a limited number of achievements in areas that interest me. I have matured enough to know that these need not, and probably should not, be things such as climbing Everest or walking to the

South Pole. If they were that extreme it would be a firm indication that I continued to chase something that was ultimately impossible to attain, that is, a life permanently filled with adrenalin. Although such a life would continue to provide thrills, it would ultimately bring me much unhappiness because in the end I would fail in my quest. The elements of controlled danger in activities such as skiing couloirs and motorbike-track days give me an adrenalin fix but they are wants and not needs.

It has taken too long for me to recognise that the maxims by which I tried to live my sporting career do not work when applied to normal life. The fact that I instinctively still associate normal with mundane is to misunderstand the proper meaning of the word: that it also means healthy and occurring naturally. The truth that has escaped me is that there are enough real challenges within everyday life to occupy anybody. The difficult tasks of being a good father and husband are faced every day, and they are not made any easier by their frequency. I failed in the past to attend to important matters because I judged them to be of lesser importance than chasing my dreams. The commonplace challenges, plus the odd chance to campaign, do charity work or take an opportunity to make a difference, all these are more than enough for a normal man, which, in the end, is all that I am.

Over the years, the advice from lay and professional confidants – to 'put it all behind me' in order to achieve some sort of peace with myself – was not unreasonable or unrealistic, but to do so I had to find out what 'it' was; which was in itself difficult. I have been trying for some time now to deal with 'it', and occasionally I feel I have made huge progress. More often than not, though, I feel progress is slow. I suppose that to unravel forty-odd years could not be done any other way but I wish it were not so.

I now realise that my constant search for the one explanation that will solve all my problems is itself part of the problem. The fact is that, as far as my personal life is concerned, this 'key' probably does not exist. My legal background taught me to analyse facts and consider every detail of an issue and this led me to do the same with my past. However, doing this means that I constantly dragged experiences from my past into the present, and although they were not as viscerally felt as when they first occurred, they were nevertheless upsetting, and they could not be left to rest. I have had to learn to see them as things that I cannot alter or make better; they will always be painful. What I have to do is deal with their effects.

Crucially, I am now able to see that I should not define myself as an abused, abandoned man; rather, I am a man to whom abuse and rejection happened.

I still have to confront the lack of self-esteem and inadequacy that have been present since my childhood but I can now do so from a position of relative strength. I cannot say that I have rid myself of all negative thoughts and behaviour, and I still battle daily with Gollum about all types of things, but at least I now handle them in a more effective way. The ideal approach for me is not to fight with him but to accept his comments and then repeat the following one that Julian, a former professional counsellor of mine, wrote in one of my favourite books. 'To Gollum: thank you for your helpful and kind observations on my present predicament. Now FUCK OFF!'

# Acknowledgements

To my mother and father for your guidance and forgiveness.
To Debbie, my editor, for your professional nagging and support.
To Belinda for understanding.

# Index

(page numbers in italic type refer to Brian Moore)